State of India's Livelihoods Report 2015

Bulk Sales

SAGE India offers special discounts
for purchase of books in bulk.
We also make available special imprints
and excerpts from our books on demand.

For orders and enquiries, write to us at

Marketing Department
SAGE Publications India Pvt Ltd
B1/I-1, Mohan Cooperative Industrial Area
Mathura Road, Post Bag 7
New Delhi 110044, India

E-mail us at **marketing@sagepub.in**

Get to know more about SAGE

Be invited to SAGE events, get on our mailing list.
Write today to **marketing@sagepub.in**

State of India's Livelihoods Report 2015

Girija Srinivasan
Narasimhan Srinivasan

www.sagepublications.com
Los Angeles • London • New Delhi • Singapore • Washington DC

Jointly published in 2015 by

 SAGE Publications India Pvt Ltd
B1/I-1 Mohan Cooperative Industrial Area
Mathura Road, New Delhi 110 044, India
www.sagepub.in

SAGE Publications Inc
2455 Teller Road
Thousand Oaks, California 91320, USA

SAGE Publications Ltd
1 Oliver's Yard, 55 City Road
London EC1Y 1SP, United Kingdom

SAGE Publications Asia-Pacific Pte Ltd
3 Church Street
#10-04 Samsung Hub
Singapore 049483

ACCESS Development Services
28, Hauz Khas Village
New Delhi 110 016
www.accessdev.org

Published by Vivek Mehra for SAGE Publications India Pvt Ltd, Phototypeset in 10/13 pt Minion by Diligent Typesetter, Delhi, and printed at Saurabh Printers Pvt Ltd, Greater Noida.

Library of Congress Cataloging-in-Publication Data Available

ISBN: 978-93-515-0865-6 (PB)

The SAGE Team: Shambhu Sahu, Saima Ghaffar and Rajinder Kaur

Contents

List of Tables

List of Figures

List of Boxes

List of Annexures

List of Abbreviations

AAP	Annual Action Plan
ACF	Ambuja Cement Foundation
ADB	Asian Development Bank
ADFT	Agricultural Development Finance Tamil Nadu
ADS	Access Development Services
AFARM	Action for Agricultural Renewal in Maharashtra
AGM	Annual General Meeting
AH	Animal Husbandry
AI	Artificial Insemination
AKRSP	Aga Khan Rural Support Programme
ALC	Access Livelihoods Consulting
AMUL	Anand Milk Union Ltd
AP	Andhra Pradesh
APMC	Agricultural Produce Market Committee
APDDCF	Andhra Pradesh Dairy Development Cooperative Federation
ASA	Action for Social Advancement
ASDP	Aajeevika Skills Development Program
BAIF	Bharatiya Agro Industries Foundation
BC	Business Correspondent
BMC	Bulk Milk Cooler
BPL	Below Poverty Line
BPO	Business Process Outsourcing
BRLPS	Bihar Rural Livelihoods Promotion Society
B2B	Business-to-Business
BVD	Bovine Viral Diarrhoea
CACP	Commission for Agricultural Costs & Prices
CBO	Community-Based Organization
CBGA	Centre for Budget and Governance Accountability
CCD	Covenant Centre for Development
CCS	Centrally Sponsored Schemes
CDS	Current Daily Status
CEO	Chief Executive Officer
CET	Commissionerate of Employment and Training
CHCDS	Comprehensive Handloom Cluster Development Scheme
CIE	Cottage Industries Exposition Limited
CIF	Community Investment Fund
CIG	Common Interest Group
CII	Confederation of Indian Industry
CLC	City Livelihood Centres
CMSA	Community Managed Sustainable Agriculture
CPI	Consumer Price Index
CPR	Common Pool Resources

CRISIL	Credit Rating Information Services of India Limited
CSO	Central Statistical Office
CSR	Corporate Social Responsibility
DAY	Deen Dayal Upadhyaya Antyodaya Yojana
DBMG	Deshbandhu & Manju Gupta
DBT	Direct Benefit Transfer
DCAH	Deputy Commissioner of Animal Husbandry
DC	Development Commissioner
DCCB	District Central Cooperative Bank
DDU-GKY	Deen Dayal Upadhyaya Grameen Kaushalya Yojana
DGET	Directorate General of Employment and Training
DDUGJY	Deen Dayal Upadhyaya Gram Jyoti Yojana
DP	Displaced Person
DPIP	District Poverty Initiatives Project
DSC	Development Support Center
eFMS	electronic fund management system
EDP	Entrepreneurship Development Programme
EGMM	Employment Generation and Marketing Mission
EPCH	Export Promotion Council for Handicrafts
EU	European Union
FC	Farmers Collective
FCI	Food Corporation of India
FICCI	Federation of Indian Chambers of Commerce and Industry
FIG	Farmer Interest Groups
FMD	Foot and Mouth Disease
FMD-CP	Foot and Mouth Disease Control Programme
FPC	Farmer Producer Company
FPO	Farmers' Producers Organization
FRA	Forest Rights Act, 2006
FSA	Food Security Act, 2013
FSSAI	Food Safety and Standards Authority of India
FVTRS	Functional Vocational Training and Research Society
FWWB	Friends of Women's World Banking
FY	Financial Year
GCMMF	Gujarat Co-operative Milk Marketing Federation
GDP	Gross Domestic Product
GER	Gross Enrolment Ratio
GGRC	Gujarat Green Revolution Company
GIZ	Gesellschaftfür Internationale Zusammenarbeit
GoI	Government of India
GP	Gram Panchayat
GST	General Sales Tax
GVA	Gross Value Added
HDI	Human Development Index
HDR	Human Development Report
HIH	Hand in Hand
HR	Human Resources
IAMR	The Institute of Applied Manpower Research
IAY	Indira Awas Yojana
IBR	Infectious Bovine Rhinotracheitis

ICDS	Integrated Child Development Services
IFAD	International Fund for Agricultural Development
IFCN	International Farm Comparison Network
IFFCO	Indian Farmers Fertiliser Cooperative Limited
IFMR	Institute for Financial Management and Research
IGA	Income Generating Activity
ILO	International Labour Organization
IMR	Infant Mortality Rate
IRDP	Integrated Rural Development Program
IRMA	Institute for Rural Management Anand
IRR	Internal Rate of Return
IT	Information Technology
ITIs	Industrial Training Institutes
JAM	Jan Dhan Yojana, Aadhar, Mobile
JLG	Joint Liability Groups
KCC	Kisan Credit Card
KVIB	Khadi and Village Industries Board
KVIC	Khadi and Village Industries Commission
KVI	Khadi and Village Industry
Kg	Kilogram
KVK	Kaushalya Vardhan Kendras
LAMP	Livelihood and Microfinance Promotion Fund
MAH	Milch Animal Owning Household
MD	Managing Director
MDG	Millennium Development Goals
MDM	Midday Meal Scheme
MFI	Microfinance Institution
MGNREGA	Mahatma Gandhi National Rural Employment Guarantee Act
MIS	Management Information System
MKSP	Mahila Kisan Sashaktikaran Pariyojana
MMR	Maternal Mortality Ratio
MNC	Multinational Company
MNREGA	Mahatma Gandhi National Rural Employment Guarantee Act
MoF	Ministry of Finance
MoRD	Ministry of Rural Development
MoU	Memorandum of Understanding MT Metric Tonnes
MSME	Micro, Small & Medium Enterprises
MUDRA	Micro Units Development & Refinance Agency Ltd.
NABARD	National Bank for Agriculture and Rural Development
NABFINS	NABARD Financial Services Ltd.
NADP	National Agriculture Development Programme
NBFCs	non-banking financial companies
NCAER	National Council of Applied Economic Research
NCGTC	National Credit Guarantee Trustee Company
NCPB	National Control Program on Brucellosis
NCVT	National Council for Vocational Training
NDDB	National Dairy Development Board
NDP	National Dairy Plan
NDRI	National Dairy Research Institute
NDSP	National Dairy Support Project

NER	North Eastern Region
NFSA	National Food Security Act
NGOs	non-governmental organizations
NHDC	National Handloom Development Corporation
NITI	National Institution for Transforming India
NLM	National Livestock Mission
NMMU	National Mission Management Unit
NNI	Net National Income
NOS	National Occupational Standards
NREGA	National Rural Employment Guarantee Act
NREGS	National Rural Employment Guarantee Scheme
NRHM	National Rural Health Mission
NRLM	National Rural Livelihoods Mission
NRLP	National Rural Livelihoods Project
NSAP	National Social Assistance Programme
NSDA	National Skill Development Agency
NSDC	National Skill Development Corporation
NSDF	National Skill Development Fund
NSQC	National Skills Qualification Committee
NSQF	National Skills Qualification Framework
NSSO	National Sample Survey Organization
NULM	National Urban Livelihood Mission
NVIUC	National Vegetable Initiative around Urban Clusters
NYP	National Youth Policy
PACS	Primary Agricultural Credit Society
PACS	Poorest Areas Civil Society
PAP	Project-affected Person
PAT	profit after tax
PIA	Project Implementing Agencies
PMC	Primary Milk Collection Centre
PMEGP	Prime Minister's Employment Generation Programme
PMGSY	Pradhan Mantri Gram Sadak Yojana
PMJDY	Pradhan Mantri Jan Dhan Yojana
PMKVY	Pradhan Mantri Kaushal Vikas Yojana
PMMY	Pradhan Mantri Mudra Yojana
POP	poorest of the poor
POPI	Producer Organisation Promoting Institutions
PPP	Public Private Partnership
MSP	Minimum Support Price
PDS	Public Distribution System
PR	public relations
PRADAN	Professional Assistance for Development Action
PRC	Performance Review Committee
PRI	Panchayat Raj Institutions
PS	Principal Status
PSF	Price Stabilisation Fund
PSU	Public Sector Units
PVTG	Particularly Vulnerable Tribal Group
RBI	Reserve Bank of India

RBL	Ratnakar Bank Ltd
RBP	Ration Balancing Programme
RE	Revised Estimates
RGGY	Rajiv Gandhi Grameen Vidyutikaran Yojana
RIDF	Rural Infrastructure Development Fund
RKVY	Rashtriya Krishi Vikas Yojana
ROI	Return on Investment
RMoL	Rajasthan Mission on Livelihood
RRB	Regional Rural Banks
RTE	Right to Education Act, 2009
RTI	Right to Information Act, 2005
RSETI	Rural Self Employment Training Institutes
RSLDC	Rajasthan Skill and Livelihoods Development Corporation
RUDSETI	Rural Development and Self Employment Training Institute
SCB	State Co-operative Bank
SC	Scheduled Caste
SCMPL	Sahayog Clean Milk Private Limited
SDIS	Skills Development Initiative Scheme
SECC	Socio-economic and Caste Census
SEDI	Skills and Entrepreneurship Development Institutes
SERP	Society for Elimination of Rural Poverty
SETU	Self Employment and Talent Utilization
SFAC	Small Farmers' Agribusiness Consortium
SGSY	Swarnajayanti Gram Swarozgar Yojana
SHG	Self-help Group
SIA	Social Impact Assessment
SJSRY	Swarna Jayanti Shahari Rozgar Yojana
SL	sustainable livelihoods
SLI	Sustainable Livelihood Initiative
SMEs	small and medium enterprises
SMP	Skimmed Milk Powder
SNF	Solid Not Fat
SRLM	State Rural Livelihood Mission
SRTT	Sri Ratan Tata Trust
SS	Subsidiary Status
SSA	Sarva Shiksha Abhiyan
SSC	Sector Skill Council
ST	Scheduled Tribe
STAR	Standards Training Assessment and Reward
SVEP	Start-up Village Entrepreneurship Programme
STEPUP	Skill Training for Employment Protection amongst Urban Poor
UNDP	United Nations Development Programme
UPSS	Usual Principal and Subsidiary Status
USP	Unique Selling Proposition
UT	Union Territory
VAT	value added tax
VO	village organisation
WPI	Wholesale Price Index
YOY	Year-on-Year

Foreword

India's economy has witnessed a significant economic growth in the recent past, growing to 7.3 per cent in FY 2015 as against 6.9 per cent in FY 2014. The size of the Indian economy was estimated to be at US$ 2.01 trillion for the year 2014 as compared to US$ 1.84 trillion in 2013. This growth is powered by greater access to banking, technology adoption, urbanisation and other structural reforms.

Numerous foreign companies are setting up their facilities in India on account of various government initiatives like Make in India and Digital India. The Make in India initiative aims to boost the manufacturing sector of the Indian economy. Currently, the manufacturing sector in India contributes to over 15 per cent of the GDP. The Government of India—under the Make in India initiative—is trying to give a boost to the contributions made by the manufacturing sector and aims to take it up to 25 per cent of the GDP. This initiative is expected to increase the purchasing power of an average Indian consumer, which would further boost demand and hence, spur development. Besides this, the government has also come up with Digital India initiative, which focuses on three core components: creation of digital infrastructure, delivering services digitally and to increase the digital literacy. The *State of India's Livelihoods* (SOIL) *Report*, is about locating the impact of macroeconomic trends on the livelihoods of the poor.

Even as India continues to record fairly impressive growth rates, poverty remains widespread and disparities entrenched. It is these complexities that the 2015 edition of the SOIL Report tries to capture by exploring wide-ranging themes and the role of different actors in the context of livelihoods of the poor.

The opening chapter namely 'Overview: Taking Stock', explores the macroeconomic context of livelihoods which is seen to have improve gradually over the last two years or so. It also takes stock of other aspects of livelihoods apart from income enhancement by tracking the HDI and the progress on Millennium Development Goals. It looks at the significant changes in the pattern of funding by state governments for supporting different projects and programmes, resulting in key reductions to departments and programmes relating to livelihoods. It also touches briefly on livelihoods in agriculture and allied sectors as well as wage employment.

Chapter 2 namely 'Policy and Financing Framework for Livelihoods', provides an annual policy update centering the discussions around budget, policies, legislation and programmes relating to livelihoods like the Land Acquisition Bill, National Food Security Act, RRB Amendment Act and Labour Laws. Other developments such as the transitioning of erstwhile Planning Commission to NITI Aayog, National Policy on Skill Development and Entrepreneurship, Deen Dayal Upadhyaya Antyodaya Yojana and setting up of Price Stabilisation Fund for Horticultural Crops are also touched upon.

Chapter 3, 'Some Important Programmes in Livelihoods: Searching for Focus?', examines how some of the flagship programmes such as the Mahatma Gandhi National Rural Employment Guarantee Scheme, National Rural Livelihoods Mission, National Urban Livelihoods Mission and the Food Security Programme are designed, run and monitored.

Chapter 4, 'Dairy-based Livelihoods', provides a deep dive into the dairy sub-sector which is a key livelihood for a large number of rural households.

Chapter 5 ('Producer Companies') carries forward the conceptual and systemic underpinnings of producer companies in the Indian context covered in last year's report and makes an effort to dialogue with producer companies, their boards, members and other stakeholders, especially the promoting institutions in different states including some of the resource agencies.

Chapter 6, 'Skilling India: An Aspirational Challenge', puts the spotlight on skill development by presenting a picture of the present education and employment scenario, framework of initiatives to address the skill challenge, targets set for skilling by the government and a brief analysis of the major programmes for skill development and the results.

Chapter 7, 'Non-farm Sector Enterprises and Employment', looks at the key trends in the non-farm sector. Apart from an in-depth coverage of handloom, handicraft, khadi and village industries, other non-farm sector activities have been briefly touched upon.

Corporate Social Responsibility (CSR) has become a statutory responsibility for the Indian companies with the passing of the Companies Act, 2013. Chapter 8 looks at the private sector engagement in livelihoods and CSR through an analysis of CSR policies of a few companies, interventions of a few large corporates in the sphere of livelihoods, aggregate funding under CSR and challenges in the manner of companies engaging themselves in CSR. It looks at the 10 top-ranked companies in CSR and the range of activities that they engage in.

Bringing together the SOIL Report every year is an arduous task, given the complexity and diversity of issues, stakeholders and initiatives that need to be understood and analysed. While in the past we relied on a core group of authors to bring together the publication, to give the publication a greater cohesion and seamlessness across the report, a bold departure has been made during the year. ACCESS invited Girija and N. Srinivasan to write the full report. Given their great experience of many years and having earlier authored important ACCESS publications, this was well worth exploring. I'm glad that the two could pull it off and we have a well analysed report that takes into its sweep all the factors that influence opportunities for the poor. I thank them for this great effort.

I would like to take this opportunity to thank Rabobank Foundation, particularly Arindom for his continued support to the report and for reposing the faith in the ability of ACCESS to deliver on this critical sectoral report.

From within ACCESS, I would also like to thank my own team anchored by Ram for the support they provided to the process. Puja and Ila and the state teams ably supported the effort.

After a break of one year, we are going back to SAGE for publishing this report and I hope that with our combined efforts, we are able to reach an ever-increasing readership this year.

Vipin Sharma
CEO
ACCESS Development Services
New Delhi

Preface

SOIL (State of India's Livelihoods), as this report is aptly named, has a seven year history. Several scholars and practitioners of repute contributed to the previous years' reports that were brought out as edited volumes. When we agreed to author the report from end to end this year, we were aware that the venture is likely to be arduous. But little did we realise how much complex is livelihoods as a theme. While the diversity of activities and the geographical variations are well known, the differences in approaches, types of interventions and the differing flavours in understanding are usually not that well known. The livelihoods space is full of anecdotal evidence and project/programme-related information, but a picture of any single sub-sector within is available nowhere. The quality of information available varies from excellent to trivial. The making of this report has to do with putting together the available information, discussions with several authorities responsible for livelihood programmes and implementing agencies in voluntary and private sectors, besides field interactions in 11 states. While the commitment and passion is palpable in the field, strategic inputs from higher levels require strengthening. The impression that one gets is that conceptually, policy-thinking on livelihoods is short term whereas the requirements are long term. Interventions are more guided by available funds than anything else. As a result, the patience and perseverance required to make new institutions and approaches sustainable are in short supply.

We received enthusiastic support for the making of this report from a number of institutions and individuals. We thank Bharatiya Agro Industries Foundation (BAIF), Action for Agricultural Renewal in Maharashtra (AFARM), Hand in Hand, Srijan, BASIX, Access Livelihood Consulting, Catalyst Management Services, Initiatives for Development Foundation, Aga Khan Rural Support Programme, ICICI Foundation, Seva Mandir, Ambuja Foundation, Deshbandhu & Manju Gupta (DBMG) Foundation (Lupin group), Sahayog group and others. We are grateful to Al Fernandes and B.S. Suran of NABARD Financial Services Ltd (NABFINS); Girish Sohani, Bharat Kakade and Dr Ashok Pande of BAIF; T. Muralidharan and Vijay Kulkarni of CMS; Kalpana Shankar and Jeyaseelan of Hand in Hand; Ashish Mondal of Action for Social Advancement (ASA); Samson-GRAM; Vijayalakshmi Das of Friends of Women's World Banking (FWWB)/ANANYA finance; Gagan Sethi of Navjivan Foundation, Muthu Velayutham of Covenant Centre for Development (CCD); Amul Urdawareshe of Sahayog; Satya and Sarat Kumar of Access Livelihoods Consulting (ALC); Ambuj Kishore of Aravalli; Venkatesh Tagat, Vivekanand Salimath, Raosaheb Badhe, Vijay Subbiah, B.S. Shekawat and many more. More than 45 producer companies spared their time individually or in group meetings in Madhya Pradesh, Rajasthan, Maharashtra, Gujarat, Tamil Nadu, Karnataka, Andhra Pradesh and Telangana. We benefited from meeting people and organisations engaged in finding market access such as Pradeep and Sridhar of ANTS; Urmul, Ode to Earth, Raj Seelam -24 Mantra organic and others. We had excellent insights on government programmes, thanks mainly to S.P. Tucker, IAS, Special Chief Secretary (Planning), Andhra Pradesh; Rajiv Singh Thakur, IAS, Secretary, Rural Development, Rajasthan; Dr Sandhya Bhullar, IAS, Secretary, Labour and Employment, Gujarat; Ananth, Director, Animla Husbandry (AH), Telangana; Dr Dhananjay Parkale, Deputy Commissioner of Animal Husbandry (DCAH), Maharashtra; Dr G.U.K. Rao, Director, National Institute of Micro, Small and Medium Enterprises; Ishteyaque Jafri, Rajasthan Skill and Livelihoods

Development Corporation (RSLDC); C.L. Verma, Deputy Secretary, Rural Development, Rajasthan; Prashant Kumar, Executive Director, Employment Generation and Marketing Mission (EGMM), Telangana; A. Murali, IAS, CEO, Society for Elimination of Rural Poverty (SERP), Telangana; R.K. Sugoor, IFS, Joint Managing Director, Gujarat Green Revolution Company (GGRC); Mrinalini Shastry, Director, Livelihoods, SERP, AP, and many others.

NABARD provided excellent support with Dr Benugopal Mukhopadhyay and his team in Mumbai, Dr R.N. Kulkarni and his team in Bhopal, M.V. Ashok, P.V.S. Suryakumar, P. Satish, CGMs. Many others provided information and also linkages to sources of information. Our thanks are due to a number of skill and livelihood training providers like ILFS, Everonn Skill Development Limited, Functional Vocational Training and Research Society (FVTRS), Auroville, Swami Vivekananda Rural Community College, Mythili's Herbal Beauty School and Clinic, apart from others. The ACCESS teams in Jaipur, Udaipur, Hyderabad and Bhopal were of great help. The ACCESS team in New Delhi led by Ram Narayan anchored the report in many ways. Lalitha was her usual efficient self, facilitating all our field visits seamlessly. Our thanks to the advisory group members namely, Brij Mohanji, Arindom Datta, Meera Mishra, Vanita Suneja, Ashok Sircar, Sankar Datta, D. Narendranath, M.V. Ashok, Madhu Sharan and Madhukar Shukla, for their inputs about the report structure. A special thanks to Vipin who took the risk of handing over the entire report to two untested authors in SOIL. We know that we have been unable to acknowledge every institution and person who helped us. Our sincere apologies to those left out by our inadvertence.

The report just does not deal with income-generating activities but also includes some of the accompanying issues related to quality of life. It retains some of the structure of previous reports. It provides an overview, analyses the policies and funding framework through an examination of budget allocations, new policy pronouncements, large programmes initiated and legislative efforts that have a bearing on livelihoods. Four flagship programmes have taken up an assessment of performance. We have also examined the dairy sector in some depth as it provides substantial livelihood opportunities to vulnerable households. The idea is to take up one sub-sector each year for an in-depth study. A separate chapter looks at a topical theme of skill development in the country. Non-farm sector livelihoods, especially in handloom, handicrafts and village industries have been taken up for review. The aftermath of introduction of CSR obligations and private sector pro bono engagement with livelihoods have been examined. While we have sourced information from several sources, we are solely responsible for opinions expressed in the report and none else.

Being our first report, in this new format, a few rough edges are likely. We hope that in the coming years, the structure will settle down to a more comprehensive and balanced assessment of what happens in livelihoods. We need feedback from our readers in order to improve the content and the presentation of the report.

Girija Srinivasan   **Narasimhan Srinivasan**

Overview: Taking Stock

Livelihood literally is 'a means of making a living'. It encompasses people's capacities, assets, income and activities required to secure the means of living. Livelihood is sustainable when it enables people sustain a reasonable quality of life and cope with shocks and stresses that occur from time to time. Livelihood that is sustainable should help people enhance their well-being in the future without undermining the natural environment of the resource base. In the context of livelihood situation in India, several of these issues related to people's capacities, assets and opportunities will be examined. However, as stated by Sankar Datta in last year's report, livelihoods involve various other aspects of life apart from income enhancement. For example, the status of health and education, impact of climate change, government policies and strategies, and social safety nets are all a part of the livelihood situation.

The macroeconomic context of livelihoods has gradually improved over the last two years or so. The *Economic Survey*[1] says, "The macro-economy has been rendered more stable, reforms have been launched, the deceleration in growth has ended and the economy appears now to be recovering, the external environment is benign, and challenges in other major economies have made India the near-cynosure of eager investors." As per the new series of national accounts numbers, at the country level, gross domestic product (GDP) increased by 7.3 per cent in 2014–15 compared to 6.9 per cent in the previous year. Though there are some unresolved issues in changing the base year for national income statistics series from 2004–05 to 2011–12, the higher growth rate reported in GDP is a cause for optimism.[2] The *Economic Survey* concludes that GDP growth will be of the order of 8 per cent to 8.5 per cent in 2015–16.[3] This forecast is made on the basis of four factors, the first factor being the reforms that have been introduced and are being planned. The second stimuli to growth is expected to come from declining crude oil prices and the monitory easing expected to be carried out by the Reserve Bank of India (RBI) on account of moderate inflation. Thirdly, declining input costs led by a reduction in oil prices increase the profit margin and hence the investing sentiments of the corporate sector. Fourthly, declining inflation is also expected to boost household spending and borrowing for investment and consumption led by reduced interest rates.

---

[1] *The Economic Survey 2014–15*, Ministry of Finance, GoI.

[2] *The Economic Survey* says this about the new series of GDP, "These numbers seem difficult to reconcile with other developments in the economy. 2013–14 was a crisis year—capital flowed out, interest rates were tightened, there was consolidation—and it is difficult to see how an economy's growth rate could accelerate so much in such circumstances…. Regardless, the latest numbers will have to be the prism for viewing the Indian economy going forward because they will be the only ones on offer."

[3] RBI in its Monetary Policy Statement has fine-tuned its projection of growth to 7.2%.

Finally, the forecast of near normal monsoon is expected to boost agricultural GDP and the overall growth impetus.

Savings rate in the economy (Table 1.1) as a whole have been declining over the last few years, reflecting a declining capacity to invest in future. The gross capital formation rates have been seen to decline during the period, indicating that investments required to secure future livelihood development are not taking place at the expected pace. RBI noted[4] that

> the investment rate (gross capital formation as a proportion to GDP at current market prices) declined in 2012–13 and 2013–14, largely reflecting the slackening in the non-financial corporations' investment rate on account of weak domestic and external demand and other structural factors such as delay in land acquisition and environment clearances, weak business confidence and policy uncertainties.

Table 1.1:   Savings and capital formation rates

(2011–12 Constant prices)	2012–13	2013–14	2014–15
Gross savings rate as % of GDP	31.1	30	Yet to be released by CSO
Gross fixed capital formation as % of GDP	31.9	30.7	30
GDP growth rate %	5.1	6.9	7.3

Source: Central Statistical Office, Ministry of Statistics and Programme Implementation, GoI.

Figure 1.1:   Inflation behaviour–CPI year-on-year

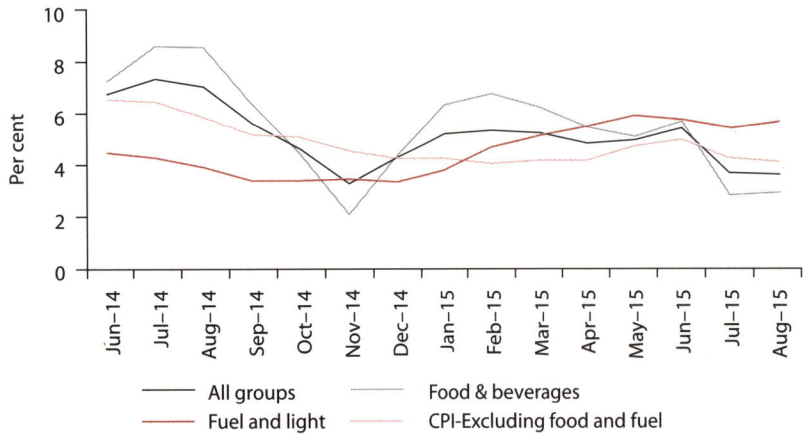

Source: Excerpted from Monetary Policy Report, September 2015, RBI.

[4] RBI Annual Report 2014–15, RBI 2015.

On the price front, inflation seems to be declining steadily since the past couple of years, thereby sustaining the value of incomes in the hands of people and leading to better quality livelihoods (Figure 1.1). In its latest Monetary Policy, RBI stated that the consumer price index (CPI) inflation had eased across the board over the first five months of 2015–16. The distribution of inflation across major sub-groups implied that the ongoing disinflation was broad-based. The easing of inflationary pressures was sufficient for RBI to reduce its repo rate by 50 basis points, bringing down the rate to 6.75 per cent.[5] Some banks have already announced a reduction in their base rate as a consequence; the resultant decrease in interest rates is expected to lower finance costs and induce investments. The expected investments that will follow the rate cut will positively impact the livelihoods situation in the country.

The votaries of trickle down theories find it difficult to explain the weak impact of robust macroeconomic growth on employment and livelihoods of the poor on the ground. While job growth has been positive, it has been at a very low rate. The high GDP numbers did not translate to high levels of employment growth (jobless growth)[6] which exacerbates the gap between the rich and the poor. A cause for concern is that new livelihoods, especially in the form of jobs are not created at a rate adequate to meet the increasing supply of labour force. The *Economic Survey 2015* points out:

> Regardless of which data source is used, it seems clear that employment growth is lagging behind growth in the labour force. For example, according to the Census, between 2001 and 2011, labour force growth was 2.23 per cent (male and female combined). This is lower than most estimates of employment growth in this decade of closer to 1.4 per cent. Creating more rapid employment opportunities is clearly a major policy challenge.

[5] The last time repo rate was at this level was in March 2011.

[6] 'GDP growth does not translate in to proportionately more jobs', *Economic Survey 2014–15*.

Table 1.2: Employment elasticity over the years

Year	Employment growth (CAGR)	GDP growth (CAGR)	Employment elasticity
1972–73 to 1977–78	2.6	4.6	0.57
1977–78 to 1983	2.1	3.9	0.54
1983 to 1988–87	1.7	4.0	0.42
1988–87 to 1993–94	2.4	5.6	0.43
1993–94 to 1999–2000	1.0	6.8	0.15
1999–2000 to 2004–05	2.8	5.7	0.50
2004–05 to 2009–10	0.1	8.7	0.01
2009–10 to 2011–12	1.4	7.4	0.18

Source: Sangita Mishra and Anup K. Suresh. June 2014. Estimating Employment Elasticity of Growth for the Indian Economy. RBI Working Paper Series. DEAR, RBI.

Employment elasticity measures the rate at which employment growth responds to GDP growth (Table 1.2). In the mid-seventies, one unit of growth in GDP resulted in 0.57 unit of growth in employment. In the period from 2004–09, the employment elasticity drastically declined to 0.01 units. Between 2009–12 and then between 2012–14, there was a continuing recovery in employment elasticity to 0.18 and 0.22 respectively. The implication is that economic growth does not automatically translate into jobs.

Quality of livelihoods

On the Human Development Index (HDI)—which is a qualitative measurement of livelihoods situation—the country has not made too much progress in terms of its global ranking. It continued to rank at 135 out of a total of 187 countries. However, there have been significant improvements reported in several areas related to the Millennium Development Goals [MDGs, (Table 1.3)]. The poverty head count ratio declined to 21.9 per cent

Table 1.3: Progress of actions under millennium development goals

Millennium development targets	State of progress
Poverty and Hunger	
Target 1: Halve, between 1990 and 2015, the proportion of people whose income is less than one dollar a day	On track
Target 2: Halve, between 1990 and 2015, the proportion of people who suffer from hunger	Slow off-track
Universal Primary Education	
Target 3: Ensure that, by 2015, children everywhere, boys and girls alike, will be able to complete a full course of primary schooling	Moderately on-track
Gender Equality and Empowerment	
Target 4: Eliminate gender disparity in primary and secondary education, preferably by 2005, and in all levels of education no later than 2015	On track
Child mortality reduction	
Target 5: Reduce by two-thirds, between 1990 and 2015, the Under- Five Morality Rate	Moderately on-track
Maternal health improvement	
Target 6: Reduce by three quarters, between 1990 and 2015, the maternal mortality ratio	Slow off-track
HIV/AIDS and disease control	
Target 7: Have halted by 2015 and begun to reverse the spread of HIV/AIDS	On-track
Target 8: Have halted by 2015 and begun to reverse the incidence of malaria and other major diseases	Moderately on-track

(Continued)

(Continued)

Millennium development targets	State of progress
Environmental Sustainability	
Target 9: Integrate the principle of sustainable development into country policies and programmes and reverse the loss of environmental resources.	Moderately on-track
Target 10: Halve, by 2015, the proportion of people without sustainable access to safe drinking water and basic sanitation	On-track for drinking water, slow in case of sanitation.
Target 11: By 2020, to have achieved a significant improvement in the lives of at least 100 million slum dwellers	Slum Dweller improvements difficult measure
Fostering partnerships in development	
Target 18: In cooperation with the private sector, make available the benefits of new technologies, especially information and communications	On track

Source: Millennium Development Goals, India Country Report, Ministry of Statistics and Programme Implementation, 2015.

as against the targeted 23.9 per cent by 2015. The poverty gap ratio significantly declined by more than a half. However, the proportion of underweight children continued to be at 33 per cent as compared to the targeted 26 per cent. School enrolments increased at the primary level to 88 per cent.

Even with all these improvements, the country did not do so well in reducing poverty and improving access to basic needs in education, health, sanitation and shelter as some of the other developing countries. The government has ambitious programmes aimed at improving livelihoods on the ground. The motto of 'Wiping every tear in every eye' towards which the government's policies and programmes have started working at is very well taken.

In this context, the problems of those who live in slums in towns and cities has to be examined to understand how the quality of life issues are dealt with. The National Sample Survey Organisation (NSSO)[7] estimated that about 8.8 million households live in about 33,500 slums. The Survey found that the situation in these slums had improved in some aspects. But with more slums cropping up, the proportion of slums that lacked basic

amenities had increased between 2009 and 2012. Sixty six per cent of the slums had *pucca* internal roads. Twenty four per cent of the slums benefited from slum improvement programme, whereas 31 per cent had not toilets and 30.9 per cent had no drainage. Garbage disposal—which should have been easier to arrange—was not available in 27 per cent of slums. Seventy one per cent slums had access to piped water and 93 per cent had electricity. But in case of water supply, electricity supply, toilet facilities and roads, the situation was better in 2009. Slum population is the most vulnerable, both in social and economic sense. Apart from dealing with income-producing livelihoods, attention to quality of life issues is also necessary.

Devolution of resources to states: Can development burden be shifted from centre?

The Union Budget of 2015–16 made significant changes to the pattern of funding state government for supporting different projects and programmes. In the process of changes to the funding patterns and devolution of revenues to states, significant reductions to key departments and the livelihood initiatives have been noticed. Agriculture, rural development and education-related

---

[7] Key Indicators of Urban Slums in India, NSS 69th Round, Ministry of Statistics and Programme Implementation (MoSPI), GOI, December 2013.

programmes have seen reduction in budget in current terms and in real terms, the cuts would be even more severe.[8] In case of health, the allocations have been marginally more than the previous year, but this too in real term, may not amount to an increased allocation of resources. From the central government's budget, the allocation of resources for areas that directly support livelihoods or strengthen livelihoods by supporting other necessary activities has been less than desired. The Centre for Budget and Governance Accountability (CBGA) in its budget analysis pointed out that, "The reduced expenditures also throw light on the lack of priority accorded to the social sector commitments of the Union government. The Union budget categorically states that due to the higher devolution of taxes to the states the Normal Central Assistance, Special Plan Assistance, Special Central Assistance and Additional Central Assistance for other purposes are subsumed in the award itself. Eight schemes have been discontinued and some Centrally Sponsored Schemes would be implemented with a changed pattern of sharing of resources, with States to contribute higher share." Given the current trends, the estimates are that the overall spend on rural and social sector by the Centre and states will actually decline. Without the pressure of tied funding, states might choose to do their own thing rather than investing in productive areas of the economy. However, the promises are that the budgetary allocations would be used with much greater efficiency on account of streamlined processes. This is something that will be watched with a great deal of interest.

Livelihoods in agriculture and allied activities

Despite the changes in contribution of agriculture to GDP, a number of households depend on agriculture for their livelihood. The Economic Census found out that

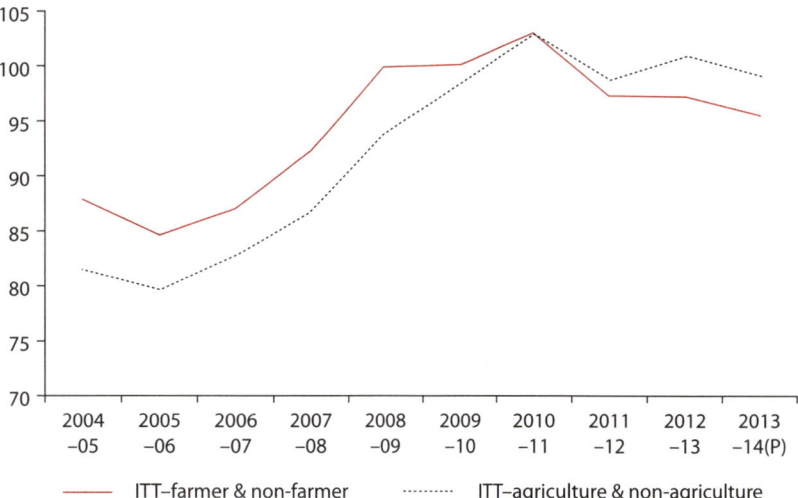

Figure 1.2: Terms of trade in agriculture

— ITT–farmer & non-farmer .... ITT–agriculture & non-agriculture

Source: Economic Survey 2014–15, Ministry of Finance, GoI.

30 per cent of rural households depended on cultivation as their source of income. Fifty one per cent depended on manual labour and they were both in agriculture and other types of labour depending on seasonality and work availability. Thus, a large part of rural people continue to depend on agriculture and allied activities for their livelihoods. However, the performance of agriculture has been lacklustre. At the farm level, there were a number of crops in which profitability was either low or negative. Farming continued to be affected by rising input costs and muted output prices. The *Economic Survey* points out that the index of terms of trade[9] in agriculture (both between farmers and non-farmers, agriculture and non-agriculture) which was moving in favour of the farmers has reversed the trend in the last four years (Figure 1.2).

Murthy and Misra (2012)[10] found that the economics of paddy farming was adverse in Andhra Pradesh (AP) over the last few years. The increasing input costs

---

[8] See Chapter 2 for a more detailed discussion on this aspect.

[9] These are calculated as a proportion of the prices received to prices paid. When prices received are more than 100, then the terms of trade in the sector are favourable for those who depend on it.

[10] Pricing of Paddy, A Case Study of Andhra Pradesh by R.V. Ramana Murthy, University of Hyderabad and Rekha Misra, RBI, published by DEAP, RBI 2012.

Table 1.4:   Profitability of paddy production in Andhra Pradesh

Year	Grade	Cost of production (₹/qtl.)	MSP proposed by agrl. Dept (₹/qt)	MSP fixed by GOI (₹/qtl.)
2008–09	Common	921	1,382	900+50 (Bonus)
	Grade-A	963	1,445	930+50 (Bonus)
2009–10	Common	1,038	1,557	950+50 (Bonus)
	Grade-A	1,093	1,640	980+50 (Bonus)
2010–11	Common	1,092	1,646	1,000
	Grade-A	1,121	1,682	1,030
2011–12	Common	1,270	1,905	1,080
	Grade-A	1,355	2,033	1,110

Source: Pricing of Paddy, A Case Study of Andhra Pradesh by R.V. Ramana Murthy and Rekha Misra.

and marketing costs were not covered by the minimum support price (MSP) fixed. Further, in the absence of active procurement in the state, farmers got much less than the MSP (Table 1.4). The study also commented that the cost calculations of Commission for Agricultural Costs & Prices (CACP) were understated and not realistic, leading to lower MSP.

The Situation Assessment Survey of Farmers[11] revealed that in five states, farmers reported that the income was less than their expenditure (Table 1.5). These were averages across all classes of farmers. In case of small farmers, the income pressure was likely to have been higher.

The truancy of monsoon in the last two years made farm-based livelihoods difficult. The increasing suicides of farmers apart from signalling high levels of distress in

Table 1.5:   Deficit in income to meet expenditure

State	Monthly deficit in income to meet expenditure
Bihar	1,900
Tripura	1,500
Uttarakhand	1,000
Uttar Pradesh	1,300
West Bengal	1,900

Source: Key Indicators of Situation of Agricultural Households in India, NSSO 70th Round.

[11] Key Indicators of Situation of Agricultural Households in India, NSSO 70th Round, MoSPI, December 2014.

some pockets of the country also put pressure on the government. The aspects that small farms will benefit most from will be focus on water, productivity, risk mitigation and markets. While in the current year, the Government of India (GoI) has made irrigation a priority, the Rashtriya Krishi Vikas Yojana (RKVY) has been put on the back-burner. The crop-per-drop initiative and optimising water use will go a long way in improving agricultural production and promoting cost efficiencies through better input use. But transferring the National Agriculture Development Programme (NADP) to states may not result in positive outcomes. Given the variability in implementation rigour and efficiency in different states, support to agriculture might suffer in a number of states. Crop insurance has not been popular as it was not effective as a risk mitigant. The weather-index based insurance has been gaining some ground in recent years, but still has a long way to go. Across the country, crop insurance covers about 15 per cent of acreage and less than five per cent of the value of crops produced. Instead of focusing on the risks and access to viable markets, money and effort is expended on credit and other input supplies. Livelihoods in agriculture require a value chain-based approach that minimises risks with a market orientation. There are locations, and crops in which it had been possible to orient production towards a market and thus stabilize livelihoods.

Producer collectives as an option for aggregating farmers and providing them with complete solutions for input, technology and marketing seem promising. The pace of registration of producer companies has increased in the last two years with support from organisations such as Small Farmers' Agribusiness Consortium (SFAC), National Bank for Agriculture and Rural Development (NABARD) and a number of promoting organisations. These institutions have a long learning curve and attempts to shorten the duration of learning will result in failures. The support systems and initial funding should be adequate to support the initial period of five to eight years, depending on location and characteristics of members. A review of the support mechanisms and funding arrangements is necessary.

Wage employment

As indicated earlier, the services sector has expanded exponentially. The new economy jobs in communication, health, education, information technology (IT) and logistics have opened up several avenues. Start-ups, small enterprises, own account self-employed services and wage employment have been vigorously increasing in mobile-based services, financial services, television and media-related services, as also courier and logistics. The e-commerce revolution is making a number of career options possible and thus generates livelihoods of a different nature. Some of these jobs do not require very high levels of skills but adequate training to develop a raw person into a semi-skilled one. Preparing the work force for the new economy's jobs is a critical requirement. The need for incremental people to be employed in security services, courier services, mobile-related services, cable TV-related services is projected to be very high. Some of these require minimum technical skills. In others, right aptitude is required. Identifying people for these sectors and building their capacities is a challenge. In a separate chapter on skills development, some of the issues in building skills are covered in greater detail. The initiative to upgrade the skills of a large number of people in the country is thus a very timely and appropriate one. We must ensure that the funds allocated and the efforts taken are well spent and result in meaningful livelihoods.

A cause for concern is that new livelihoods, especially in the form of jobs, are not created at a rate adequate to meet the increasing supply of labour force. The *Economic Survey 2015* points out:

> Regardless of which data source is used, it seems clear that employment growth is lagging behind growth in the labour force. For

example, according to the Census, between 2001 and 2011, labour force growth was 2.23 per cent (male and female combined). This is lower than most estimates of employment growth in this decade of closer to 1.4 per cent. Creating more rapid employment opportunities is clearly a major policy challenge.

The phenomenon of jobless growth is heard of more frequently now than in the past. Economic growth in terms of GDP does not translate into jobs. The declining employment elasticity over the years in India (Table 1.2) has been attributed to increasing labour productivity, shifting of labour from low productivity sectors to high productivity sectors and investment decisions that focus on non-labour intensive sectors. The Planning Commission task force for the 12th five year plan projected an employment elasticity of 0.31 in the best case and 0.24 in the worst case scenarios and came up with projections ranging from 59 to 28 million new jobs over the period 2012 to 2017, depending on the varying GDP growth and factor productivity assumptions. The task force highlighted some basic issues in the light of changes taking place in the structure, location and nature of employment. The first of these is the migration taking place from agriculture to non-agriculture work and from rural to urban areas as these jobs carry better wages. This is a transformative change but whether the new jobs that replace the old ones are 'decent work' is an issue to be dealt with. Employment security and income security issues have to be addressed for the migrant people. The second issue is that of transition of labour from informal jobs in unorganised sectors to informal jobs in organised sectors. This is a welcome change as it improves the quality of employment and usually based on a contract that is enforceable. The third type of change is the shift from unorganised sector jobs or informal jobs to formal, organised sector jobs. This is the best possible outcome but given the profile of employment in different sectors, this is likely to happen to a small percentage of labour force.

While it is easy to hire and maintain informal and unorganised sector jobs and these jobs account for most of the employment in the country, in terms of gross value added (GVA), the formal, organised sector has a much higher share. The Planning Commission task force for the 12th five year plan observed, "Unorganised manufacturing contributes to 85 per cent of total manufacturing employment in the Indian economy, while organised manufacturing's contribution is only 15 per cent (2004–05). On the other hand, for GVA, the contribution of the organised segment is the exact opposite, that is, 78 per cent, while the share of the unorganised segment of manufacturing is 22 per cent of total GVA in manufacturing in the economy. Similarly, in non-manufacturing industry (i.e., gas, electricity, mining and construction), the share of the unorganised segment is 69 per cent in employment but only 32 per cent in GVA. On the contrary, for GVA, the contribution of the organised segment is 68 per cent for GVA while the unorganised segment employs 69 per cent of all workers engaged in non-manufacturing industry. For services, the contributions to employment and GVA of the organised and unorganised segments are very different as well. Organised services contribute 27 per cent of all employment in services, but twice as much to total GVA produced by services in the economy. Unorganised services, on the other hand, are very significant in terms of employment generation (73 per cent of all services' sector employment), but contribute much less (45 per cent) than organised services (55 per cent) of all service sector GVA." The inference is that, creation of unorganised sector jobs and informal jobs depends on the prospects of growth in the sector in which they are situated and can disappear at the first signs of a downturn.

Skill development is an important part of government's strategy for dealing with creation of employment for the increasing labour force, increasing productivity for the employers and for realising the potential of demographic dividend. But the resources required to build skills in the projected numbers are far too large. The projected demand for labour in some official documents may be exaggerated. For the present, the structuring of meaningful curriculum, identifying good training providers and enhancing their skills, finding private sector collaborations for placement in jobs and improving the environment for microenterprises creation are the priorities. Over the next two years, the nature of challenges in skilling for employability will unfold and that would be the right time to refine strategies. Private sector's involvement in skill building of the youth has been significant as seen in several programmes. Skill development offers the corporates a significant opportunity to fulfil the CSR mandate recently stipulated.

The government is aware of the minimum needs to keep poverty away and raise minimum wage levels under its programmes. The states have followed suit and raised minimum wages across sectors and skill levels. Despite such action, the growth rate in rural wages has registered a decline. The decline has been almost secular for about four years now. A comparison with the CPI shows (Figure 1.4) that it declined between 2010 and 2012, but again reversed the trend and started increasing. However, the wage levels have been on a decline (Figure 1.3). While the *Economic Survey 2014–15* concludes that this will lessen the overall inflationary pressures in the economy, the pressure on the fragile incomes of the poor households should be a matter of concern.

The policies of the State should influence investments towards sectors where employment elasticity is high. To encourage investments in labour intensive industries and global scale units, the Labour Laws require a review. The existing Labour Law framework, while exhaustive and painfully intrusive, does not protect the interests of labourers. Investments in labour productivity are critical. The recent momentum given to skilling labour is a step in the right direction. Apart from skilling labour, issues in Contract

Figure 1.3:   Rural wage growth

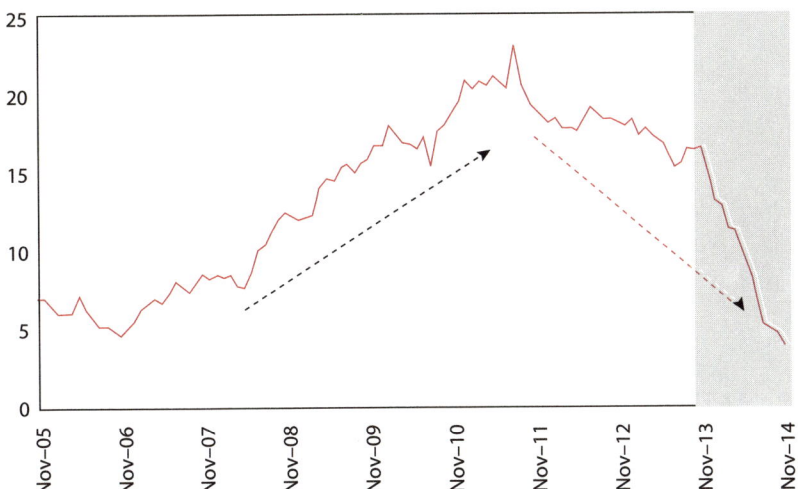

Source: Based on Labour Bureau data. Excerpted from *Economic Survey 2014–15*, Ministry of Finance, GoI.

Figure 1.4:   CPI for rural labourers

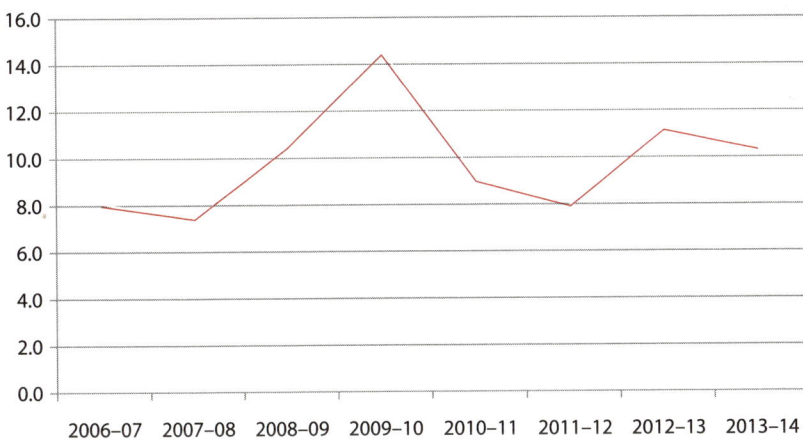

Source: Labour Bureau, GoI.

Labour Legislation should also be reviewed to ensure that workers get a fair deal and 'decent work'. In case of microenterprises and own account units, facilitating access to markets (whether for inputs, outputs, credit or technology) is a prime requirement and not Subsidy Schemes that keep the enterprises barely alive on artificial support systems.

Public finances

Government's spending: Shifting from subsidies to productive areas

The spending by government has, over the last many years, shifted from non-plan expenditure to non-productive areas. While most of these expenditures are unavoidable, there have been profligate tendencies in some ill-designed large programmes. The investments in productive capital stock have to increase. This requires that the government finds resources that can be invested to boost capital formation. The high subsidy budget carried on for several years now is limiting the capacity for investments in future growth and development.

Of the subsidied food, fertiliser and oil subsidies accounted for ₹2,539 billion in 2014–15 and the current year's budget rightly slashed it down by about 10 per cent (Table 1.6). But the Food Subsidy Bill is as

Table 1.6: The subsidy bill 2015–16

Head	Budget provision (₹ billions)
Food (including NFSA)	1,244.19
Fertiliser	729.68
Petroleum	300.00
Interest subvention to industrial units in Andhra Pradesh and Telangana	1.00
Interest subsidy to LIC for Pension Plan of senior citizens	1.02
Interest subvention for providing Short Term Credit to farmers	130.00
Interest subsidy to banks under export promotion	16.25
Interest subsidies to khadi and village industries	0.26
Scheme for extending financial assistance to sugar undertaking in 2014	8.00
Susidy on import of pulses	0.10
Total	2,430.50

Source: Based on Budget documents of Union Budget 2015–16, MoF, GoI. There are a few other subsidies which are not listed here because the amounts involved are not significant.

yet unquantified as the full impact of the National Food Security Act (NFSA) implementation will be known by the middle of the current fiscal year 2015–16 (Table 1.6). If the NFSA is implemented as envisaged, the Subsidy Bill could be about five times more than what is provided on a conservative estimate[12] (Chapter 2 has a detailed analysis of the NFSA and its implementation). The cutting down of subsidies, targeting their destination and building leakage free channels of delivery are the major tasks before the government. This will free resources for investing in productive areas of the economy that can support enterprises, employment and livelihoods. According to the *Economic Survey*[13] this also

> requires proactive support from the government in the form of a well-functioning, well-targeted, leakage-proof safety net that will both provide minimum income and protect against adverse shocks. This is also true in rural India where economic conditions for farmers and labourers are under stress. The policy issue now is no longer whether but how best to 'provide and protect…'

[12] The food security bill could be as high as ₹7,500 billion.

[13] The economic survey 2014–15, Ministry of Finance, Government of India.

The JAM trinity[14] is to be used to cut down the delivery costs and leakages in benefits transfer from government to target households (Box 1.1). The operational modalities of direct benefit transfer (DBT) to banks accounts has already been tested in case of cooking gas subsidies, where the government has shifted from subsidising the gas at the purchase point to providing cash equivalent directly to the identified consumers. The pace of Aadhar registration in some states, the Supreme Court's ruling that takes away the element of compulsion in production of Aadhar numbers for entitlements and the dormancy of recently opened bank accounts for several reasons, are likely to prove as dampners for the immediate roll-out of JAM-based DBT.

Box 1.1: *Cutting down subsidy expenditure through smart IT-based delivery*

Cash transfers can also augment the effectiveness of existing anti-poverty programmes like the Mahatma Gandhi National Rural Employment Guarantee Act (MGNREGA). A recent study reported evidences from AP where MGNREGA and social security payments were paid through Aadhar-linked bank accounts. Households received payments faster with the new Aadhar-linked DBT system and leakages decreased so much that the value of fiscal savings—due to reduced leakages—was eight times greater than the cost of implementing the programme. Much of the leakage reduction resulting from biometric identification stems from fewer ghost beneficiaries. Indeed, the government is realising the gains from DBT areas by paying cooking gas subsidies directly into the bank accounts of 9.75 crore recipients. Today there are about 125.5 million Jan Dhan bank accounts, 757 million Aadhar numbers and approximately 904 million mobile phones. It is possible to envisage that when the JAM trinity becomes linked, the goal of periodic and seamless

[14] The Jan Dhan Yojana, Aadhar, Mobile numbers form this trinity.

Credit Rating Information Services of India Limited (CRISIL) in its Budget Analysis[15] notes:

Direct benefit transfer, or DBT, will likely prove to be a game changer in food subsidy….DBT will help bring millions of poor households that currently do not have access to PDS into the food subsidy net. At fiscal 2016 prices, the cash transfers under the DBT will amount to almost ₹5,800 per year for a family of five, which will implicitly raise their disposable income. At first glance, ₹5,800 may seem small, but it is higher than the reported total annual expenditure (food+non-food) of the poorest 5 per cent of the rural households and more than half the annual expenditure of the poorest 10 per cent of urban households. Given the high marginal propensity to consume at lower income levels, such a significant unconditional cash transfer will undoubtedly raise discretionary spending of the recipient households, providing a consumption boost the economy.

However, the JAM trinity by itself cannot lead to sustainable livelihoods as it just provides a pipeline to specific individuals for transfer of payments. Improvements in the economic situation of the account holders depend on transfer of welfare funding to the people. Welfare payments can only go some distance in sustaining livelihoods. The people may require a more sustainable footing of either employment or enterprise.

Taxes and debt

The government policies and programmes result in a favourable environment for livelihoods to survive and prosper. The policies favour those who are vulnerable, with the support of those who can afford to help the government to fulfil its responsibility. The taxation policies pursued over the last few years show distinct tilt towards indirect taxes that are regressive and moving away from direct taxes. As part of the reform measures, the tax regime should also be reviewed in its entirety. The tax GDP ratio should increase with a greater direct tax collection effort so that vulnerable people do not have to pay disproportionately out of meagre incomes towards taxes. The public debt situation is said to be under control with the fiscal responsibility cast of governments. Rough estimates show that the average debt per capita in the country in March 2015 was about ₹47,800 (Table 1.7). Seen against the per capita net national income of ₹74,104, the debt burden amounts to eight months of income. The Situation Assessment Survey[16] brought out that a farmer on an average has a surplus of (income above expenditure) ₹2,400 a year. The public debt burden in an average farmer's case works out to be 20 years of the surplus. The fact that public debt has to repaid by the people out of their earnings should influence the design and implementation of policies and programmes.

The past year had not been one of performance in the field. But it was rich with new programmes and policies and fine-tuning of existing programmes. The year seems to have been used up in carrying out reality checks of what is needed to be done in the different sectors. Some actions such as rolling out the Jan Dhan Yojana

Table 1.7: Debt burden on citizens

Aspect	2015
Total debt (₹ billion)	57,945.33
Population (billion)	1.21
Per capita debt (₹)	47,889
Per capita net national income (NNI) (₹)	74,104

Source: Authors.

---

[15] CRISIL Budget Analysis, CRISIL Research, February 2015.

[16] Key Indicators of Situation of Agricultural Households in India, NSSO 70th Round, MoSPI, December 2014.

and the accompanying insurance schemes, setting up of Micro Units Development & Refinance Agency Ltd. (MUDRA) bank, dismantling of Planning Commission, instituting the National Institution for Transforming India (NITI) Aayog and galvanising the public service machinery into action, took most of the time. The erstwhile flagship programmes such as National Rural Employment Guarantee Scheme (NREGS) and National Rural Livelihoods Mission (NRLM) that actually worked in the livelihoods space did not get enough attention. The Skill India Initiative tries to bring under one umbrella all the issues relating to employment and enterprise creation. Looking ahead, there is hope that with the spadework having been done, the government will get down to the nitty-gritty of delivering results on the ground.

The rest of this report is divided into seven chapters to examine the livelihoods-related policies, budget and legislation, some large and important livelihoods sustaining programmes, skill development efforts, non-farm sector livelihoods, private sector's engagement in livelihoods of the poor and functioning and functionality of producer collectives. A special chapter on dairying—a major livelihood sub-sector—tries to delve into the various aspects of the dairy value chain. A concluding piece tries to summarize the different suggestions and looks at the way forward.

Policy and Financing Framework for Livelihoods

Budget, policies, legislation and programmes

The government has the declared mission of 'wiping the tear from every eye' of the poor population in the country. It also promised maximum governance through corruption-free government and leakage-proof processes for delivery of development services and benefits to people. Over the last 15 months, government has taken several actions in line with its promise. The government recognises challenges arising from limited fiscal space, business environment and volatility in global finance and trade. A possibility of oil price hike and continuing deterioration in global trade environment are potential threats. In agriculture specifically, the government recognised the declining capital formation rates and the deteriorating terms of trade as problems to be addressed. Amidst the challenges, there are also opportunities offered by the young workforce, a start-up culture that thrives on information and communication technology (ICT), a strong domestic market and a promise of good governance. The government is not only planning the future in economic terms alone but also doing it in many other ways as reflected in the Swachh Bharat Abhiyan (clean India), Digital India (to make government services available electronically), Shramev Jayate (dignity of labour) and Beti Bachao, Beti Padhao (save girl child, educate girl child) campaigns. There are signs of easing the regulatory barriers for entry and operation of business. The policies and programmes of the government have to be seen in the context of new hope tempered with an understanding of the challenges.

Union budget 2015–16

In a bid to improve the macro situation, the government formulated a budget[1] with the key strategy of promoting cooperative federalism under which the state governments would be provided more of public revenue resources so that they could decide on the priorities of development in their respective areas. The Budget seeks to improve the operating environment for agriculture and also create greater opportunities for self and wage employment for those not engaged in agriculture. The government has a very clear vision of where in the long run it would like the country to move to. In the Budget, the Finance Minister has talked about a vision to be realised by 2022. This vision—outlined in the Union Budget 2015 (Box 2.1)—envisages access to education, health, electricity and connectivity, both physical and electronic, as well as jobs. The Budget seeks to improve agricultural productivity and incomes and charges industries with creation of jobs, skilling of youth being the responsibility of the State. The resources required to realise

[1] This was the first full budget of this government. The last budget was for a part of the year and prepared in great haste.

Chapter 2

Box 2.1: *Making India a global power*

Vision of India

(i) A roof for each family in India. Complete 2 crore houses in urban areas and 4 crore houses in rural areas.

(ii) Each house in the country should have basic facilities of 24-hour power supply, clean drinking water, a toilet, and be connected to a road.

(iii) At least one member from each family should have access to the means for livelihood and, employment or economic opportunity, to improve his or her lot.

(iv) Substantial reduction of poverty and elimination absolute poverty.

(v) Electrification, by 2020, of the remaining 20,000 villages in the country,

(vi) Connecting 1,78,000 unconnected habitations by all weather roads. completing 1,00,000 km of roads and building 1,00,000 km of new roads.

(vii) Providing medical services in each village and city.

(viii) Educating and skilling our youth through quality education. Upgrade over 80,000 secondary schools and add or upgrade 75,000 junior/middle, to the senior secondary level.

(ix) Increase in agricultural productivity and realization of reasonable prices. Increase the irrigated area, improve the efficiency of irrigation systems, promote agro-based industry and secure reasonable prices for farm produce.

(x) Ensure connectivity to all the villages and remove rural-urban divide

(xi) The Skill India and the Make in India to create jobs for youth.

(xii) Encourage and grow entrepreneurship and support new start-ups.

(xiii) Develop Eastern and North Eastern regions to be on par with the rest of the country.

By the time of the 75th year of Indian independence, Amrut Mahotsav of our independence is reached, we have to achieve all of the above, so that India becomes a prosperous country; and a responsible global power.

Source: Reproduced from the Union Budget speech, 2015–16.

---

this vision are massive and not necessarily of the financial kind. The ideas, technology and human resources needed to be mobilised to realise this vision are of a larger order and hopefully planning for this would be equally robust. The Prime Minister (PM) also announced the 'Make in India' campaign to stimulate manufacturing growth and expand gainful employment opportunities. Twenty five sectors have been selected for skill enhancement and job creation so that manufacturing growth in these sectors contributes to nation building. This announcement by the PM was followed by easing of procedures for licenses and approvals and increased investment limits for foreign entities. In a significant move, the government allowed up to 49 per cent foreign investments in defence-related manufacturing units and 100 per cent foreign investments in railways-related units. The Budget gives a fillip to the Make in India campaign which focuses on select sectors with growth and employment potential. The government is concentrating on ensuring ease of doing business. For example, to reduce the barriers at entry stage for industries, a critical initiative is troubleshooting that is being undertaken by the Project Monitoring Group (PMG) in the Cabinet Secretariat. The Group actively engages with central and state governments to debottleneck projects that are stuck on account of environment clearances, land acquisition or other state/central level clearances in major infrastructure sectors, both Public and Private sector.

Significant theme of current year's budget is democratic federalism under which most of development and social sector responsibilities have been pushed towards the state governments. The Centre retains the core minimum of larger programmes with significant impact potential. Also, the Centre provides assistance to national schemes that have a legislative backing such as food subsidy and the NREGS. The restructuring of the state-centre financial relationship proposed by the 14th Finance Commission had been utilised for a thorough overhaul of the development schemes supported by the central government. Twenty four planned schemes have been discontinued from coverage by the Centre for revenue expenditure. A large number of significant and flagship schemes from the past formed a part of this list such as the RKVY, NRLM, National Urban Livelihoods Mission (NULM), Indira Awaas Yojana (IAY), cattle development schemes, Mission for Integrated Development of Horticulture (MIDH), National Livestock Mission (NLM), National Mission for Sustainable Agriculture (NMSA), Dairy Vikas Abhiyan, Veterinary Service & Animal Health Programme, National Afforestation Programme (NAP), etc. All these schemes are now expected to be taken over by the states and funded out of increased devolution of tax revenues made available by the central government. As part of its revamp, the Centre has also discontinued some schemes from the current year onwards. Some of these schemes were found useful in the past for supporting certain areas that impacted livelihoods. Backward Regions

Grant Fund (BRGF), National Mission on Food Processing (NMFP) and Rajiv Gandhi Panchayat Sashaktikaran Abhiyan (RGPSA) as also the National e-Governance Plan (NeGP), are some of the important programmes which potentially had an impact on livelihoods. Their discontinuation might impair current livelihoods on the ground as well as impact future options for the youth. The Model School Scheme that aimed at setting up 6,000 model schools across the country has also been dropped, despite reduced access to education among the poorer households even in those areas where stoppage of the scheme is likely to have an adverse impact.

One of the significant (and somewhat disturbing) features of the Budget is reduction in the Central Plan Outlay for the rural sector. In 2009–10, the total actual expenditure of Ministry of Agriculture was of the order of ₹158.56 billion (Table 2.1). It increased to ₹266.23 billion in the year 2014–15. The Budget for 2015–16 estimates Ministry of Agriculture's budget at ₹249.10 billion and this includes the extra allocations made during the year for setting up a national agricultural market. However, the

Table 2.1: Sector-wise central plan outlays

Central plan outlay					(in ₹ crore)
					Variation between BE 2015–16 and BE 2014–15
	2013–14 (Actual)	2014–15 (BE)	2014–15 (RE)	2015–16 (BE)	
Sectors–central plan	1	2	3	4	5
Agriculture and allied activities	17,788	11,531	10,199	11,657	126
Rural Development	51,757	3,082	1,877	3,131	49
Irrigation and flood control	441	1,797	896	772	−1,025
Energy	182,388	166,275	154,878	167,342	1,067
Industry and Minerals	33,433	40,209	39,397	43,113	2,904
Transport	103,959	116,202	106,242	193,417	77,215
Communications	16,209	13,009	13,027	12,032	−977
Science, technology and Environment	13,535	18,792	14,821	19,023	231
General Economic Services	26,064	26,318	17,303	20,333	−5,985
Social Services	150,736	79,411	64,284	81,003	1,592
General Services	7,263	7,906	3,887	26,559	18,653
Grand Total	**603,573**	**434,532**	**426,811**	**578,382**	**93,850**

Source: Budget documents of Ministry of Finance, GoI.

Table 2.2: Combined current and capital expenditure of centre and states on agriculture and rural development (₹ billion)

	1990–91	2000–01	2005–06	2009–10	2010–11	2011–12	2012–13	2013–14
Agriculture allied	117.14	308.21	584.27	1,270.91	1,446.43	1,509.11	1,886.62	2,128.27
Of which rural development	51.47	147.28	367.67	741.58	835.98	850.15	1,021.24	1,146.18
Net agriculture and allied	65.67	160.93	216.60	529.33	610.45	658.96	865.38	982.09
Irrigation major	32.78	120.71	248.64	346.05	346.70	363.27	430.34	505.75
Irrigation minor	14.82	28.88	53.44	100.93	121.26	130.45	170.36	203.45
Total irrigation	47.60	149.59	302.08	446.98	467.96	493.72	600.70	709.20
Capital expenditure on agriculture	6.67	37.11	55.42	164.24	126.06	173.41	195.42	237.87
Agriculture and irrigation	113.27	310.52	518.68	976.31	1,078.41	1,152.68	1,466.08	1,691.29
Total budget expenditure	1,526.01	5,448.32	9,292.06	18,103.75	21,060.41	23,478.32	27,284.07	31,916.55

Source: Indian Public Finance Statistics 2013–14, Economic Division, Ministry of Finance, Government of India; Agricultural Statistics at a Glance 2014, Ministry of Agriculture.

focus on agriculture and rural development over the years seems to have been declining (Table 2.2).

The Budget allocations for agriculture, rural development and irrigation—which form the core of support to livelihoods—declined from 11.6 per cent of the total budget allocation in 2009–10 to 2.7 per cent in 2015–16. While the allocations in 2015–16 may be explained by the greater devolution of resources to states, it is difficult to explain the decline in 2014–15 during which the allocation to these sectors was only three per cent. The Budget allocations also have to be seen in the context of contribution of agricultural sector to GDP which is around 15 per cent. The data relating to Budget expenditure by states and Centre on agriculture, allied activities, irrigation and rural development was examined. The analysis shows that as a percentage of total budgetary expenditure, agriculture and allied services got an allocation of 10.8 per cent in 1991. While over the years, the level has been fluctuating, it declined to 8.89 per cent in 2013–14. In fact, during the last five years from 2009–10, it remained above the level of 10 per cent.

Similarly, as a proportion of GDP, the expenditure on agriculture and rural development sector put together did not exceed three per cent since the last five years (Figure 2.1). The maximum level of 3.1 per cent was reached in the year 1990–91. After that, during the next twenty five years, it breached the three per cent level only once in 2008–09. The feeling one gets is that, despite all the pronouncements in favour of farmers and their livelihoods, agriculture and rural development do not get the desired funding support in the form of development programmes that improve production, productivity and incomes. Some of the money intended to support farmers, perhaps, is accounted for under the Ministry of Finance for subsiding the cost of farm credit and other ministries for input subsidies on power, fertilisers, etc. The linkage between subsidised farm credit and improved farm livelihoods is nebulous. Money being fungible, the subsidised credit is perhaps excessively drawn by larger farmers with banking access and diverted for other purposes and really not applied in agriculture per se. The diversion of resources inequitably, impacts the small and marginal farmers who either do not have access to the banking system or even when they have it, can obtain very small amounts of credit. The *krishkonnati* is mostly continuation of earlier programmes and the addition of new irrigation programmes.

What is clear from the Centre's move is that the responsibility to cater to the needs of social sector, socially disadvantaged sections as well as rural economic development has been placed on the states. But whether these expectations will be realised just because higher revenue devolutions to states have

Figure 2.1: Budget expenditure on agriculture and rural development

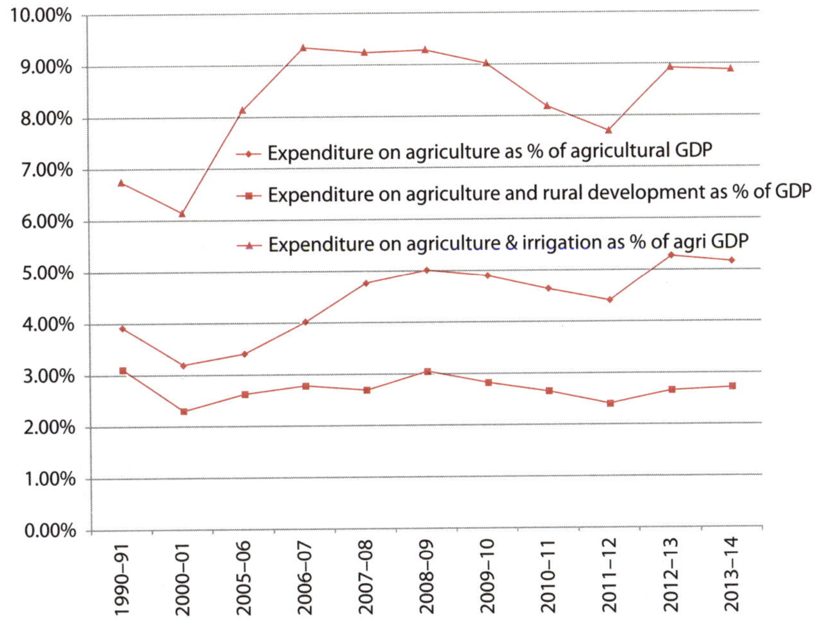

Source: Authors' working based on data from Indian Public Finance Statistics, Ministry of Finance, GoI and CSO data on GDP.

been proposed is to be examined. Data analysis for the years 2011–15 showed that on an average, the states spent between 35 per cent to 40 per cent on social sector programmes. If the states continued to allocate funding at the normal current proportion for social sector, it would have been around 40.5 per cent of their total budget as was seen in the year 2014–15. At this level, the incremental spending on social sector by the states, based on the additional resources devolution would be an increase of 0.12 per cent of GDP. But the decline in the central government's budget for the concerned sectors is of the order of 0.24 per cent of GDP.[2] In net terms, the shifting of burden of development programmes related to livelihoods and social security to states is likely to result in lesser expenditure and thus lesser development impact, at least in the short term. Two important schemes were spared the Finance Minister's axe. These are the food subsidy scheme (under the NFSA) and the NREGS

(under NREGA). Neither of these two schemes could be passed on to the states nor the funding could be reduced on account of the statutory nature of the schemes as they are born out of central legislation. A detailed assessment of the current position of implementation of these two statutory programmes is carried in the next chapter.

The Budget also mentions the key approaches to be followed in strategising the reforms and the consequent growth impetus. *Economic Survey 2014–15* says, "Wiping every tear from every eye also requires proactive support from the government in the form of a well-functioning, well-targeted, leakage-proof safety net that will provide both minimum income and protect against adverse shocks." This is also true in rural India where economic conditions for farmers and labourers are under stress. The policy issue, according to the *Survey*, is no longer 'whether' but 'how' best to provide and protect. Continuing its emphasis on the need to achieve growth, the *Survey* states that economic growth is good for the poor because it raises the income directly and generates resources to invest in public

---

[2] Based on 'Of Bold Strokes and Fine Prints', Analysis of Union Budget 2015–16, Centre for Budget and Governance Accountability (CBGA), 2015.

services and safety nets. Indirectly, growth improves the prospects and the opportunities and encourages individuals to invest in their own human capital. The Union Budget 2015–16, on its part, described the five major challenges facing the country. These are agricultural incomes under stress, increase in investment in infrastructure, decline in manufacturing sector's performance, resource crunch at the Centre on account of higher devolution of tax revenue to states and maintaining fiscal discipline.

In agriculture, the Budget specifically aims at focussing on micro irrigation and setting up corpus of ₹250 billion for Rural Infrastructure Development Fund (RIDF). The NREGS has been allocated ₹50 billion more than the last year. The NREGS was also restructured (Box 2.2) last year to focus more on creation of lasting assets that improve production and productivity.

In the social sector, government is laying considerable store on the Direct Benefits Transfer scheme (DBT) that delivers government benefits to the beneficiary's bank account directly. As of July 2015, 175 million PMJDY accounts have been opened by banks and savings of more than ₹220 billion have been mobilised. While 46 per cent of these accounts carry zero balance, overall

---

Box 2.2: *Amendment to Schedule I of the NREG Act*

Sixty per cent of the works to be taken up in districts must be for the creation of productive assets linked to agriculture and allied activities. The creation of community assets, in addition to individual assets, is allowed for vulnerable communities. The ratio of the cost of wages and the cost of materials for a project was to be maintained at 60:40 for all projects collectively at the block level. At the block level, for projects not implemented by the Gram Panchayat at this ratio is flexible. At the district level, the ratio of 60:40 needs to be maintained for projects not implemented by the Gram Panchayat.

Source: Based on the amendment carried out to the NREG Act.

---

average balance held in these accounts is around ₹1275. While 10.6 crores of these accounts are rural, the remaining 6.9 crore accounts are urban. This places the government in a position to directly channel the benefits to remote rural areas through the banking system. The Budget 2015–16 and the *Economic Survey 2014–15* talk about the JAM trinity that was the focus of debate in the press and media. The PMJDY bank accounts, the Aadhar- based authentication processes and the mobile payment systems together are supposed to provide the impetus for building a leakage-free-and-speedy payment system that will enable the government to directly provide payment benefits to the accounts of the beneficiaries. While the number of PMJDY accounts opened and the positive business environment around the mobile payment system are encouraging, issues are in the functionality of bank accounts opened under the PMJDY. According to the field information, a number of these accounts are still not functional. The accounts that have been opened are more in a compliance mode to satisfy the programme targets of the government and the RBI rather than providing effective services to customers. These accounts are like cost centres for the banks and providing even minimum services to most of these accounts across the country will cost the banks significantly. The appointment of agents to deal with these accounts through efficient IT platforms is a potential solution but entails significant initial investment in both the IT platforms as well as in an agent's recruitment and training. The licensing of 10 entities for operating small finance banks and 11 entities for payments banks can be a game changer in channelling payments and remittance services. The new class of banks can mobilise savings (limited amounts in case of payments banks) and thus offer customers a superior service value proposition than mainstream banks. The much awaited small banks licenses will also lead to increased services to the hitherto excluded people. A new initiative in risk mitigation for vulnerable households has been the Pradhan Mantri Suraksha Bima Yojana that offers an insurance cover of ₹2.00 lakh on payment of a premium of ₹12. This is expected to improve access to insurance for the lay person and is linked to the PMJDY bank accounts.

On employment and for the youth, a few new initiatives have been announced in the Budget. One of these is the Nai Manzil scheme for empowering the minority youth. The Swachh Bharat Abhiyan has a target of building 60 million toilets across the country which is a welcome measure from several angles but may have a limited direct impact on livelihoods. The national common market for agricultural commoditiesis an idea that is being studied with a view to roll it out after sorting out the legal issues. This may help farmers in getting better access to the markets and ensuring better price discovery and dissemination. The Self-employment and Talent Utilization Scheme (SETU) has also been announced as one of the important means for promoting enterprises. Deen Dayal Upadhyaya Grameen Kaushalya Yojana (DDU-GKY) has been a part of the NRLM in order to promote employment amongst rural youth through suitable skilling. These measures enhance wage employment and self-employment opportunities for the youth. What is on the anvil are the labour reforms for which the changes to law made in Rajasthan are seen as a useful model. The push to complete the Aadhar registrations in order to set up a dedicated payment mechanism has been hampered somewhat by the Supreme Court's ruling that Aadhar should not be made compulsory for government benefits. The introduction of General Sales Tax (GST) to replace the differing commercial taxes regime in different states is likely to have a positive effect on improving the business environment in the country.

Several studies that looked into the Budget and its directions have pointed out a few areas of concern. One significant area of concern is the shift in the focus of taxation from the rich towards the poor. The share of direct taxes is about 30 per cent of the total taxes collected and 70 per cent is from the indirect taxes. Indirect taxes burden the poor disproportionately and are regressive in nature. The second connected issue is the lowering of direct taxes which reward the rich. The third issue is the reduction in tax revenue as a proportion of GDP. Direct taxes which were 5.8 per cent of GDP in 2009–10 increased marginally to 6 per cent in 2013–14. Indirect taxes during the same period increased from 9.6 per cent to 11.9 per cent. In terms of comparative growth rate, indirect taxes increased by more than ten times that of the direct taxes and thus had a much larger adverse impact on the poor people. So the continuing high taxation of the poor and low taxation of the rich is a critical issue in how we protect the livelihoods of the vulnerable. The second major concern pointed out in the comments on the Budget relates to low attention paid to the farmers' income and to improve the sustainability of farm-based livelihoods. Theoretically, creation of a national market may improve the incomes but as a clear income enhancer, its impact is likely to be felt over a long run rather than during a short run.

The continuing rationalisation of subsidies is a welcome development. One of the drivers of the overhaul of development schemes that impact livelihoods has been the realisation that public expenditure should be rationalised and made optimal. The *Economic Survey* 2015 states that, "the upcoming budget should initiate the process of expenditure control to reduce both the fiscal and revenue deficits. At the same time, the quality of expenditure needs to be shifted from consumption, by reducing subsidies, towards investment. "But withdrawal of some of the subsidies should result in higher and better quality support of other kinds to the affected people so that on net terms, they are not worse off. Subsidy schemes for items such as fertilisers, power, irrigation and credit are either heavily weighted in favour of institutions that market these inputs or the larger farmers who have a much better access to these products and services (Annexure 2.1 contains an analysis of the poor's share in some subsidy schemes). In order to meet the goal of serving the excluded poor, these schemes need to be restructured in a manner that the benefits actually reach the poorer people. When existing subsidies are withdrawn, the resulting gaps should be dealt with in a manner that the poor do not suffer. This is an aspect which requires to be worked upon.

As regards financial outlays, the Finance Minister has tried to compensate for the reduced budget spending with loans from financial institutions for rural infrastructure, agriculture, microenterprises and microfinance (Table 2.3). A slew of allocations (not from the Government Budget but mostly out of priority sector lending shortfall related contributions from banking system) have been announced as has been the practice since the last decade. The legitimacy of including finances that are not a part of the Budget and create an illusion of funding development programmes has to be questioned.

The RIDF, Long Term Rural Credit Fund and the PMMY are likely to have a positive impact on the ground by addressing gaps as well as coverage of underserved people. On agricultural credit flows, there are issues of concentration in some states and unequal access where small farmers lose out. While

nominally, agricultural loans should fully support livelihoods through either production or investments, the subsidy element in crop loans has increased the demand for credit in some quarters and the loans are not always applied for cropping. The Credit Guarantee Fund of ₹30 billion announced for the MUDRA bank will be welcomed in the microenterprise space. While the details are to be known, availability of a dedicated fund of ₹200 billion for small enterprises with a guarantee facility is bound to kick-start a number of enterprises. For the purpose of the Scheme, banks have been asked to provide loans named MUDRA loans to customers who fall under the definition of small customers. At the end of August 2015, banks reported a disbursement of ₹220 billion. The target for the year 2015–16 is ₹122 trillion.

Legislative initiatives

Land acquisition bill

Pending passage of the Bill on land acquisition, an ordinance on land acquisition was promulgated twice. But in the absence of parliamentary support for the Bill (both from the opposition as also some of the allies) the ordinance was allowed to lapse recently. While before the Parliament the Bill sought to ease the processes of acquisition and reduce the time taken for acquiring land for a variety of purposes, there was trenchant criticism on two key aspects. The apparent neglect of social impact concerns and a summary manner of acquisition—waiving off informed consent from the owners of the land—were thought of as draconian. There have been debates in which the inefficient processes in the current acquisition law delay the project start-up that depends on the land and attendant cost-overruns have also been highlighted (Box 2.3). The need for a quick and efficient legal framework that makes land available within a reasonable price for development purposes—where people including owners of the land benefit—has been underlined time and again. Objections have been

Table 2.3: Allocations made outside the budget

Purpose	Amount (₹ billion)
Rural Infrastructure Development Fund (NABARD)	250
Long Term Rural Credit Fund (NABARD)	150
Short Term Cooperative Rural Credit Refinance Fund (NABARD)	450
Short Term RRB Refinance Fund (NABARD)	150
Pradhan Mantri Mudra Yojana (PMMY) corpus (MUDRA Bank)	200
Target for agricultural credit	8,500

Source: Union Budget 2015–16.

to acquisition of fertile land, waiving off the social impact analysis, disenfranchising people of their livelihoods without viable alternatives and perceived unfair compensation. Farmers' organisations have been against the Bill in its present forms as also several non-governmental organisations (NGOs). From livelihoods perspective, loss of land invariably causes disruption of a familiar livelihood and places vulnerable in jeopardy. It is not just the landowner who suffers in the process of acquisition but others also who depend on the land for their employment, either as tenants or as labourers. When the acquiring entity is not sensitive, the promised rehabilitation becomes a mirage. It has been estimated that there are about 60 million displaced persons/project-affected persons (DPs/PAPs) since independence till 2000 and as per the government's sources, at least 75 per cent of them have not been rehabilitated. The High Level Committee set up by the Government of India[3] estimated that of the total displaced due to development projects, 47 per cent was tribal population. Typically, the tribal population does not have the resources or access to information to present its case. The Committee observed in its report:

The 2013 Act already has a provision for safeguarding food security and states that multi-crop irrigated land will not be acquired, except as a last resort measure. Further, the State Government is to set limits on the acquisition of such land under this law. States are also required to set a limit on the area of agricultural land that can be acquired in any given district. However, there is no mention of the need to protect tribal land and community resources. Hence, a suitable provision is required to be incorporated in the Act, to safeguard tribal land and community resources in Scheduled Areas and disallow acquisition by a non-tribal, including private companies.

- The definition of 'public purpose' in the new law is very wide and will only lead to greater acquisition and displacement in Scheduled Areas. The exercise of 'eminent domain' and definition of 'public purpose' should be severely limited.
- Government agencies acquiring land with the ultimate purpose to transfer it to private companies for stated public purpose, should be kept outside the ambit of the new law, as the Public-Private Partnership mode of acquiring land is simply a backdoor method of alienating land in violation of the Constitutional provision to prohibit or restrict transfer of tribal land to non-tribals in Scheduled Areas.

Box 2.3: *Painless land acquisition*

Even as the pros and cons of the Land Acquisition Bill are being debated, Government of Andhra Pradesh has the real and immediate problem of finding about 45,000 hectares of land for building its new capital city. The Government apparently has found a way out. The proposal is to make all farmers stakeholders in the new capital, so that they voluntarily 'pool' their land with the city's development agency. Once the city is developed in a decade, they will get back almost 30 per cent of their pooled land as highly-priced city land. This return of one-third of the land after ten years makes the farmers see land pooling as the means of getting wealthy. The Government of Andhra Pradesh has also offered the farmers a monthly payment per acre as high or higher than the ongoing leasing rate for farmland. Loans taken for agriculture of upto ₹1.5 lakh will be waived off. Landless labourers will get a monthly pension of ₹2,500. Skill-development centres have been opened to train farmers in new occupations. The Employment Guarantee Scheme is supposed to provide work every day of the year. If this model works out, it will be a painless alternative and with willing participation of the landowners.

Source: Based on newspaper reports.

---

[3] Report of the High Level Committee on Socio-economic, Health and Educational Status of Tribal Communities of India by Professor Virginius Xaxa, Ministry of Tribal Affairs, Government of India, May 2014.

Food security (NFSA)

The Government of India appointed a committee to explore the restructuring of the Food Corporation of India (FCI) which had submitted its report. The committee recommended a higher buffer stock, reducing coverage of people under the FSA from 67 per cent of the population to 40 per cent higher food grain release for vulnerable households under the public distribution system (PDS) and removing the subsidies on fertilisers (Box 2.4).

There has been criticism that there is lack of political will to implement the NFSA and several administrative actions have been taken to weaken the food entitlements that secure lives. A more detailed coverage of the issues in implementation of the food security measures is provided in the following chapter.

Regional Rural Banks (RRBs) Amendment Act

The RRBs were set up to cater to the needs of excluded populations in the rural areas, especially for credit. Across the country, 196 banks have been established and over the last five years, RBI has taken up a plan for consolidation of these banks into larger entities, covering more districts and customers. The merged entities would require additional capital to expand their businesses and customer outreach. The RRB Amendment bill proposes to raise their authorised capital from ₹5 crores to ₹20 billion. The share capital of RRBs is currently held by the central government, state governments and various sponsor banks. The Amendment proposes to allow the banks to raise equity from other willing investors as well. In effect, this would mean that the private sector shareholders could also hold equity in RRBs and depending on the extent of shareholding, elect directors to the board and participate in governance. However the Centre's and the sponsor banks' equity cannot go below 51 per cent of the total equity, thus retaining the public sector character of the RRBs. The enhanced equity will enable RRBs to do inclusive banking by taking more customers and expanding credit to different types of livelihoods and enterprises.

Labour laws

The Factories (Amendment) Bill 2014 is pending before the Lok Sabha after which it will go to the Rajya Sabha. The Bill seeks to remove the restrictive provisions that prevent women from being employed in certain types of industries and also working in night shift (Box 2.5). The Bill stipulates safety and health restrictions for employment of pregnant women, persons with disabilities in certain industries and so on. The Bill intends to improve the working conditions, promote health and safety in the factories and impose additional responsibilities on

---

Box 2.4: *Gist of recommendations of high level committee*

Food security and public distribution: In order to avoid high leakages in the distribution system, the implementation of the National Food Security Act (NFSA) should be limited to states that have done end-to-end computerisation of their food management system. The Committee also recommended that the coverage of the NFSA be reduced from the current 67 per cent to 40 per cent of the population.

The allocation of food grains to priority households should be increased from 5 kg per person to 7kg per person. Pricing for high priority families should be adjusted to be about 50 per cent of MSP.

Move to cash transfer: FCI should gradually move from a food grain distribution system to a cash transfer system. This can begin from larger cities.

Cash subsidy for fertiliser of ₹7000 per ha and discontinue fertiliser subsidy in present form.

Source: High Level Committee Report on the Restructuring of FCI by Shanta Kumar, GoI, 2015.

Box 2.5: *Easing labour laws: The Rajasthan model*

Rajasthan State Government has initiated comprehensive labour law reform. The State Government relaxed the Trade Union Act, Industrial Dispute Act, Contract Labour Act, as well as the 1948 Factories Act and 1961 Apprenticeship Act to spur economic development and attract foreign investment to the state. The following are the key changes made:

1. Industrial establishments employing up to 300 workers are now allowed to retrench employees without seeking prior permission of the Government.
2. The threshold of the number of employees required for the purpose of applicability of the Factories Act has been increased from 10 to 20 (in electricity-powered factories) and from 20 to 40 (in factories without power) thereby putting small factories

in Rajasthan outside the purview of the Factories Act.
3. Membership of 30 per cent of the total workforce needs to be recorded for a union to obtain recognition, up to 15 per cent, a move that will halt productivity losses due to industrial dispute.
4. As against the existing threshold of 20 contract labourers/workmen, the Contract Labour Act will be applicable only to those establishments and contractors in Rajasthan who employ 50 or more contract labourers/workmen in the preceding 12 months.

There were adverse reactions from labour unions and the amendments were termed as anti-labour and pro-employer.

Source: Based on amendments and news reports.

---

the employers to secure conducive working conditions. The Apprentices (Amendment) Bill was passed in November 2014. The Bill empowers the government to specify the number of apprentices to be taken by an employer in designated trades and optional trades. Other legislation on the anvil in labour-related themes are (a) Labour Code on Wages Bill (b) Small Factories Bill and (c) Amendments to Child Labour Laws.

Other developments

NITI Aayog

NITI Aayog was established on 1 January 2015 to replace the Planning Commission. NITI Aayog provides strategic and technical advice to states regarding different aspects of policy. NITI Aayog will

- Involve states in deciding national development priorities, sectors and strategies;
- Foster cooperative federalism through state initiatives and mechanisms;
- Develop plans at the village level and scale them up to higher levels of government;
- Design strategic and long-term policies and programme frameworks and monitor their progress and efficacy; and

- Focus on technology upgradation and capacity building in order to implement the programmes and initiatives.

The prime minister is the chairperson of the Aayog. Its Governing Council has all the chief ministers and lieutenant governors as its members. The Regional Councils are formed with with all chief ministers of the states and lieutenant governors of union territories(UTs), experts and specialists with relevant domain knowledge as special invited members. The Aayog is yet to settle down with a clear organisational structure and work procedures as it is just a few months old.

In February 2015, the government announced the formation of three sub-groups within the NITI Aayog. These sub-groups aim to: (a) study the 66 Centrally Sponsored Schemes (CCS) and recommend which ones to continue, to transfer, or to cut down (b) recommend how the NITI Aayog can promote skill development and skilled manpower in states and (c) decide on institutional mechanisms to be evolved in implementing the Swachh Bharat scheme. The Government of India (Allocation of

Business) Rules were amended in March 2015 to provide space to the NITI Aayog in place of the erstwhile Planning Commission. The amended Business Rules state that the NITI Aayog is the successor of the Planning Commission. In terms of roles, the work allocation seems to envisage the NITI Aayog as being (a) a thinktank, (b) a catalyst in collaborative work, research and studies with other public and private sector knowledge institutions, (c) arbiter of inter-sector and inter-departmental conflicts and (d) evaluator of policies and programmes.

While there has been skepticism in some quarters on what the NITI Aayog will do differently, its lack of direct accountability to the Parliament[4] and lack of adequate organisational structure and staffing, the Aayog is still very young and will be able to deal with structure and staffing issues in time. The Aayog is similar in nature to the Planning Commission in terms of accountability to the Parliament. The Aayog does not have the powers to allocate funds to states or approve projects/programmes. Hence, it will not thrust its ideas on the states and will not be a top-down institution, which must be welcomed by the state governments. The usefulness of the Aayog in economic policy-making depends on the kind of personnel that man it and the freedom to voice its opinions in public.

National policy on skill development and entrepreneurship[5]

The government issued a draft policy for consultation and inputs. The Policy estimates that about 120 million youth will have to be provided with skills of various types over the period from 2015 till 2022. The vision articulated in the policy is "to create an ecosystem of empowerment by Skilling on a large Scale at Speed with high Standards so as to ensure Sustainable livelihoods for all citizens and to place India in the committee of front ranking entrepreneurial and innovative nations." The mission as enunciated in the draft is as follows:

- Create a demand for skilling across the country;
- Correct and align the skilling with required competencies;
- Connect a supply of skilled human resources with sectoral demands;
- Certify and assess the alignment with global and national standards; and
- Catalyse an ecosystem wherein opportunity-based and innovative entrepreneurship germinates and grows, leading to the creation of a more dynamic entrepreneurial economy.

The Policy's objectives on skill development rightly focus on the youth's mindshift to make vocational and skills training an aspirational choice and to convince employers that skilled manpower is the key to productivity. The other objectives are to ensure that the gap in skills of human resources (HR) in various spheres of economic activity is filled with skilled manpower and to focus on result-based approaches where employability of trained people is prioritised, to create quality training and skilling infrastructure, to introduce quality assurance and certification for skill standards and to build an IT platform in which the demand for skills and skilled manpower can find its match. In entrepreneurship, the objectives go beyond training and advocacy for enterprise creation. It seeks to create a suitable environment for business, build support network for mentors, resource persons and foster the spirit of social entrepreneurship to serve the vulnerable people.

The newly formed Ministry of Skill Development and Entrepreneurship implements the Policy and monitors the results. It is helped by the National Skill Development Agency (NSDA), National

---

[4] Ministry of Planning is accountable to the Parliament for the work of the NITI Aayog as per the Business Rules.

[5] Source: Draft National Policy on Skill Development and Entrepreneurship, Ministry of National Policy on Skill Development and Entrepreneurship, May 2015, Government of India.

Skill Development Corporation (NSDC) and Sector Skill Councils. National Commission on Entrepreneurship has been set up to "guide entrepreneurship movement in the country, unleash entrepreneurship and youth power in pursuit of wealth creation, employment generation and productivity improvement by judiciously harnessing technology and resources". The National Skill Development Fund (NSDF) takes care of funding requirements. Private and public contributions to the fund are invited. The corporate sector is also invited to fund skill development initiatives out of their CSR budget, either directly or through the NSDF. All governments across various sectors reserve a part of their budget for skill development support, either directly or through the NSDF. The end users are also required to bear a part of the costs. A guarantee fund mechanism has been set up in the name of National Credit Guarantee Trustee Company (NCGTC). This fund guarantees loans for skilling and enterprise development.

The Policy brings to one place all the issues and actions related to skills and enterprise development. It seems heavily weighted towards skills development. Unless enterprises come up, skilled people cannot find employment. Beyond the National Commission on Entrepreneurship, there is no other concrete measure on enterprise space. One of the major problems in enterprise creation is equity for start-ups and first stage expansion post start-ups. Financing for enterprises in the Policy documents is all about loans. The proposal on "revisiting bankruptcy rules and facilitating counselling and advisory service to troubled firms" are very critical and relevant for enterprises.

Deen Dayal Upadhyaya Antyodaya Yojana

The central government announced the Deen Dayal Upadhyaya Antyodaya Yojana (DAY) in September 2014. The scheme proposes to increase the livelihood opportunities for the poor through skill development. The new scheme covers all the 4,041 statutory towns as compared to the previous scheme that covered only 790 cities. An amount of ₹10 billion was allocated for the urban component of DAY during 2014–15. Out of this, ₹5 billion was to be spent on skill development of over 5,00,000 urban poor. The urban component of the scheme focuses on the following:

- Imparting skills to individuals to make them employable (at a cost of ₹15,000 to ₹18,000 per person);
- Promotion of self-employment by setting up individual microenterprises and group enterprises with interest subsidies (loans at 7 per cent);
- Training urban poor by imparting market-oriented skills through City Livelihood Centres (CLCs);
- Enabling urban poor from Self-Help Groups (SHGs) for meeting financial and social needs with a support of ₹10,000 per group;
- Development of vendor markets; and
- Constructing permanent shelters for the urban homeless and providing other essential services

Price stabilisation fund (PSF) for horticultural crops

A price stabilisation fund of ₹5 billion for select horticultural crops has been announced. The Fund is operated by the SFAC. Initially, the fund was used to deal with problems in potato and onion crops. If necessary, the fund can also take up other crops at a later date. This intervention is expected to regulate price volatility through procurement by state/UT governments and central agencies of selected produce, maintenance of buffer stocks and regulated release into the market. The Fund can also be used to provide interest-free advances to central and state agencies to procure crops from the farmers immediately after harvest in order to stabilise prices. Any profits made out of dealings in crops with the help of the Fund is ploughed back into the fund.

Any losses arising from procurement and marketing operations are also borne by the Fund. However, the Fund does not to seem have a pro-farmer slant. The procurement is on behalf of the consumers and with the objective of keeping retail prices affordable by procuring crops during harvest when the prices are low. The scheme states, "When retail prices of notified agri-horticultural commodities are anticipated to increase substantially, then their procurement could be undertaken from farm gate/mandi to reduce the cost of intermediation and made available at a cheaper price to the consumers." If the crops were aggregated and stored in buffer stock on behalf of the farmers, then the higher realisations could have been passed on to the farmers. There is an inherent conflict in the scheme as consumers are preferred over farmers, that too by the Ministry of Agriculture.

Deen Dayal Upadhyaya Gram Jyoti Yojana (DDUGJY)

The ongoing rural electrification programme has been revamped and relaunched as the DDUGJY. The components of the revamped scheme are (a) separation of agricultural and non-agricultural electricity feeders to improve supply for consumers in rural areas, (b) improving sub-transmission and distribution infrastructure in rural areas, and (c) electrification of rural areas by carrying forward Rajiv Gandhi Grameen Vidyutikaran Yojana (RGGVY) targets. The scheme—over the next seven years—is estimated to be at ₹823.08 billion. The Centre is projecting funds support of ₹689 billion. In 2015–16, an allocation of ₹45 billion has been made. The implementation of this programme on time will positively impact the livelihoods in some of the remote villages.

There are a number of programmes that have been announced over the last one year (Annexure 2.2). Some of these have new content and ideas while others are a continuation of the earlier programmes with marginal changes and a new name. The promise is that the programme implementation will be improved vastly and intended benefits will accrue to the target people.

In summary, the Budget and programmes point to a sense of urgency in creating a better business environment, focusing on enterprise promotion and employment creation, balancing the requirements of both demand and supply sides, easing credit constraints and following a bottom-up process with a strong slant towards providing more fiscal space for the states to take responsibility for development. While urgency in delivery is clearly needed, it should not turn into haste. Revamping the existing laws and programmes should be carefully analysed for both positive and negative fall outs. The decision taken should be objective; whatever produces greatest good for the greatest number should be pursued. The signals given out by smaller allocations for rural development programmes and perceived weakening of entitlements of poor such as in the case of food security should be dealt with by communication of what is in store. Whether the assumption that states will spend adequately for developmental activities will be realised, whether without the Planning Commission, states will be able to formulate their own programmes and implement the same, are other questions for which answers are awaited with some concern. Finally, one hopes that the government has got its balance right between reforming subsidies, announcing new programmes for the poor and rationalising tax revenues in favour of indirect taxes.

ANNEXURE 2.1
How much subsidies reach the target

Product	Producer subsidy	Consumer subsidy	Fiscal expenditure (Cr.)	Fiscal expenditure (percent of 2011–12 GDP)	What share of benefits accrue to the poor?
Railways	N/A	Subsidised passenger fares[1]	₹51,000	0.57	The bottom 80 per cent of households constitute only 28.1 per cent of total passenger through fare on railways
Liquefied petroleum gas	N/A	Subsidy (now via DBT)	₹23,746	0.26	The bottom 50 per cent of households only consume 25 per cent of LPG
Kerosene	N/A	Subsidy via PDS	₹20,415	0.23	41 per cent of PDS kerosene allocation are lost as leakage, and only 46 per cent of the remainder is consumed by poor households
Fertiliser & nitrogenous commodities	Firm and nutrient specific subsidies to manufacturers. Import of urea regulated by the government	Maximum	₹73,790	0.82	Urea and P&K manufacturers derive most economic benefit from the subsidy, since fanners, especially poor farmers, have elastic demand for fertiliser
Rice (paddy)	Price floor (minimum support price)	Subsidy via PDS	₹129,000	1.14	15 per cent of PDS rice is lost as leakage. Households in the bottom 3 deciles consume 53 per cent of the remaining 85 per cent that reaches households
Wheat					54 per cent of PDS wheat is lost as leakage. Households in the bottom 3 deciles consume 56 per cent of the remaining 46 per cent that reaches households
Pulses	Price floor (MSP)	Subsidy via PDS	₹158	0.002	The bottom 3 deciles consume 36 per cent of subsidised pulses
Electricity	Subsidy	Capped below market price	₹32,300	0.36	Average monthly consumption of bottom quintile = 45 kWh vs top quintile = 121 kWh Bottom quintile captures only 10 per cent of the total electricity subsidies, top quintile captures 37 per cent of subsidy
Water	N/A	Subsidy	₹14,208	0.50	Most water subsidies are allocated to private taps, whereas 60 per cent of poor households get their water from public taps
Sugar for sugar cane farmers, subsidy to mills	Minimum price	Subsidy via PDS	₹33,000	0.37	
Total			₹377,616	4.24	48 per cent of PDS sugar is lost as leakage. Households in the bottom 3 deciles consume 44 per cent of the remaining 52 per cent that reaches households

Source: Excerpted from the *Economic Survey 2014–15*, Ministry of Finance, Government of India.

ANNEXURE 2.2
New initiatives announced over the last 15 months

Economic growth and development	1. The National Institution for Transforming India (NITI Aayog) 2. Make In India 3. Digital India 4. Smart City Programme 5. The National Urban Development Mission 6. Mission Housing for All
Anti-poverty	1. Pandit Deen Dayal Upadhyaya Shramev Jayate Karyakram: skill and confidence development 2. Deen Dayal Upadhyaya Antyodaya Yojana 3. Mission Housing for all: skill development and enterprise promotion 4. Micro Units Development and Refinance Agency Bank (MUDRA Bank): financing for microenterprises and microfinance customers
Children and youth	1. MyGov.in Online Platform 2. Digital India 3. Make In India 4. National Policy for Skill Development and Entrepreneurship 5. National Sports Talent Search Scheme 6. Swachh Vidyalaya Abhiyan: clean schools 7. Padhe Bharat Badhe Bharat: literacy and schooling 8. Pandit Madan Mohan Malviya National Mission on Teachers and Teacher Training 9. Rashtriya Avishkar Abhiyan: nurturing science, technology and maths learning, fostering innovations
Agriculture and rural livelihoods	1. Enhanced Compensation for Distressed Farmers Due to Crop Damage 2. Deen Dayal Upadhyaya Gram Jyoti Yojana: rural electrification 3. Soil Health Card Scheme 4. Pradhan Mantri Krishi Sinchai Yojana: irrigation scheme 5. Rashtriya Gokul Mission: protection and improvement of indigenous cattle breeds
Women	1. Beti Bachao, Beti Padhao Abhiyaan: educating girl children 2. Sukanya Samriddhi Account: deposit scheme for the girl child for higher education or marriage 3. Swachh Bharat Mission: clean India
Financial sector	1. Pradhan Mantri Jan Dhan Yojana: financial inclusion 2. Gold Monetisation Scheme 3. Pradhan Mantri Suraksha Bima Yojana: insurance 4. Pradhan Mantri Jeevan Jyoti Bima Yojana: insurance 5. Atal Pension Yojana

Source: Listing by the authors using public domain information.

Some Important Programmes in Livelihoods: Searching for Focus?

The GoI has a number of schemes that deal with livelihoods directly or indirectly. Some of the larger programmes that might be called Flagship Programmes implemented across the country are the Mahatma Gandhi National Rural Employment Guarantee Scheme, National Rural Livelihoods Mission, National Urban Livelihoods Mission and the Food Security Programme under the National Food Security Act. This chapter is an examination of these programmes as to how they are designed, run and monitored.

I. Mahatma Gandhi National Rural Employment Guarantee Scheme

NREGS was launched through an Act of Parliament in 2005 to address low level of employment in the rural areas and seasonal unemployment caused by short agricultural seasons.[1] NREGS has been a boon to unemployed and underemployed rural poor where vagaries of monsoon and low level of economic activity in certain regions played havoc with their lives. In rural areas those households that registered for a job under the Scheme were employed (manual labour not requiring any skills) to implement works planned by the gram panchayats. At the end of 2014–15 the scheme reported 273.2 million workers enrolled for jobs. Of this, 91.5 million were considered active (defined as persons that have worked at least for a day in the current year or the previous two years). Even with such liberal definition of one day of work under NREGS in three years, the number of active workers is about 33 per cent of those registered. Two-thirds of those registered did not work for even a day in three years and hence are not considered active. Whether the NREGS is not useful for two-thirds of the registrants and if so why, are questions that should be answered.

As mentioned in the last year's report, the *Economic Survey* of 2014–15 made a strong pitch for revamp of the NREGS programme in the light of several limitations that had developed such as lack of participation of Panchayati Raj Institutions (PRIs), poor monitoring, intangibility of assets created and low benefits arising from the executed works. There have also been other issues relating to leakages with the full quantum of wages not reaching the intended households and elite capturing of the Scheme's benefits. However, the government committed to continuing the programme but with modifications. Budget Speech 2015 says, "We will ensure that no one who is poor is left without employment. We will focus on improving the quality and effectiveness of

---

[1] NREGS is based on the Employment Guarantee Scheme run by the Government of Maharashtra from 1965 and then made statutory by the EGS Act in 1979. An assessment of the Maharashtra scheme can be seen in http://www.odi.org/sites/odi.org.uk/files/odi-assets/publications-opinion-files/1698.pdf.

Table 3.1:   NREGS: A snapshot (2014–15)

Number of persons registered	275.7 million
Number of active workers	91.5 million
Revised budget 2014–15	₹330.00 billion
Budget for 2015–16	₹346.99 billion
Number of persons demanding work	73.1 million
Number of persons allocated work	72.9 million
Number of persons who took up work	62.2 million
Number of person days of work provided	1662.7 million
Average number of days worked per household	36
Number of households gaining 100 days work (% to total)	2.49 million (5.4%)
Wages paid to workers	₹248.39 billion
Average income per household	₹6,000

Source: NREGS MIS, MoRD, GoI.

activities under MGNREGA. I have made an initial allocation of ₹34,699 crores[2] for the programme". The budget allocation in 2015–16 is marginally higher than the allocations made in 2014–15 at ₹339.89 billion.[3]

During 2014–15, ₹248.39 billion were paid out as wages to about 62.2 million persons from 41.4 million households (Table 3.1). Eighteen per cent of the households were able to earn more than ₹10,000 during the year from NREGS.[4] But 56 per cent households had received less than ₹5,000 during the year. The average wage received by an individual worker was about ₹6,000. These numbers quite clearly bring out that NREGS wages played a critical role in at least 44 per cent of participating households with life-sustaining incomes. The scheme, at the same time, seems to suffer from inefficiencies in some states. The share of wages paid is at 67 per cent of total expenditure at the country level; roughly 2 out of every 3 rupees spent on the scheme reaches the

workers. But in some states such as Bihar (46 per cent), Gujarat (57 per cent) and Karnataka (58 per cent), a higher proportion is spent on material and administration components. States such as Kerala, Tripura and Tamil Nadu have managed to keep other expenditures very low and managed to utilise 92 per cent, 84 per cent and 79 per cent respectively of their funds towards wages.

The outcome from deployment of such a large number of people in wage labour has been an area of considerable debate. While a number of projects in irrigation, agriculture-related infrastructure, roads and community infrastructure have been taken up, completion of work has been slowing down over the years (Figure 3.1). The last two years in particular have seen a drastic decline with 60 per cent and 40 per cent of the work reported as completed compared to 94 per cent works completed in 2009–10. Whether this decline in completion rates is on account of large public works that can be completed over a longer period of time is not clear.

Different types of economic, social and welfare infrastructure have been taken up as part of the NREGS works (Table 3.2). Road connectivity projects have been prioritised followed by water harvesting and soil and water conservation and renovation of traditional water bodies. Water has been a major theme in NREGS with drought proofing category of works also concentrating mostly on water conservation.

Many works taken up have been of a temporary nature that have to be redone again

---

[2] While there is a marginal increase in the budget allocation, over the years the budgets have not factored in the increased minimum wages. As a result even with higher allocations, only a lesser number of days of work can be offered.

[3] Even as this chapter was being drafted, the GoI had announced additional 50 days of extra work per household during 2015–16 in drought affected areas.

[4] See annexure at the end of the chapter for more state-wise details.

Figure 3.1: NREGS falling work completion rates (%)

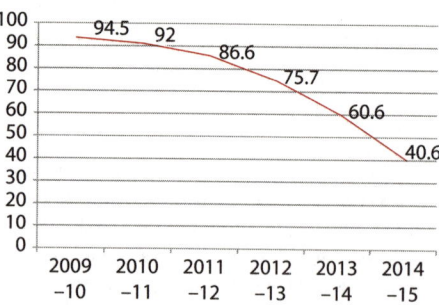

Source: NREGS MIS sourced from MoRD website.

Table 3.2: Works taken up in 2014–15

Work category	Number of works	Amount of expenditure (₹ crores)
Anganwadi	11,856	81.26
Bharat Nirman Rajeev Gandhi Sewa Kendra	44,519	741.61
Coastal areas	1,106	1.89
Drought proofing	1,562,424	1,784.51
Fisheries	12,907	77.71
Flood control and protection	325,788	1,367.61
Food grain	1,107	14.25
Land development	947,488	2,898.35
Micro irrigation works	601,385	1,602.45
Other works	356,926	584.55
Play ground	4,663	28.67
Renovation of traditional water bodies	448,905	4,108.24
Rural connectivity	1,795,721	10,966.62
Rural drinking water	15,683	33.78
Rural sanitation	4,259,602	1,079.37
Water conservation and water harvesting	1,332,100	4,655.34
Works on individuals land (Category IV)	2,507,701	3,615.61
Total	14,229,881	33,641.89

Source: Presentation to the Programme Review Committee, NREGS, from MoRD website, GoI.

one or two years later. Even the roads are mostly earthwork roads without black topping. Renovation of existing tanks typically entails deepening, desilting and strengthening of bunds, but all involve earthwork. Means and methods of ensuring that works completed under NREGS become long term assets to improve productivity, create employment opportunities and provide access to basic needs over a sustained period of time, should be explored.

The Accountability Initiative pointed out[5] that the budget allocation in the current year has been marginally more than the previous year and in real terms this may be actually less compared to the funds provided in 2011–12. The timing of fund releases has slowed down considerably in 2014–15 leading to crowding of works towards the end of the year and consequently creation of a lower number of man days. Several states

had been short funded. In the year 2013–14, the state governments spent much more than the total funds released by the Centre, resulting in an outstanding liability of ₹55.12 billion in the beginning of 2014–15. A redeeming feature has been the creation of a high proportion of employment having been generated in the most backward districts. Fifty five per cent of the MGNREGS workers were women in 2014–15. Most states achieved the threshold of 33 per cent women being employed. However, four states viz. Uttar Pradesh, Jammu & Kashmir, Nagaland and Assam failed to achieve this 33 per cent threshold of women's participation during the year 2014–15.

The Scheme, however, does not seem to enjoy the whole-hearted support of the policy establishment. In an article,[6] Jagdish Bhagwati and Arvind Panagariya (currently the Vice Chairman of NITI Aayog) described

---

[5] Budget Briefs, Volume 7 Issue 6, MGNREGS, GoI, 15/16- Accountability Initiative, Centre for Policy Research, New Delhi 2015.

[6] Excerpted from an article in *Times of India* by Jagdish Bhagwati and Arvind Panagariya, 23 October 2014.

NREGS as highly inefficient in transferring income to the poor. The calculations on expenditure incurred under the Scheme showed that 30 per cent of the expenditure was incurred on materials and 70 per cent on wages. Looking at minimum wages of ₹130 and overall expenditure of ₹186 including material had to be incurred to employ one worker per day. They argued that the workers had other opportunities but at lower wages from which they shifted to NREGS work. It is assumed that a net increase of ₹50 per day is achieved when job card holders cease to do the other work and do work under NREGS. In effect for an incremental income of ₹50 in the hands of a person, the government spends ₹186. After taking in to account the leakages, government is estimated to spend five rupees to deliver one rupee of benefit under the scheme to people as wages. While the calculations seem to indicate that NREGS is a highly inefficient mechanism of providing employment, one also notices that the value of assets created and their impact on the ground have not been considered at all. It has been assumed that the work done under NREGS does not produce any other benefits apart from the increased income for the duration of work given. The restructuring of Scheme is on the basis that the work done under NREGS can be gainfully utilised to create long-term beneficial impact through focussing on infrastructure that can add to production and productivity such as in irrigation, afforestation, soil conservation and the like. Applying the asterisk of efficiency as argued in this article, perhaps no government-funded projects can ever be justified. Moreover, where projects do not create local employment and eventually do not create tangible benefits for lack of involvement of people and lack of consultation with the local villages, the benefits might seem negligible.

The efficiency of the Scheme has so far been measured in terms of number of person days of employment generated, number of households that were covered and number of households which could actually benefit

from the 100 days of work during the year (originally promised in the legislation). As per the reports available, almost all those asking for work were provided the same, though the assurance of 100 days of work to each household each year has been observed more in the breach. However, of the 270 million registrants, only 72 million demanded work under the Scheme. Even if 'active workers' are considered, against 91.5 million persons considered active, less than 80 per cent demanded work. The reason why demand for work under the Scheme is low should be studied. The higher wages prevailing in rural areas is a possible dampener that limits demand. As observed elsewhere, more women come forward for work in many locations as wages of males are higher in these areas and hence wean away male labour to lucrative alternative employment. But this does not explain why allocations are made to states where the demand might be very limited and why a larger allocation cannot be made to other states with potentially higher demand for work.

The comfort in reporting that more than 99 per cent of households that demanded work (Figure 3.2) had been provided work is false and diverts attention from changes needed to improve the Scheme. Why only a limited number of households demand employment is a critical question. The falling rates of employment provision to households in terms of person days also points to problems of adequacy in work generation. Social audits in several blocks

Figure 3.2: Per cent of households given jobs

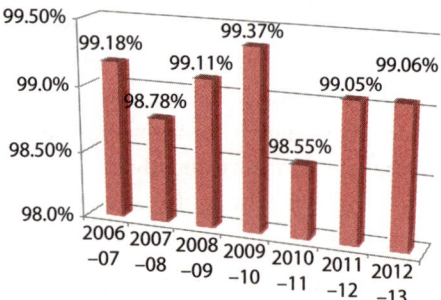

Source: NREGS MIS sourced from MoRD website.

Figure 3.3: Per cent of households with 100 days employment

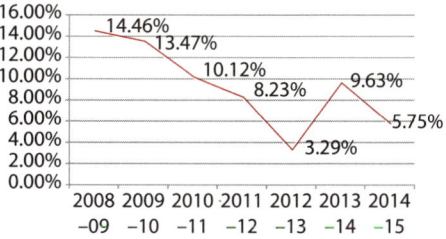

Source: NREGS MIS sourced from MoRD website.

Figure 3.4: Average number of days per household

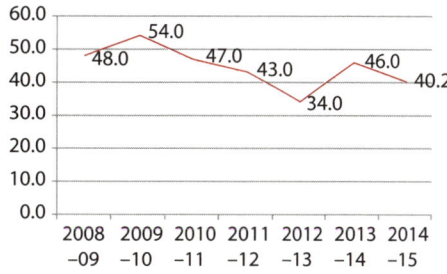

Source: Graph by authors based on data from NREGS MIS.

reported that apart from low wages and delayed payments, work is not available when people need it most. The proportion of households to which 100 days of employment was provided fell to as low as 3.29 per cent in 2012–13 and again to 5.75 per cent in 2014–15 (Figure 3.3). A national programme that *guarantees* 100 days employment, fulfilling the guarantee only to 5.75 per cent households requires a serious re-examination. Back of the envelope calculations show that *to provide 100 days of work to all households that demanded jobs during 2014–15, the wage budget would have cost ₹767.25 billion.*[7] The current allocations are less than 50 per cent of the required budget and reflect gross underfunding. Given the fiscal space, it does not seem feasible to fulfil the statutory guarantee in the near future.

In 2014–15, 1662.7 million person days of work had been provided under NREGS. There has been a steady decline in the number of days of work generated under the scheme from 2012–13 onwards. The average number of days of employment provided per household also has been declining steadily. From a peak of 54 days per year per household in 2009–10, it has declined to 40.16 days in 2014–15 (Figure 3.4).

There is considerable variation in the scheme implementation efficiency across states (Annexure 2 at the end of the chapter provides comparative data of states on

some aspects of scheme implementation). Fourteen states allocated far more person days of work than budgeted. At the country level, the person days allocated during 2014–15 was 109 per cent of the budget. States such as AP, Kerala and Puducherry allocated 200 per cent to 350 per cent of the budgeted person days. At the other end of the spectrum, states of West Bengal, Jammu and Kashmir, Madhya Pradesh, Bihar, Meghalaya and Manipur allocated between 50 per cent and 9 per cent of the budget to the households (Figure 3.5).

While the budget itself was low in some of these states, in others the budget was substantial. Allocations in excess of budget led to cornering the NREGS resources by a few states (Table 3.3). The top five states in terms of person days allocated took up more than 70 per cent of all India person days allocated.

There was a gap between the work allocated to households against demand and actual work taken up by households. Unsuitable timing seems to be a major factor for this gap as per social audits.

Wage Payments

While IT systems have been in place to deal with timely payment of wages, delays continue to plague the scheme. In 2014–15, 27 per cent of all wage payments were made in time. About 72 per cent of all payments were delayed beyond 15 days (Table 3.4). Sixteen per cent of payments were delayed by more than three months. Though there is a provision for compensation to beneficiaries for

---

[7] Calculations by the authors. Based on ₹165 per day wage and 4.52 million households demanding work in 2014–15.

Figure 3.5:   Person days allocated as per cent of budget

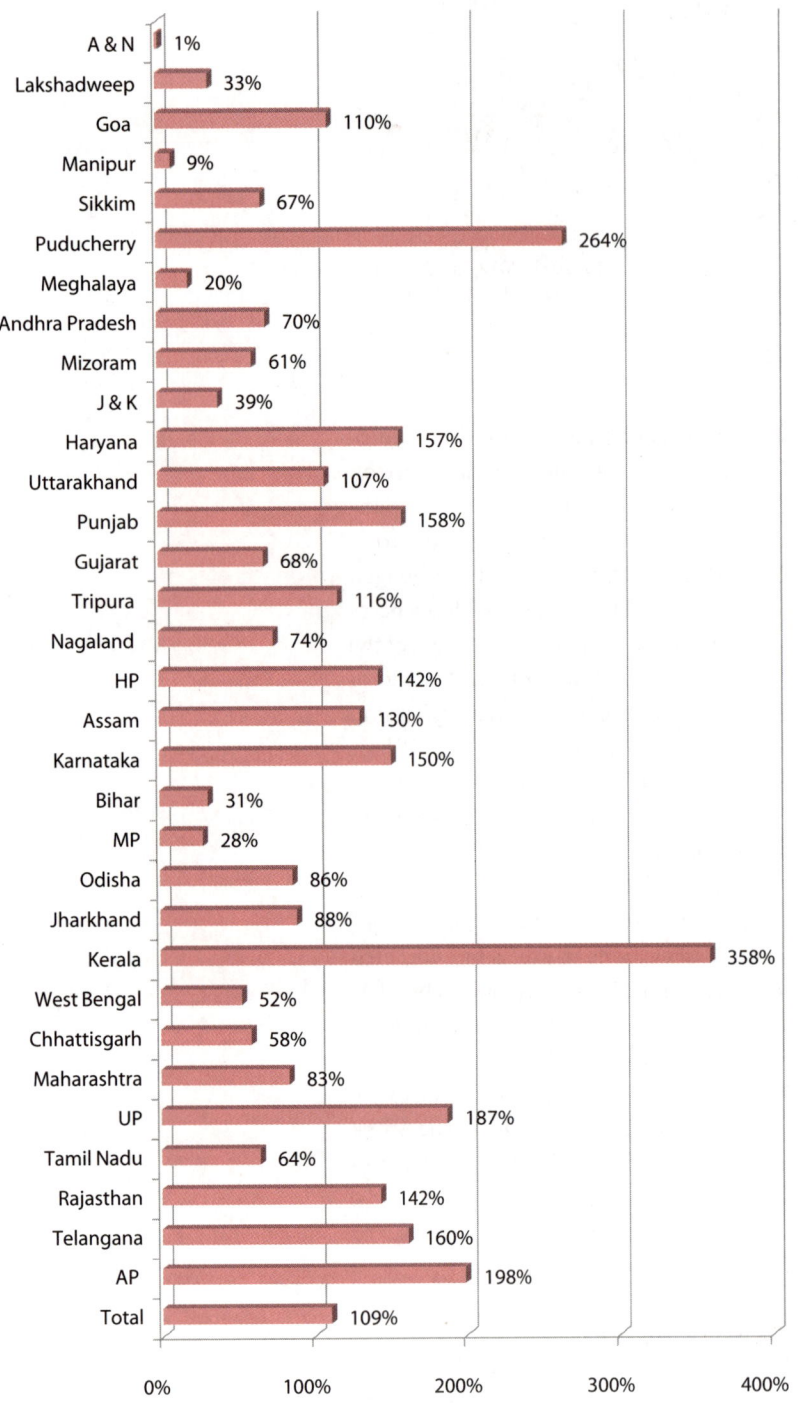

Source: NREGS MIS sourced from MoRD website.

Table 3.3:   Work budgeted and allocated

States	Person days budgeted for the state	Allocated to households by state	State share of all India person days allocated
Andhra Pradesh	1,263.34	2,504.84	26%
Telangana	932.88	1,495.08	14%
Rajasthan	994.84	1,411.07	14%
Tamil Nadu	1,396.84	892.62	9%
Uttar Pradesh	427.69	799.5	8%
India	8,925.38	9,772.14	

Source: NREGS MIS, MoRD, GOI.

Table 3.4:   Delay in wage payments (₹ crores)

Total wages paid 14–15	Paid in time	Delayed by more than 30 days	Delayed by more than 90 days
23,302.82	6,296.12	11,385.89	3,788.20

Source: NREGS MIS sourced from MoRD website.

A number of initiatives have been taken to reduce delays in wage payments. More than 90 million workers have been facilitated to open banks accounts so that payments can be electronically credited to the workers' accounts. The accounts are also being seeded with Aadhar numbers so that verification of credentials of customers and crediting of the correct accounts is done without loss of time. The JAM trinity propounded by the Ministry of Finance intends to take the electronic payments further by crediting mobile wallets. While mobile ownership might not be a problem, Aadhar seeding of accounts has been progressing somewhat slowly. Of the total job registrants, 25 per cent have Aadhar numbers and of the active workers, 51 per cent have seeded Aadhar numbers. Aadhar registration in states where National Population Register has the responsibility has been proceeding slowly, and this is the main cause of gaps in Aadhar seeding under the NREGS.

The major challenges identified by the Ministry of Rural Development (MoRD) in implementation of NREGS were low awareness and public participation, low level of capacity of functionaries, concerns on quality

these delayed payments under the Act and almost every state had delayed wage payments, only six states paid any compensation amounting to ₹74.9 million, of which Maharashtra alone paid ₹73.4 million.

utility and durability of assets, delays in wage payments, shortage of implementation staff, lack of adequate planning, lack of outcome-based monitoring, inadequate coverage of persons with disabilities and of women in some states, ineffective social audit and lack of information technology infrastructure for monitoring and report. The *Economic Survey 2014* argued for significant changes to NREGA and the Scheme (Box 3.1). The changes that have been brought about relate to greater involvement of the panchayats in implementation as also in monitoring of the programme and linking the programme to works that result in creation of productive assets in agriculture and allied activities. An amendment to Schedule 1 of the NREG Act has been carried out which states, "for all works taken up by the gram panchayats, the cost of material component including wages of the skilled and semi-skilled workers shall not exceed 40 per cent at the gram panchayat level. For works taken up by agencies other than gram panchayats, the overall material component including wages shall not exceed 40 per cent at the district level".

Several new initiatives have been announced by the department to improve the scheme implementation (Figure 3.6). These have been listed as intensive participatory planning, emphasis on agriculture and allied activities, greater focus on convergence with the state convergence plan, use of line departments to provide technical supervision, outcome orientation in implementation of projects, a provision for payment of

Figure 3.6: Work taken up as per cent of allocation

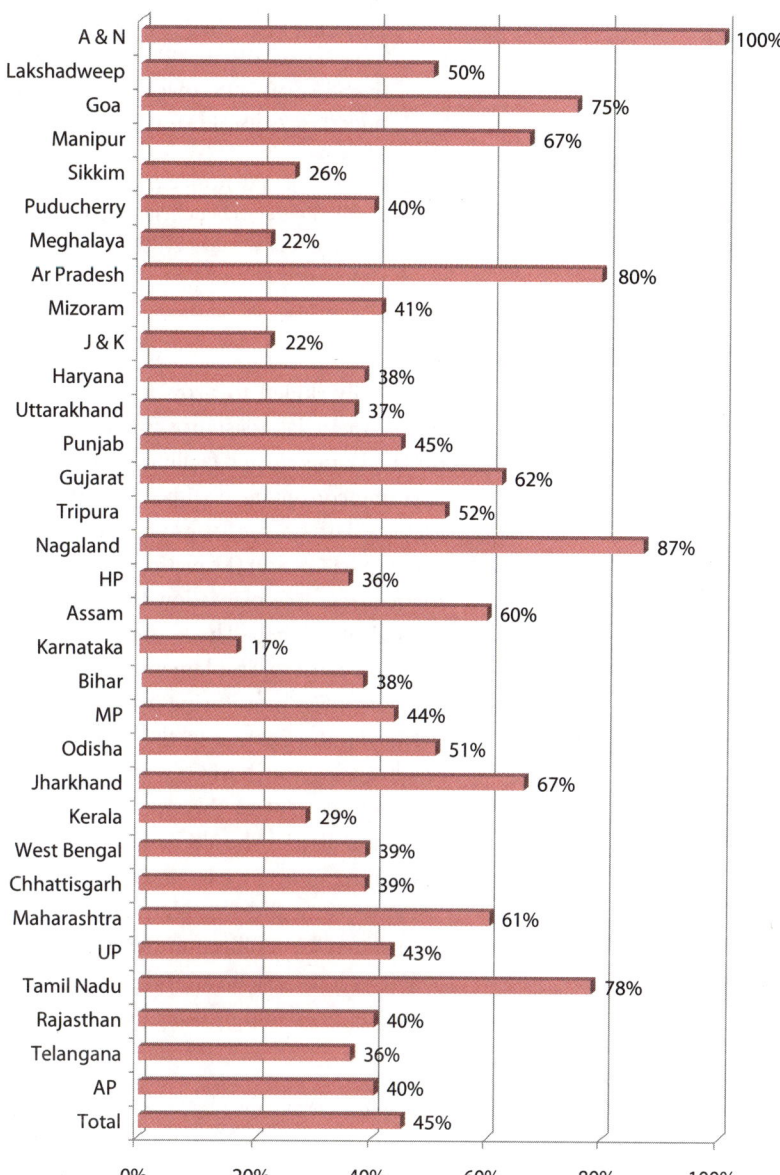

Source: NREGS MIS sourced from MoRD website.

Box 3.1: Economic survey 2014 *on NREGA*

Though the Act is panchayat-centric and demand based, on the ground there is lack of principal role in planning, execution and monitoring by the PRI's especially the gram sabha.

- The awareness level in the gram sabha/PRIs is very low, resulting in lack of ownership, ill-conceived planning and shelf of projects, and weak or even no social audit.

- The need for community projects is becoming less important as such works have already been completed or are on the brink of saturation or on account of lack of common interest in public works. Individual activities on farms are preferred by beneficiaries.
- Delayed measurement of works leads to delayed wage payment. This is also owing to lack of technical staff.

- In some places, only female workers are interested in availing of work as market wage for males is much higher, resulting in only small works of lesser utility being undertaken instead of big and tangible projects.
- Need to avoid projects with single or small number of beneficiaries and the use of Mahatma Gandhi NREGA funds in a supply-driven mode.

So there is an urgent need to revamp the Mahatma Gandhi NREGA to prevent its misuse and make it a development-oriented programme creating tangible and meaningful assets and infrastructure including tourism-related infrastructure or some large agriculture-related activities.

Source: Excerpted from *Economic Survey 2013–14*, Ministry of Finance, Government of India, 2014.

technically skilled to provide supervision, special financial assistance for social audit units, placing cluster facilitation teams for ensuring convergence with other schemes, creating dash boards for providing information in NREGA Soft (IT platform) and a plan for roadside tree plantation for promoting ecological balance. These changes in programme content, implementation process and improved monitoring are expected to bring about a change in the utility of the results arising from NREGS work (Figure 3.6).

Sixty per cent of the work to be taken up in the district should be for creation of productive assets such as land development, water security and tree plantations, which means that ₹250 billion under MGNREGS will flow into agriculture-related activities. A special provision of three per cent of the

value of work has been created for technical supervision of the work done. This has been introduced to ensure that technical manpower guides the planning and execution of physical work which otherwise does not get done in a manner that is sustainable. The labour to material ratio for work taken up by agencies other than gram panchayat will be reckoned at the district level. This change is likely to facilitate a flow of ₹80 billion for essential infrastructure such as minor irrigation. The third change envisaged is focus on convergence with other departments resulting in better technical guidance, increased professionalism and more resources for the work that is carried out. A participatory planning exercise was carried out to create a shelf of projects with quantified physical outcomes (Table 3.5)

Table 3.5: NREGS works based on participatory planning for 2015–16

Work category name/work sub category name/work type	New works identified during planning exercise			
	No. of new works	Unit	Estimated outcome	Estimated cost (in lakhs)
Water	4,19,548	Hec.	30,57,527	4,96,841.93
Irrigation	3,92,619	Hec.	9,18,924	8,10,094.56
Afforestation/horticulture	5,13,618	Hec.	6,15,374	6,19,280.47
Agriculture	3,90,922	Hec.	2,02,077	3,07,214.04
Allied sector	4,06,568	Nos.	2,39,375	1,66,457.11
Roads	4,02,789	KM.	1,80,216	95,525.85
Sanitation	6,37,091	Nos.	6,37,091	47,155.01
GP Bhawan/BNRGSK	4,775	Nos.	13,101	15,861.84
IAY/Housing Scheme	53,632	Nos.	53,632	8,935.49
Other works	8,68,030	Nos.	8,68,030	54,767.93
Grand Total	40,89,592			26,22,134.23

Source: Brochure on NREGS, MoRD, GoI 2015.

in line with the changes envisaged in the scheme. The changes show that in departure from the past, roads are not prioritised. Agriculture related works have a large share of about 70 per cent and afforestation has a share of 23 per cent of the financial allocation. There is a conscious attempt to focus on sustained impact on production, productivity and vulnerability reduction arising from climate-related stress.

MoRD has specifically initiated action on the following aspects to improve performance and worker friendliness of the NREGS in 2015–16. These are:

- Protecting entitlements of workers
- Avoiding delays in payment
- Conduct of social audit as per the Rules
- Mobile-based monitoring on pilot basis
- Expand electronic fund management system (eFMS) and introduce eFMS in all gram panchayats
- Skilling MGNREGA workers under other compatible schemes

Social audits

Social audit of MGNREGS has been brought in as an integral part of the scheme so that community groups and volunteers after due training are able to verify the work carried out, expenditure incurred, payments made to workers and other aspects of the scheme. While the social audit took a while to gain ground, since the last two years social auditors seems to have been carrying out a number of audits. While consolidated information is not available, the audit reports are available in the website of MoRD in an easily retrievable form. In AP and Telangana, for example, the social audits have established that ₹23.1 million have been spent in deviation from the Scheme's norms and rules (as agreed by the government). It has been established that of this, ₹10.3 million have been misappropriated. This led to 281 FIRs being filed with the police and termination of services of more than 7,200 staff. In Bihar, the social audits found cases of fraudulent entries in books, measurements recorded in books being different from actual quantity of work done and non-maintenance of books in some cases. In Maharashtra, of the 5,825 works verified, 19 per cent were found to be deficient. In Tamil Nadu, the people contacted during the social audit process had grievances relating to

- low wages
- inability to get work when they needed it
- delayed wage payment
- issues with bank payments
- worksite facilities not being provided
- not being able to get job cards
- old people and women with children being discouraged
- no grievance redressal system

The major findings of social audit across different works in Tamil Nadu were

- poor quality of work and poor asset creation like poor planning, poor selection of work and poor monitoring, quantity not commensurating with the wages disbursed
- registers not maintained properly or no updations
- incomplete and wrong data at ***mgnrega. nic.in***
- significant fake entries and overwriting in job cards, NMR, etc.
- discrepancies between job cards, muster rolls, registers and online data
- technical staff not visiting the worksites
- poor documentation like books not maintained well, no photos in the Asset Register and no completion of reports.

A major concern is that all states still do not seem to take social audits seriously. The latest position regarding social audits put out by MoRD indicates that out of 28 states, 17 are yet to adhere to the Social Audit Rules. In many states, the processes of recruitment of personnel for social audits, training, etc. are ongoing since a long time. The need is for an early roll-out of social audits and a well laid out protocol for corrective measures.

The Rural Employment Guarantee Scheme is a thoughtful legislative effort to ensure that poor families in rural areas have access to gainful employment, especially when the agricultural prospects turn poor. In this, it has been a positive contributor to the income of rural households and thus ensured a minimum level of economic security. Studies carried out have referred to the beneficial impacts of economic security offered by the Scheme. The impact—as found by several different studies—is that NREGS provided about 7 per cent to 17 per cent of household income, made work available in seasons when no other work was easily available and stabilised income flows, positively impacted consumption expenditure with increasing nutritious food intake, thus leading to positive health outcomes on account of better incomes, higher asset accumulation and increased propensity to save. The most significant impact is on the wage levels which increased in the rural areas. The higher wage benchmarks set by NREGS resulted in higher income levels even when people worked on other-than-NREGS-jobs. The challenge is to sustain the momentum gathered by the Scheme and save it from becoming a mediocre effort. The declining generation of number of days of employment and reduced average number of days of employment provided to each household seem to indicate that the Scheme is running out of steam. The last two years' numbers on the Scheme's progress reflect fatigue arising from implementation of the Scheme year after year in the same format, involving millions of families and the elaborate monitoring and accounting arrangements. The recent changes announced certainly would go a long way in improving the effectiveness, relevance and utility of the works completed with the help of NREGS. However, while restructuring the programme to orient it towards results that would provide long term benefits to local communities, there must be a continuing emphasis on creating employment for a greater number of people and satisfying all households that actually demand employment. The manner in which the accounting is done for households that demand employment and also the work

provided to such households needs careful scrutiny. Given that the national unemployment rates have not declined and more and more persons enter into the labour force year after year, a fall in the number of households demanding employment from NREGS does not strike a positive chord. The Scheme, as intended, should fulfil its assurance that those who need 100 days of employment during a year are actually provided the same. The budget allocations seem inadequate to fulfil the guarantee given to the rural poor by law. Despite all reservations about the efficiency of producing incremental incomes in the hands of people at policy levels, NREGS needs to be persisted with. The problems around the Scheme should be dealt with appropriate strategies and management, ensuring that it actually delivers positive benefits on the ground. NREGS is a unique social safety net that requires people to contribute in order to access benefits. Its uniqueness in avoiding overt subsidies even when providing welfare net should not be lost in the process of its revamp.

II. National rural livelihoods mission

NRLM is the flagship programme of the Government of India for promoting poverty reduction by building strong institutions for the poor, particularly women, and enabling these institutions to access a range of financial services and livelihoods services. NRLM had its origin in the Swarnajayanti Gram Swarozgar Yojana (SGSY) that was launched in the year 1999 after termination of the much maligned Integrated Rural Development Programme (IRDP). NRLM is an attempt to provide sustainable livelihood in the rural areas of the country and is considered a significant improvement over the SGSY.

The experience from SGSY suggests that the current below poverty line (BPL) list has large inclusion and exclusion errors. To widen the target groups beyond the BPL list and to include all the needy and poor, NRLM undertakes community-based process i.e., participation of the poor in the process of identifying those target groups which are approved by Gram Panchayats. NRLM ensures adequate coverage of vulnerable sections of the society such that 50 per cent of the beneficiaries are SC/STs, 15 per cent are minorities and 3 per cent are persons with disability, while keeping in view the ultimate target of 100 per cent coverage of BPL families. The recent Socio-economic and Caste Census (SECC) is perceived to provide reliable data on poverty level, income level and excluded groups. NRLM has advised the state units to make the SECC findings, the basis of their planning.

NRLM believes that institutions of the poor such as self-help groups (SHGs) and their village organisations (VOs) and higher level federations at cluster and block levels are necessary to provide space, voice and resources for the poor and to reduce their dependence on external agencies (Box 3.2). In addition, NRLM would promote specialised institutions like livelihoods collectives, producers' cooperatives/companies for livelihoods promotion to deliver economies of scale, backward and forward linkages and access to information, credit, technology, markets etc. Thus the project would provide support to create and strengthen livelihoods through training, capacity building, enterprise development and placement in jobs after suitable vocational skills training.

Self-help groups and federations

Poor women are mobilised into homogenous groups of 10 to 20 and guided to build social capital through bonding, training and skill building. The groups are encouraged to save some small amounts at regular intervals (weekly, fortnightly or monthly as decided by the groups). Over a six-month-period, the groups are trained to become disciplined financial intermediaries that provide loans to other group members out of these savings. The SHGs are linked to a bank at this stage through a savings bank account.

The groups are provided with revolving fund assistance once they demonstrate their resolve to function as cohesive units after the first six months. Microcredit planning is initiated after six months of the group, where in, each member of a SHG makes a household investment plan and the Micro Credit Investment Plan is an aggregation of all the household investment plans of all the SHG members. The Plan addresses the members' investment needs for income generation and is a process-oriented document which is to be re-visited periodically. The Plan ascertains the credit demand of the group for different purposes. Subsequently, a community investment fund is contributed at village organisation to enable the groups to take livelihood initiatives either individually or as a group.

The project personnel facilitate a bank loan for the group that enables members to take up the activities they had proposed in the plan. Beyond this, women farmers are trained under Mahila Kisan Sashaktikaran Pariyojana (MKSP) to become better farmers and thereby improve their income levels.

Box 3.2: *A typical block outcome*

Expected outcomes in a typical intensive block which is supported for 10 years.

- 13,500 poor families (90 per cent of NRLM target group) in the block mobilised into 1200 SHGs
- Federations of SHGs at village level – 120 VLFs, Cluster level federations – 4 CLFs and 1 Block level federation formed/ strengthened.
- Each household would have borrowed at least ₹1 Lakh as loan in multiple doses, and another ₹1 – ₹2 lakhs from their own savings and community funds (provided by the project).
- Around 10,800 households (80 per cent) pursuring at least two sustainable livelihoods, initiated by the project.
- 4,500 most vulnerable households, benefited from special food security and vulnerability reduction intervention.

Source: Website of MoRD.

For the landless, skill training and placement in jobs is carried out directly by the project staff or through the Rural Self Employment Training Institutes (RSETIs). NRLM thus has an elaborate institutional architecture to create institutions for the poor and to ensure flow of finance to meet needs of the members of SHGs. The financial inclusion vision of NRLM is much clearer than its livelihood approach.

Over the last four years in which NRLM has been functional, a number of achievements have been reported (Table 3.6).

At present, (August 2015), NRLM covers 398 districts and 2,756 blocks. 2.4 million SHGs have been formed covering more than 27.8 million households. The programme has been supported by the World Bank through its National Rural Livelihoods Project (NRLP). NRLP's aim is to intensively support implementation of NRLM in 100 districts and 400 blocks of 12 high poverty states and to create best practice sites and local immersion locations for NRLM to build on. The reported credit mobilisation is very high, given the fact that in most states the SHGs are in their initial years. The credit facilitated in erstwhile AP for many years for a number of groups had been the highest in the country across states. AP's data on credit provides an exaggerated picture of credit flow.

The progress during 2014–15 has been slower and the Ministry in its Outcome Budget commented that there had been a delay in transition of states to NRLM and they were in the process of establishing systems for fund disbursal in intensive blocks. Funds were primarily provided to new/revived SHGs that had received initial capacity building. A large number of SHGs in the non-intensive blocks had also been assisted and the information pertaining to them would be tracked after the establishment of management information system (MIS) in these blocks. Under NRLM, the targets are defined in terms of SHGs and the households of SHG members. The concept of assisting individual Swarozgari has been discontinued in favour of concerted focus on groups.

Although the target for assisting new SHGs has been achieved (Table 3.7), the targets for facilitation of bank loans to SHGs has not been achieved to a significant extent. Regarding skilling of youth and placing them in jobs, the progress has been tardy. Only one- third of the target was met in 2013–14. In 2014–15, the target has

Table 3.6: Progress since Inception till March 2015

i.	Number of districts where implementation has started	352
ii.	Number of blocks where implementation is underway	2,639
iii.	Number of SHGs promoted	21.7 lakhs
iv.	Households covered	250 lakh
v.	Number of Village Organisations (VOs) formed	1.3. lakh (10–20 SHGs per V.O)
vi.	Number of Cluster Level Federations (CLFs) formed	2,829 (25–40 VOs per CLF)
vii.	Total amount of Revolving Fund released to SHGs	₹243 crore
viii.	Total amount Community Investment Fund released	₹400 crore
ix.	Total amount of credit mobilised	₹63,950 crore

Source: Excerpted from 'Achievements of the Ministry of Rural Development' 2015, GoI.

Table 3.7: Targets and achievements

Deliverable	Target (lakhs) 2013–14	Target (lakhs) 2014–15	Achievement (lakhs) 2013–14	Achievement (lakhs) 2014–15	Share of AP, Telangana, Tamil Nadu, Kerala and Karnataka 2014–15
Number of new SHGs assisted	1.87	1.00	1.03	1.15	
SHGs facilitated for bank credit	–	16.92	–	10.39	6.97 (67%)
Amount of bank credit (₹ crore)		28,851		21,396	17,750 (82%)
Rural youth to be skill trained	4.00	2.10	1.37	0.51	–
Rural youth to be placed		1.58		0.29 (Nov 2014)	
Women farmers' coverage under MKSP	–	24.50	–	32.22	29.08 (90%, (Tamil Nadu is not part of this)

Source: Outcome Budget 2014–15, MoRD, GoI, 2015.

been scaled down considerably, possibly on account of other programmes aimed at skill development. Against the reduced target too, achievements have lagged far behind, especially in placement of trainees. Capacity building of women farmers' under MKSP is one of the livelihood supporting initiatives under NRLM. The number of women farmers covered cumulatively has exceeded the target. A review of the achievement reveals that the southern states have been at the forefront of the SHG movement, accounting for 82 per cent of all credit facilitated in the country.

A mid-term assessment carried out found that 60 per cent of the households mobilised belong to the disadvantaged section of the population i.e., SC and ST. Across states, between 75 per cent to 90 per cent of the SHGs were *Panchsutra* compliant (Box 3.3).

The average savings per member amounted to ₹1,260 by December 2014. Sixty four per cent of all groups had been provided with the revolving fund assistance. Forty two SHGs out of 2.75 lakh SHGs that were in existence by December 2014 had been provided with community investment funds (CIFs). One of the primary objectives of NRLM is to facilitate bank credit linkage for the groups. Of all groups that had been in existence for six months, 35 per cent were able to access bank credit. However, the mid-term assessment also found that more than 50 per cent of the sample SHGs selected for a survey had idle funds of ₹10,000 or more.

The latest impact assessment of the World Bank (April 2015)[8] has rated the project development objectives and implementation progress as moderately satisfactory while rating the overall risk as substantial, thus raising it from 'moderate' risk rating in the previous report. The higher perceived risk arises from the shift in emphasis in implementation of the programme. The World Bank which had sanctioned a loan of $1 billion cancelled half the loan and scaled it down to $500 million on account of slow progress, thus resulting in slow disbursements. The World Bank in its review came to the conclusion that most of the states had reached the critical stage from which they were poised to go to the next level and deal with livelihoods of the poor, taking up social development activities. The lead time taken from the launch of NRLM to the take off stage is four years, with which the admittedly lengthy process of social mobilisation is too long.

The state-wise position of expenditure on NRLM is provided in Table 3.8. Of the 27 states, only seven managed to spend a satisfactory level of 75 per cent of the funds made available. Thirteen states could not spend even 50 per cent of the available funds. There were a number of mainstream states which were unable to gather the required momentum in the implementation progress.

Box 3.3: *Quality dimensions of SHGs*

Panchsutra: The five principles for a good SHG

Regular Savings
Regular Meetings
Regular accounts' book-keeping and accounting
Regular repayments
Adherence to rules and regulations of the SHG

Source: Excerpted from NRLM Brochure, MoRD, GoI.

Table 3.8: Low level of spending by states (₹ crore)

State	Total available fund	Expenditure (2014–15)	Per cent of expenditure (%)
Andhra Pradesh	38.63	20.56	53.23
Gujarat	43.28	10.46	24.17
Haryana	19.33	17.33	89.65
Jammu & Kashmir	63.28	45.61	72.08
Jharkhand	128.61	31.7	24.65
Karnataka	36.42	18.51	50.82
Madhya Pradesh	62.53	32.2	51.5
Punjab	14.15	6.77	47.84

(Continued)

[8] Quoted from Implementation Status and Results Report, the World Bank, April 2015. Sourced from www.worldbank.org.

(Continued)

State	Total available fund	Expenditure (2014–15)	Per cent of expenditure (%)
Tamil Nadu	186.48	161.34	86.52
Uttar Pradesh	208.48	38.59	18.51
Assam	136.06	29.53	21.7
Manipur	2.07	2.07	100
Mizoram	2.8	2.8	100
Tripura	8.64	4.15	48
Bihar	692.5	383.27	55.35
Chhattisgarh	57.9	13.42	18.07
Himachal Pradesh	8.05	4.25	52.84
Kerala	25.2	25.17	99.87
Maharashtra	126.46	96.84	76.57
Odisha	165.41	45.28	27.38
Rajasthan	35.31	5.54	15.7
Uttarakhand	15.71	3.23	20.53
West Bengal	41.33	39.9	96.55
Arunachal Pradesh	3.35	0	0
Meghalaya	10.72	2.15	20.08
Nagaland	9.23	9.23	100
Sikkim	1.08	0	0

Source: Based on NRLM MIS, MoRD website.

The performance of NRLM in its livelihood activities seems to be wanting. Most of the initiatives taken under NRLM relate to forming of groups and linking them with banks. There have not been many livelihood-related initiatives as part of NRLM. The mid-term assessment of NRLP carried out by the National Mission Management Unit (NMMU) in March 2015 has made no reference to livelihood initiatives in the entire report. In the Outcome Budget of 2015–16, the MoRD points to capacity building of women farmers and also to enterprise development initiatives of rural self-employment training institutes as part of livelihood intervention of NRLM. The NRLM design is based on the AP Model of SHG-based interventions and has created people-based multi-tier institutional structures that can handle financial services efficiently and can effectively channel different other services. However, this efficient delivery channel has been used more for channelling subsidies

and bank credit rather than organising and transforming people's livelihoods except in a limited way in AP. A number of initiatives carried out by the Mission in the livelihoods space relate to capacity building of women farmers, infrastructure and marketing support, skill development for self-employment and wage employment, rural self-employment training through rural self-employment training institutes (RSETIs) and also organising marketing fairs. A reading of the available reports shows that livelihood-related initiatives are very limited compared to financial-inclusion initiatives. The clarity visible in financial architecture, seed funding and facilitation of loans is not seen in case of livelihoods initiatives. *Economic Survey* of 2013–14 observed:

> The SGSY/NRLM has been working satisfactorily in activities like tailoring, home-made products like *agarbattis*, locally consumable items, pottery and hospitality services. However, careful assessment of demand and supply of the end-product through meticulous planning and putting in place the backward and forward linkages is necessary. For this, proper time-bound identification and development of growth centres at block levels is needed. The mismatch in the scope of activities and large amount of investments made in infrastructures like buildings and equipments need to be looked into.

While some states were able to mobilise groups at a faster pace, a number of states were not able to complete the mobilisation phase (Figure 3.7). In a number of states such as Punjab, Haryana, Uttarakhand and Himachal Pradesh, the progress was very low.

The Mission is yet to prove its national character by expanding to all parts of the country and by making financial architecture work for the benefit of the rural households. A critical aspect of the NRLM is that it is skewed more towards the southern states, especially the state of AP. In terms of budget allocation and expenditure, AP has had a lion's share since the last four years out of the total NRLM expenditure. Especially under the credit and interest subvention for

Figure 3.7: SHGs'-promoted state-wise comparison

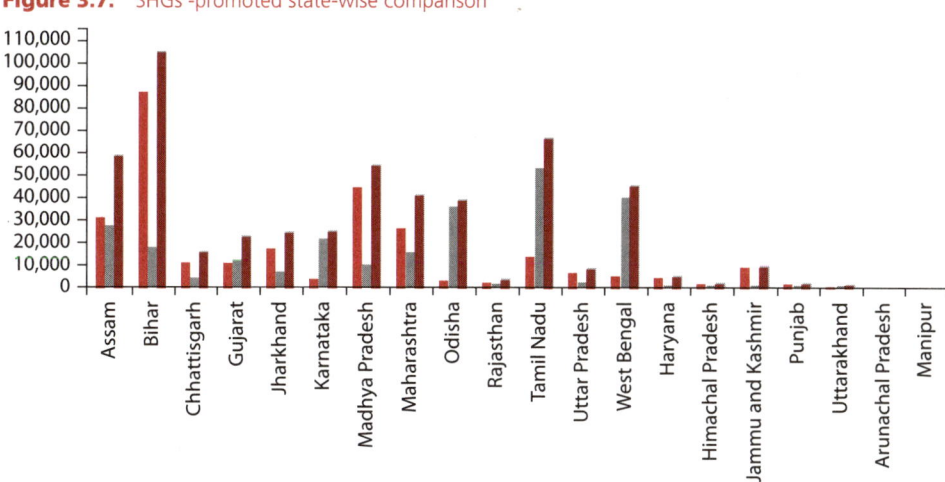

Source: Mid-term Assessment of NRLP–National Mission Management Unit, NRLM; MoRD, GoI, 2015.

credit, AP has taken the lion's share of the total allocation. The Outcome Budget for the year 2014–15 has a target of ₹120 billion of bank credit for SHGs in AP and Kerala, and only ₹2 billion for all the other states. Out of a total of ₹4.76 billion provided by way of interest subvention on SHG bank loans in 2013–14 and 2014–15, ₹3.69 billion went to AP.

Southern states have had more than a fair share of NRLM funds and support as they were early movers in the SHG movement. In credit, 67 per cent of the groups that accessed credit in 2014–15 were from the southern region and had a share of 82 per cent of the total credit amount facilitated. The Subvention Scheme on credit was introduced in the year 2014 under NRLM. The subsidy amounts too have been flowing in to southern states as the programme is slow to make headway in other states. Of the total interest subvention amount of ₹4.76 billion disbursed in 2013–14 and 2014–15, ₹4.40 billion has been received by southern states (92 per cent). Of the total 1.65 million groups that were eligible for subvention, 80 per cent (1.33 million SHGs) were in the southern states. Under MKSP, of the total 3.2 million women farmers covered, AP (including erstwhile Telangana) accounted for 2.62 million women farmers. The achievement in AP alone was higher than the targeted coverage

of 2.45 million. In the rest of the states, not much by way of livelihood initiatives have been reported. Thus, NRLM—in the first four years of its existence—has been focussed on the southern states and mostly on the state of AP. The distribution of NRLM benefits has been highly skewed, which is untenable given the mission of "organizing and supporting the poor to come out of poverty". As a national programme and a matter of priority, it should have also focussed on other states with preponderant poor population and not just continued to fund one state or region.

There have been problems in the credit arrangements made for SHGs under NRLM. By end of March 2015, there were 2.63 million SHG loan accounts with banks with an outstanding loan amount of ₹342.49 billion. Roughly, one-third of these accounts were in default. Approximately, ₹48.45 billion i.e., 14 per cent of the total credit was defaulted. In the southern states too, significant defaults were reported. In a total of 13 states, the defaults were in more than 50 per cent of the accounts and in 10 states, 50 per cent or more of the loan amounts were in default. At such high levels of default, banks find it difficult to continue the credit facilities. While the "*Panchsutra*" is an inalienable part of the programme of SHG mobilisation and support, the disseminated principles of financial discipline do not seem to have percolated to the groups. While involuntary loan default can arise on account of reasons beyond the borrower's control, mass default where one-third of the groups default, is difficult to justify. The quality of training and handholding, and rigour of appraisal of planning by groups and their loan proposals seem too weak. The roles of different resource persons dealing with groups and VOs have to be reviewed. The contents of their jobs should be redefined and strengthened to ensure that groups do not become financially undisciplined. Further, when the loans are clearly linked to viable livelihoods, the tendency to default declines on account of better incomes. There have been no monitoring reports that reflect any review of livelihoods created, incomes generated and sustainability of households ensured. The programme review committee at the central level does not call for and therefore does not review the number of livelihoods created, the incremental incomes realised and households that have crossed the poverty line.

The more successful part of NRLM is the self-employment training. The RSETIs have reported a placement rate of around 60 per cent as explained in Chapter 6. However, the RSETIs had been formed under a separate programme and were not an integral part of the NRLM. It is difficult to conclude that NRLM has been able to integrate the training and placement of candidates with the rest of the livelihood initiatives under rural livelihoods.

Changes have been proposed to the planning and implementation processes of NRLM from the year 2015. MoRD has advised the states to ensure that

- Gram Panchayat Poverty Reduction Plan is prepared with an integrated poverty reduction approach for each household;
- all panchayats are covered under intensive approach of NRLM;
- SECC data is used as the basis of planning and monitoring in social mobilisation phase;

- conjunctive use of resources is made under programmes of various ministries and panchayat untied grants;
- households without shelter, destitute, manual scavengers, Particularly Vulnerable Tribal Groups (PVTGs) and legally released bonded labourers are included as top priority, that is approximately 16.48 lakh households as per SECC;
- NRLM SHGs are linked integrally with PRIs for improving transparency, accountability and leakages in implementation;
- MIS is focused on monitoring of poor households.

The changes aim at improving demand-responsive planning, inclusion of marginalised sections of the poor, better alignment of groups with PRIs and convergence of efforts of different departments and agencies of government to provide best outcomes in the hands of groups.

Despite its democratic character and creation of people's institutions, the programme does not live up to its promise of creating and stabilising livelihoods. Some of the income increases reported have been meagre and do not justify the large mobilisation and the budgetary support the programme enjoys. Prime Minister's Employment Generation Programme (PMEGP),[9] since 2008–09 and with a much smaller budget allocation, has managed to find gainful employment to 2.55 million persons through creation of 290,000 microenterprises (Chapter 7 on non-farm sector has a detailed review of PMEGP). The grant and credit support in NRLM are also not focussed on livelihoods and incomes. As stated earlier, the revolving fund has remained idle in a number of SHGs and there is little monitoring to ensure that the CIF grants are actually applied for

---

[9] Prime Minister's Employment Generation Programme is run by KVIC, KVIBs and the District Industries Centres. It focuses on setting up micro-enterprises.

improving livelihoods. The programme has to rethink about its focus and strategy. The NRLM should focus more clearly on differentiated livelihood strategies that are relevant in different local areas. The less developed states and those with a large population of poor should be prioritised. Monitoring should not restrict itself to outputs but outcomes also in terms of vocations, livelihoods and incomes. With several other schemes underway on financial inclusion, NRLM with its high costs is perhaps not needed to create groups which default to banks. NRLM is badly needed to create, strengthen and sustain livelihoods and not for creating groups that would borrow without adequate ideas on how to apply the money for productive purposes.

The central government which had been the prime mover so far has passed on the implementation responsibility to the states. During the restructuring of centre–state finances, the central government thought it fit to reduce the Centre's support for NRLM and confined this only to capital expenditure with revenue expenditure to be borne by the states out of their share of increased devolution of taxes. A number of states in the past moved very slowly on implementation, even when full funding was assured. With funding now having been restricted, whether states will move full steam on a programme where Centre is seemingly losing interest remains to be seen. There is a serious risk of investments made so far, becoming infructuous unless the states own the mission and take the necessary steps. The changes in funding pattern are likely to adversely impact the states' willingness to invest more amounts in creating the HR capacities and infrastructure necessary for implementation of NRLM in more blocks.

Greater focus is now on skill building in people with a view to provide them jobs and enterprise opportunities not just in local areas but also in other urban locations. The increasing urbanisation and the low-income opportunities in agriculture necessitates shifting of labour force from low paid unskilled jobs to viable, skilled jobs and self-employment opportunities. NRLM looks to move towards this direction. Two new programmes have been announced, one aimed at village entrepreneurship in the non-farming sector (Start-up Village Entrepreneurship Programme, SVEP) and second at skill development for youths resulting in skilled jobs (Deen Dayal Upadhyaya Grameen Kaushalya Yojana, DDU-GKY) under NRLM. DDU-GKY will fit in with the thematic content of Skill India Initiative of the government. This programme (DDU-GKY) trained 86,000 candidates and placed 52,000 in jobs during 2014–15. Details are discussed in a later chapter on skill development. With such sub-projects and programmes, NRLM is facing a distinct shift in its orientation. However, the ***introduction of subsidised loans for NRLM women SHGs, prioritised credit access over developing and stabilising livelihood ideas that needed funding and thus distorted the focus on basic objectives of NRLM***. Skill development leading to enterprises or jobs is a valid and relevant way of dealing with issues of livelihoods for vulnerable people. Often this results in migration. For those who do not want to migrate, other parts of NRLM should be strengthened so that they can continue in the rural areas with viable livelihoods. For this to happen, the NRLM should develop comprehensive and differentiated approaches for livelihood development that respond to the demand arising from microcredit plans. Cluster-based value chains that convert demand into effective livelihoods, provision of backward and forward linkages, technical know-how, training and making people's organisation develop competencies in serving members' livelihood resource needs are aspects that NRLM should work on. The SHG formation and federation creation should no longer occupy the centre stage of NRLM work; the mobilisation of people is just a means to achieve the ultimate objective for improving livelihoods. The focus should shift from 'means' to 'end'.

III. National urban livelihoods mission

The National Urban Livelihoods Mission (NULM) was launched in September 2013 under the 12th Five-Year Plan. The mission replaced the then existing Swarna Jayanti Shahari Rozgar Yojana (SJSRY). The focus of NULM is on organising the urban poor into SHGs and creating opportunities for skill development leading to wage and self-employment opportunities. The mission also envisages focus on enterprises through facilitation of bank credit to budding entrepreneurs (Table 3.9). NULM is supposed to cover all district headquarters, towns and other towns with a population of 100,000 or more. Primarily, NULM targets the urban poor and the urban homeless. The six major components under NULM are social mobilisation and institution development, capacity building and training, skill training and employment, self-employment, support to urban street vendors and shelter for the urban homeless. It also supports innovative and special projects and has planned a robust monitoring and evaluation system. NULM is a clone of NRLM in all key aspects except in the profile of livelihood opportunities which are different in urban areas.

Effectively, two years of review of NULM are available for this report. The allocation made under NULM in the last two years was ₹9.50 billion (2013–14) and ₹10.03 billion (2014–15). Enterprises' potential in the urban areas has to be unleashed and the urban local bodies have been chosen as the implementation agencies for NULM.

The three major aspects on which NULM works are that of skill development, facilitation of credit and support to street vendors. NULM seeks to converge the efforts of other government departments in areas of education, health, enterprise development, social assistance as well as livelihood skills. Private sector partnership is encouraged especially in creation of jobs and job placements after skills training. NULM mimics the processes and structures of NRLM to a large extent. The urban poor are mobilised into SHGs. These groups are federated into area level federations. The SHGs are provided with a revolving fund assistance of ₹10,000 after six months of satisfactory working. The area level federations are also provided with corpus fund assistance of ₹50,000. Cluster level CLCs are being set up (upto a maximum of eight per city depending on its size). These centres will provide support to project households, groups and federations in their livelihood initiatives. In capacity building to project households, priority has been accorded to rag pickers, beggars and construction workers who usually find it very difficult to have a meaningful livelihood. The overall cost of capacity building has been capped at ₹50,000 per person including the cost of placement in a job.

The self-employment programme is addressed at both individual and group level. Individuals can avail bank loans of upto ₹200,000 and group microenterprises can avail ₹1 million at 7 per cent rate of interest (subvented by the government). In case of women SHGs, a further rebate at

Table 3.9: NULM achievements

Aspect	Target for 2014–15	Achievement (till 10 March 2015)
Budget	₹10. 03 billion	Revised estimate ₹7.33 billion
Number of urban poor to be imparted skill training	5,00,000	1,56,947
Number of urban poor to be assisted for microenterprises (individual and group)	60,000	23,194
Number of SHGs to be formed	40,000	36,787

Source: Annual Report of Ministry of Housing and Urban Development, 2014–15.

3 per cent rate of interest can be provided if loans are repaid on time. Effectively, women SHGs can borrow at 4 per cent rate of interest of if they maintain credit discipline. Five per cent of the budget of NULM has been earmarked for specifically supporting initiatives relating to street vendors. This amount is used for creating capacity building in the local body for pro-street vendor planning relating to spaces, markets and storage for street vendors. Further, the amount can also be used for creating and linking social security options to street vendors. So far, no further assessments or evaluations have been done after NULM came into being about 2 years back. The challenges to NULM are similar to those faced by NRLM in mobilisation, skill building and also establishing viable livelihood opportunities. There are some special issues on account of the project being located in urban areas. Housing, access to basic necessities such as water, education and health, might be a harder task in urban areas where poor people tend to live together in slums.

The numbers put out by the Department of Urban Development do not give a sense of how well the Mission's objectives are being achieved. The magnitude of urban poverty and vulnerability among migrants and slum dwellers, the size of NULM allocations and scope of work seem inadequate. The drastic reduction in the targets during 2014–15 does not seem to be an encouraging sign. In the year 2015, the Centre has decided to support only capital expenditure undertaken by the states in NULM and not the current expenditure (as in the case of NRLM). This change in funding pattern is likely to affect implementation as the state governments have to implement this through local bodies for which they have to make allocation of funds from the states' resources. However, with a significant part of NULM being skill building and loan facilitation for setting up of microenterprises, the other programmes of the government, especially the National Skill Building Initiatives and also the

Prime Minister's Mudra Yojana under which loans for microenterprises are supposed to be given, will take care of some of the issues that might come up in NULM implementation. The states will thus lose interest in a programme in which Centre's support is low. NULM as a stand-alone programme does not appear to have any validity. There are other larger programmes on skill development, social security nets and loan facilitation for enterprise development under which the tasks of NULM can easily be done. It might be a good idea to dispense with this programme in case no new ideas to make it worthwhile are on the anvil.

IV. National Food Security Act (NFSA)

The Act is a critical piece of legislation in stabilising livelihoods through assuring food security to poor and vulnerable people. It mandates that up to 75 per cent of rural and 50 per cent of urban residents receive five kilogram of highly subsidised grains each month. For the 'poorest of the poor' households called Antyodaya, the entitlement is 35 kg a month. It further mandates universal maternity benefits and a free daily meal for pregnant and lactating mothers, school meals for all children from six to 14 years in government and government-aided schools, feeding children below six years in Integrated Child Development Scheme (ICDS) centres and an additional meal for malnourished children. The total number of NFSA beneficiaries is fixed at 813.4 million and 119 million of this are estimated to be the poorest of the poor (based on number of Antyodaya ration cards issued). The NFSA prescribed a 365-days time limit for selecting the households for subsidised grains. Twelve states have already completed the identification of eligible households and started implementation. The government has extended the time limit to 30 September 2015 for other states to commence implementation. But it is not likely that all states will be able to comply with the new deadline. If the government is unable to ensure implementation across the country soon, it may have to move for amendment of the Act in the Parliament for a realistic timeframe.

The government has been subsidising food grains supplied through the Public Distribution System (PDS) over the years. In 2012–13, the food subsidy expenditure incurred was ₹897.4 billion and increased to ₹1132.65 billion in 2013–14. The allocation for 2015–16 is of ₹1199.19 billion. Rough estimates indicate that if all eligible people are issued with five kilogram of wheat per month (where the subsidy is lower than rice), the allocation of funds may increase six times from the current year's level to ₹7500 billion![10]

The Shanta Kumar Committee which was set up primarily to review the restructuring of Food Corporation of India (FCI) also considered the implementation and operationalisation of NFSA. It recommended that (a) GoI should defer the implementation of NFSA in states that have not done an end-to-end computerisation, have not put the list of beneficiaries online for anyone to verify, have not set up vigilance committees to check pilferage from PDS, (b) coverage of population should be brought down to around 40 per cent, (c) BPL families and some even above that be given seven kilogram of grains per person and (d) while Antyodaya households can be given grains at ₹3/2/1 per kilogram for the time being, pricing for priority households must be linked to MSP. These recommendations appear to have been implicitly accepted as reflected in the subsequent actions of the government.

The civil society makes out a case that the government is working towards weakening the provisions of the NFSA by repeated postponements in the deadline for implementation of NFSA; acceptance in stealth of recommendations of the Shanta Kumar Committee to replace distribution of food grains with cash through pressure on state governments to initiate pilots for DBT in PDS; putting limit on the MSP and procurement. Further, the cuts in budget allocations for mid-day meals and ICDS (cut by 50 per cent) and non-implementation of universal maternity entitlements add to the perception that government is not serious about implementation of NFSA provisions.

A working paper published by ICRIER[11] finds that NFSA in its existing form may be unimplementable.

> There are wider apprehensions that the Act will fail to deliver on the promises made. The bigger operational challenges include-ensuring the adequate supply of grains every year, lowering per person entitlement or population coverage particularly when the population is expanding, unpreparedness of the implementing states, slowing down the natural process of agricultural diversification by increasing the relevance of rice and wheat in the system.

Therefore, the authors of the paper suggested that there should be no haste in carrying out the NFSA implementation process without satisfying its pre-conditions in each state. The challenges in physically moving a large stock of grains—first during procurement and then during delivery through the distribution system—are daunting. Instead of investing in an elaborate system of procurement and distribution grains, the target population can be given the financial means to buy food from the market. This

---

[10] Authors calculations based on data in Evolution and Critique of Buffer Stocking Policy of India, Working paper 283, Shweta Saini and Marta Kozicka, ICRIER 2014. Assumptions: 800 million beneficiaries, 5 kg of wheat per month, Central Issue Price at ₹415 per quintal (BPL price), economic cost of wheat for FCI ₹1994 per quintal; subsidy of ₹15.80 per kg.

[11] The National Food Security Act (NFSA) 2013-Challenges, Buffer Stocking and the Way Forward, Working Paper 297, by Shweta Saini and Ashok Gulati, ICRIER 2015.

would ensure that people get support for food security and that delivery of financial means is done without extraordinary casts, thus fully avoiding leakages. The working paper concludes that

> trying to achieve an equity objective (extending economic access to food for the poor) by using a price policy instrument is also inconsistent with the basics of economics. The answer going forward lies in substituting the present system of physically distributing grains with conditional/unconditional cash transfers.[12]

As in the case of NREGS, fulfilling the legislative mandate of ensuring food security to the defined target population might be beyond the fiscal capacity of the government. The target of food security programme should be more sharply defined on well laid out criteria that establish the need. As the ICRIER paper argues, providing cash or food coupons might be a better way of enabling the target households to become food secure. Engaging in physical supply of food under NFSA will be expensive and wasteful.

The review of major programmes in livelihood space establishes that while progress is being made, there is a considerable scope to improve (Annexure 3.1). The programmes require a clearer vision of the results to be achieved and look for alternative means for achieving it, given the emerging context of technology-based service delivery systems. The very limited collaboration with voluntary and private sectors in all these programmes is difficult to understand. While voluntary sector understands grass root delivery of services, private sector can bring technology and cost efficiencies. A critical aspect of both NREGS and NFSA is that the intended coverage is ambitious while the public finances are not in a position to fund the entire extent of expenditure required to fulfil the parliamentary mandate. Rethinking on how to creatively deal with the government's responsibility is badly needed. As for the two Livelihoods Mission, it is time for them to begin focussing on livelihoods.

---

[12] The National Food Security Act (NFSA) 2013. Challenges, Buffer Stocking and the Way Forward, Working Paper 297, by Shweta Saini and Ashok Gulati, ICRIER 2015.

ANNEXURE 3.1
NREGS income range-wise distribution of households across states

State	No. of households having earning (in ₹)		
	Upto 5,000	5,001–10,000	10,000 and more
Andhra Pradesh	1,850,261	885,092	561,087
Arunachal Pradesh	1,28,444	6,840	885
Assam	741,731	171,137	62,925
Bihar	737,292	255,567	167,353
Chhattisgarh	1,116,302	455,751	183,267
Goa	4,682	1,758	785
Gujarat	309,699	127,063	78,068
Haryana	122,326	49,695	47,486
Himachal Pradesh	214,459	139,195	100,578
Jammu and Kashmir	185,518	104,052	42,872
Jharkhand	566,384	293,688	262,075
Karnataka	490,543	342,007	301,583
Kerala	462,938	348,198	573,228
Madhya Pradesh	1,411,864	743,068	649,820
Maharashtra	591,269	255,670	315,731
Manipur	386,990	79,270	2,798
Meghalaya	132,281	129,605	89,729
Mizoram	194,008	58	0
Nagaland	318,867	84,692	2,297
Odisha	858,447	369,568	270,171
Punjab	202,496	63,463	23,646
Rajasthan	2,179,286	1,067,439	442,677
Sikkim	26,297	17,401	13,172
Tamil Nadu	2,760,024	1,876,867	1,021,269
Telangana	1,507,494	640,716	312,990
Tripura	31,135	65,522	486,717
Uttar Pradesh	2,416,791	951,836	589,972
Uttarakhand	282,236	132,310	44,677
West Bengal	3,049,245	1,419,622	757,674
Andaman and Nicobar	5,468	3,089	4,768
Dadra & Nagar Haveli	0	0	0
Daman & Diu	0	0	0
Lakshadweep	257	190	30
Puducherry	29,329	939	29
Total	23,314,363	11,081,368	7,410,359

Source: NREGS MIS from MoRD website.

ANNEXURE 3.2
Comparative performance of states (NREGS)

State	2014–15 year over year growth person days generated	Average days per household	Per cent of households completed 100 days	Work completion rate	Per cent of registered SC/ST household provided employment	Per cent of wage paid within 15 days
Goa	149.62	23.87	1	55	21	42.03
Maharashtra	118.66	52.93	14	62	18	26.47
Jharkhand	103.91	40.8	7	81	30	67.91
Tripura	98.39	87.96	43	92	94	69.23
Madhya Pradesh	95.35	42.03	5	85	35	16.48
Telangana	92.18	42.5	6	62	41	35.22
Rajasthan	91.67	45.74	7	72	46	40.64
Manipur	89.35	21.58	0	44	97	88.49
Uttarakhand	89.1	32.37	1	74	34	32.37
Andhra Pradesh	84.24	47.18	11	71	38	41.33
Gujarat	78.82	35.37	3	77	17	45.74
Meghalaya	77.52	47.65	9	62	73	6.84
Odisha	75.14	36.44	5	63	26	19.46
Uttar Pradesh	74.86	33.52	2	72	27	18.45
West Bengal	73.9	33.14	3	68	49	4.22
Tamil Nadu	72.87	47.36	5	85	69	27.45
Assam	70.65	21.81	1	71	25	29.8
Kerala	67.97	42.65	7	73	56	15.51
Himachal Pradesh	67.46	42.12	4	83	41	19.28
Karnataka	60.48	39.65	3	63	19	11.67
Sikkim	54.79	42.51	5	72	69	43.95
Haryana	52.25	28.29	2	90	29	17.14
Arunachal Pradesh	52.11	14	0	6	71	33.48
Nagaland	49.21	22.29	0	68	95	19.22
Punjab	48	22.38	0	76	28	3.81
Chhattisgarh	42.79	31.79	2	72	43	28.67
Bihar	40.98	34.05	2	58	8	17.75
Jammu and Kashmir	35.55	36.4	2	46	34	14.77
Mizoram	32.62	22.47	0	83	106	98.31

Source: Compiled by author from NREGS MIS MoRD website.

Dairy-based Livelihoods*

Chapter 4

I. Dairy farming in Indian rural economy

India ranks first in milk production, accounting for 17 per cent of the world's production. During 2013–14, milk production peaked at 137.69 million tonnes, thus becoming an important livelihood and secondary source of income for 70 million rural households engaged in dairying. Seventy per cent of the workforce in dairying are women.[1] The average year-on-year (YOY) growth rate of milk at 4.04 per cent vis-à-vis the world average of 2.2 per cent shows sustained growth in availability of milk and milk products for the growing population.

Indian agricultural system is predominantly a mixed crop–livestock farming system, where dairying forms an important livelihood activity for most of the farmers, supporting agriculture in the form of critical inputs, contributing to the health and nutrition of the households, supplementing incomes, offering employment opportunities and finally in times of emergency, livestock as an easily saleable asset provides liquidity to manage the risks. It acts as a supplementary and complementary enterprise.

The following points characterise India's dairy farming and its relevance to inclusive growth:

- About 70 per cent of India's milk production is contributed by small and marginal farmers. Seventy million of the reported 147 million rural households depend on dairy in varying degrees for their livelihoods. Farmers of marginal, small and semi-medium operational holdings (area less than 4 hectare) own about 88 per cent of the livestock. The base line study[2] of National Dairy Plan (NDP) implemented by National Dairy Development Board (NDDB) in 14 major dairying states shows that 35 per cent of the surveyed households are milch animal owning households (MAHs). Out of these MAH, 23 per cent are landless, 41 per cent marginal farmers, 27 per cent small farmers, 6 per cent medium farmer and only 1 per cent are large farmers.
- Livestock is more equitably and evenly distributed than land and other livelihood assets (Table 4.1). Small and marginal farmers own more than 75 per cent of milk producing animals in the country, but only about 40 per cent of farmland.

---

* This chapter benefits from discussions with several stake holders including the government, NGOs, producer companies and co-operatives. The authors are grateful to BAIF for organising a round table on small holder dairy farming for this chapter where dairy farmers, representatives of dairy co-operatives, sector experts, private companies and government representative participated. Rich learnings of these discussions form part of the chapter.

[1] GoI, 2015, Economic survey 2014–15, http://indiabudget.nic.in/es2014-15/echapter-vol2.pdf, seen on 12 August 2015.

[2] The base line study was carried out in 2012–13 and covered 14,992 households in 1,257 villages in 420 *talukas* of 14 states.

Table 4.1:   Landholding of households in different land-based activities

Characteristic	Self-employed in		
	Cultivation	Livestock farming	Other agricultural activities
(1)	(2)	(3)	(4)
Estimated no. of hhd (00)	670,121	27,328	54,236
% of hhd	42.92	1.75	3.47
% area of land owned	81.41	1.47	1.48
Average area owned per hhd (ha)	1.104	0.489	0.248

Source: Key Indicators of Land and Livestock Holdings in India, NSS 70th round, December 2014, NSSO, MoSPI, GoI.

Box 4.1:   *Indian dairy vis-a-vis the global dairy*

Productivity: India tops in milk production world-wide. The average productivity of milking animals has increased but is significantly lower than the global standards. While milk productivity is 2,041 litres per annum in India, other countries such as Israel, US, UK and Australia have a productivity of 11,415 litres, 9,591 litres, 7,535 litres and 5,471 litres per annum respectively.

Cost of production: According to the International Farm Comparison Network (IFCN), research on benchmarking the cost of milk production in 46 countries and the level of cost per 100 kg of milk production for South Asia including India is less than $30, whereas the levels for USA, Brazil and Oceania are $35 to $40. For the European Union (EU), the Middle East and China, it is $40 to $50. Indian dairy farmers are competitive globally due to low cost input systems and cheap labour.

Benefit to dairy farmer: Indian dairy supply chain has been recognised globally as the most efficient, passing on about 80 per cent share of consumers' rupee to the dairy farmer vis-a-vis around 30 per cent to 35 per cent in some of the developed countries (however, this 80 per cent is questionable since interactions with farmers and dairies showed that the farmers are able to get only 50 per cent to 60 per cent share of consumer rupee and in some circumstances even lower. This is discussed later in the chapter).

Farm size: While other countries rely on medium-to-large-sized farms, in India milk contribution is made by both small and marginal farmers. The average herd size in UK, Australia and New Zealand is 126, 268 and 402 animals respectively.

Source: Making Indian Dairy Farming Competitive: The Small Farmer Perspective, A White Paper, Yes Bank, 2015.

- Dairying is a part of the farming system and not a separate enterprise for small and marginal farmers. Feed is mostly residue from crops, whereas cow dung is an important organic source of nutrition for the crops (Box 4.1). The manure availability leads to lower production costs.
- Further, a large proportion of dairying activities at the household level are carried out by women. The base line study of NDP shows that women's share of total time spent in dairying is 64 per cent; while women spend more time on activities done at home, men spend more time on activities outside home. Despite their considerable involvement and contribution, significant gender inequalities also exist in access to technologies, credit, information, inputs and services, probably because of inequities in ownership of productive assets including land and livestock.
- Dairying provides a source of continuous cash flow, whereas income from agriculture is seasonal and lumpy. This regular source of income has a huge impact on minimising risks arising from lack of liquidity in the household.

• Contribution of livestock, especially dairying, to family income ranges from 20 per cent to 50 per cent and poorer the family, greater is the contribution.

Dairying is a livelihood option for those who hold limited land. The NSSO survey data clearly establishes the fact that those in livestock farming are likely to have much less land than those engaged in crop cultivation. In other words, dairy farming is the key livelihood for more vulnerable households.

II. Emerging demand–supply imbalances

The growth rate of milk production varied from an average of 4.3 per cent per annum in the 1990s to 3.7 per cent per annum in the 2000s, achieving five per cent growth in the years 2010–11 and 2011–12 but fell to 3.5 per cent and 3.9 per cent during 2012–13 and 2013–14. Buffaloes and cows contribute 51 per cent and 45 per cent of the total milk production respectively (Figure 4.1). Production in top milk-producing states such as Uttar Pradesh, Andhra Pradesh and Rajasthan is largely contributed by buffaloes' milk. Tamil Nadu is the largest producer of cow's milk, having 11 per cent share of the total cow's milk in the country out of which 89 per cent is produced by cross-bred and exotic cows.

Indigenous milch cattle (48 million) and milch buffaloes (51 million) make up for 82 per cent of the country's total milch population, in contrast to the cross-bred cows (19.5 million) at 18 per cent.

While livestock population has been declining, milk production has been increasing (Table 4.2). While this can be due to improvements in the productivity of animals and culling of non-productive animals, there are some apprehensions that the enhanced production figures may be due to adulteration of milk.

Domestic demand for milk and milk products continues to grow, spurred by

Figure 4.1: Milk production trends

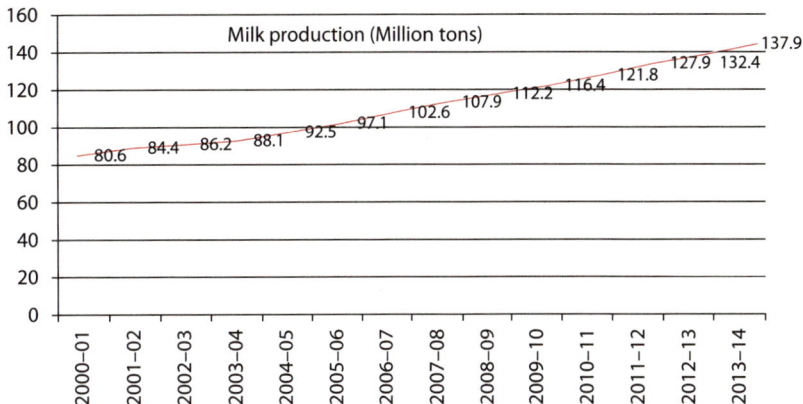

Source: Basic Animal Husbandry and Fisheries Statistics 2014, Department of Animal Husbandry, Ministry of Agriculture, GoI.

Table 4.2: Livestock population

S. No.	Species	Livestock census 2003 (no. in millions)	Livestock census 2007 (no. in millions)	Livestock census 2012 (no. in millions)	Growth rate (%) 2007–12
1.	Cattle	185.2	199.1	190.9	−4.10
2.	Buffalo	97.9	105.3	108.7	3.19
3.	Yaks	0.1	0.1	0.1	−7.64
4.	Mithuns	0.3	0.3	0.3	12.88
	Total Bovines	283.4	304.8	300.0	−1.57

Source: Annual Report 2014–15, Department of Animal Husbandry, Dairying & Fisheries; Ministry of Agriculture, Government of India.

rising incomes and changing food preferences. According to the Government of India estimates, milk demand is projected to grow to at least 180 million tons by 2021–22. Meeting this demand from domestic supply would require production to grow at 5.5 per cent per annum. If India fails to achieve substantial production growth, the country would need to resort to significant imports from the world market which has the potential to cause prices to spurt since India is a large consumer. Hence, increasing milk production and improving productivity of dairy farmers to meet the projected domestic demand is a key development challenge facing the Indian dairy sector.

III. Government funding for the sector

As a proportion of the total outlay for agricultural sector, the share of livestock fell from 11.2 per cent in the 2nd Five-Year Plan to 3.6 per cent in the 9th Five-Year Plan but increased to 9.3 per cent during the 11th Five-Year Plan and about 12 per cent in the 12th Five-Year Plan period. Working group of the Planning Commission recommended a budgetary outlay of ₹315.60 billion for the 12th Five-Year Plan for animal husbandry and dairy sector to achieve a growth rate of 6 per cent. However, actual allocation for the 12th Five-Year Plan period is ₹120.19 billion. Allocation of funds to the Department of Animal Husbandry, Dairy & Fisheries as a proportion of the overall allocation to agricultural sector has been inadequate over the last several Plan periods in spite of rising contributions of the livestock sector to GDP. The growth needs of a sector with high potential are not being fully supported. Overall public spending is equivalent to less than three per cent of livestock GDP and about 0.2 per cent of total public expenditures. Thus, the budget support for dairy has not been commensurate with its contribution to growth and GDP.

The revised expenditure by the GoI on animal husbandry sector in 2014–15 is about 40 per cent of the budget spent in 2013–14. The allocation for the current year too is well below the level of expenditure achieved in 2012–13. The states are expected to spend higher amounts for animal husbandry as a number of livestock programmes have been made the responsibility of the states in the aftermath of the financial devolutions arising from the 14th Finance Commission (Table 4.3).

Bulk of the public investment for livestock development comes from the state governments. The central government contributes about 10 per cent to the total investment. However, interactions with some of the state departments and also an analysis of the past trends[3] reveal that about 90 per cent to 95 per cent of the state's budget goes towards recurrent expenditures to meet salaries and other operating expenses. Limited budget is available for investments that improve production, productivity and value addition in the field.

According to the report of the Working Group on Animal Husbandry and Dairying for the12th Five-Year Plan, the 11th Five-Year Plan had a total of 29 schemes (21 in animal husbandry, six in dairy, one under the special package for suicide-prone districts and one under the externally aided project). The centrally sponsored schemes of animal health and disease control and National Project for Livestock Development accounted for a major share of the total outlay for animal husbandry. The overall performance of most of the schemes has not been up to the desired levels due to funding pattern, poor flexibility etc. Most of these schemes were stand-alone with meagre financial outlay.

The GoI launched the NLM in 2014–15 with an outlay of ₹24 billion for growth of the livestock sector. The NLM focuses on improving the availability of quality feed and fodder, risk coverage, effective extension, improved flow of credit and organisation of livestock farmers. The new government laid emphasis on indigenous animal development and launched the Rashtriya Gokul Mission. It made a modest beginning to revitalise the indigenous milk production system with an outlay of ₹5 billion to be implemented during the 12th Five-Year Plan.

Overall, both central and state governments have to increase their capital and programme expenditure on dairy sector. The dairy sector, however, has attracted considerable private investment in processing, value addition and marketing.

Table 4.3: Budget allocations for livestock sector

	Actuals 2013–14	Budget 2014–15	Revised 2014–15	Budget 2015–16
Department of Animal Husbandry, Dairying & Fisheries (₹ Billion)	17.49	11.33	9.09	11.33

Source: Department of Animal Husbandry, Dairying & Fisheries, Ministry of Agriculture, GoI.

[3] The World Bank.2010. India–National Dairy Support Project NDSP. Project Appraisal Document, http://documents.worldbank.org/curated/en/2010/04/12157650/india-national-dairy-support-project.

Table 4.4: Factor conditions

Herd	
Herd inventory	Very large number of indigenous animals with low productivity and a small portion of cross-breeds
Breed	Lack of policy focus on strengthening indigenous breeds
Feed	Very poor awareness of quality feed, which hinders productivity
	Farmers not interested in quality feed because of the low price of milk
	Increasing feed costs
Veterinary medicine	Availability is not an issue
Veterinary medicine costs	Duplicate or cheap medicines
Human capacity	
Farmer technical capacity	Knowledge and new techniques are not accessible
Support services technical capacity	Accessibility to good quality veterinary services is an issue in many parts of the country
Organisation and managerial capacity	Organisational and managerial capacity of farmer cooperatives is very poor
Entrepreneurial capacity	Entrepreneurial capacity is hindered by a low capacity to take risks
Credit or finance market	
Formal credit mechanisms	Access to formal credit mechanisms is very poor
Informal credit mechanisms	Accessible but at very high interest
External economies	
Transmission of learning	Very poor extension support services, leading to very poor knowledge transfer
Social capital and trust	Strong social capital and trust in the village, which can sustain dairy farmer organisations if properly managed

Source: Case Study of India in Smallholder Dairy Development: Lessons Learned in Asia; FAO, Rome. 2009.

IV. Factors contributing to productivity and profitability

There are several factors such as the quality of animals, human resources and technical skills, land availability, capital, credit, extension and health care services, institutions of dairy farmers, value addition and marketing opportunities that determine the profitability of dairy farming (Table 4.4).

1. Low productivity and quality of animals

The quality of animals determines milk productivity and hence the overall production. Despite being the world's largest milk producer, India's productivity per animal is very low—at 987 kg per lactation—compared to the global average of 2,038 kg per lactation. The base line study of NDP shows that in the project area, indigenous cows, cross-bred cows and buffaloes, contribute 12 per cent, 35 per cent and 53 per cent as against their population share of 25 per cent, 26 per cent and 49 per cent respectively. Indigenous cows' productivity is low.

The average yield of milk per day per animal at national level from different types of animals during 2013–14 is given below in Table 4.5.

Table 4.5: Average yield rate of milk (kg/day)

Exotic/cross-bred cows	Indigenous/ non-descript cows	Buffaloes
6.78	2.50	4.91

Source: Annual Report 2014–15, Department of Animal Husbandry, Dairying & Fisheries; Ministry of Agriculture, Government of India.

The major causes of low productivity of milch animals are:

- Poor nutrition due to traditional feeding practices that are not based on scientific feeding methods, limited availability and affordability of quality feed/fodder and also lack of farmers' knowledge on how to better use the existing feed resources.

- Poor animal health with limited extension services. Reliable veterinary services are not available in many parts of the country.
- Low genetic potential for milk production, insufficient and ineffective cattle-and-buffalo-breeding programmes.

2. Improving genetic quality of breeds

Artificial Insemination (AI) technique has been found to be the most economical tool for breeding animals as it allows the efficient use of genetically superior bulls to improve the genetic potential of a large number of breedable cow and buffalo population. The GoI has an ambitious target of expanding the AI programme from its present level of coverage of about 25 per cent to 50 per cent of breedable bovine population by the end of the 12th Five-Year Plan.[4] The limited availability of quality AI services means that about 75 per cent of breeding in the country is through natural service which predominantly involves non-descript or inferior bulls. After more than three decades of cross-breeding, the cross-bred population is only 18 per cent in cattle.

Production of good quality, disease-free semen and effective AI services are key to a successful genetic improvement programme. Although about 25 per cent of the animals are bred using AI, only about 20 per cent per cent of the bulls in the country's semen stations have come through a genetic improvement programme.[5] Progeny-testing programmes for evaluation of bulls for

buffaloes, cross-bred cattle and indigenous breeds have not been largely undertaken because of constraints of technical man-power, small herd size and lack of interest on part of the states and absence of an effective extension network. Information on progeny-tested bulls and their performance is hardly published. To achieve improvements in the quality of animals, increasing the number of genetically improved bulls to produce high- quality semen and expanding AI services are very critical. These investments are necessary to build a foundation for increased milk production.

Dr Pande, Senior Vice President, BAIF, mentions that "Every year, 8,000 high quality bulls have to be replaced in India. Under the World Bank funded National Dairy Plan, NDDB will be able to develop about 3,000 progeny-tested bulls over five to seven years which is inadequate. The current trend in developing countries is to undertake genome testing and 70 per cent of semen used in developed countries is from genome-tested bulls. Though in India this may take a time frame of five years, a national level platform of research institutions, government departments, NGOs, to take up genome testing has to be created".

Moreover, current production of 50 million semen doses needs to be increased to around 150 million doses to cover at least 50 per cent of the breedable population. BAIF Development Research Foundation which established the Bull Mother Farm and Bull Station at the Central Research Station, Uruli Kanchan, Pune, mentions that for high-quality-disease-free semen production, the breeding bulls need to be biologically tested for TB, herpes virus etc., using reagents. For the country as a whole, the reagents used in testing are produced only at the Indian Veterinary Research Institute, Izatnagar, UP, which closed down for sometime. BAIF had to procure and store antigens in large quantities. State livestock boards also had to import antigens for their breeding farms. The GoI and state

---

[4] Annual Report 2014–15, Department of Animal Husbandry, Dairying & Fisheries; Ministry of Agriculture, Government of India.

[5] The World Bank.2010. National Dairy Support Project NDSP, Project Information Document, http://wwwwds.worldbank.org/servlet/WDSContentServer/IW3P/IB/2011/07/27/000003596_20110727150106/Rendered/PDF/NDSP0PID00Revised0July021.pdf

governments have to ensure that such basic facilities are not only set up but run reliably to ensure a steady supply of reagents so that quality semen production continues unhindered.

State Department of Animal Husbandry, the milk cooperatives and the NGOs such as BAIF, JK Trust, etc., arrange AI services. State livestock development agencies are being set up as autonomous bodies to offer services in animal breeding in the form of procurement, production and distribution of breeding inputs (such as semen and liquid nitrogen), training and promotional activities and so on. So do the trained private sector AI technicians for a fee. Most government AI centres are still stationary due to deficiency of manpower and transport facility. The conception rate under AI is poor (reported rates of 35 per cent) though some experts and stakeholders participating in the Round Table on smallholder dairy farming mention much lower rates at 18 per cent to 20 per cent; the most important reason for low conception rate is lack of well trained staff and their inability to adhere to common protocols and operating procedures. Follow up on inseminated animals, pregnancy follow up and also treatment for infertility are hardly available under the government's extension services.

NGOs and also dairy cooperatives provide AI services at the farmers' doorstep with comparatively better performance in terms of frequency and quality of services delivered. Apart from doorstep delivery of AI services through technically well- trained local resource persons, a regular follow up is instrumental in achieving 45 per cent to 52 per cent conception rate by BAIF, Sahayog and a few other private players (refer case studies 4.1 and 4.2 on pages 76 and 79 respectively). BAIF mentions that with technology improvement, pregnancy after AI can be confirmed by the first month instead of the third month, as is largely tested now. The feed can be accordingly provided to the milch animals, thus saving feed cost.

Farmers are also demanding sexed semen due to the advantages of 90 per cent guaranteed female calves, faster growth of productive herd, calves with proven genetic potential etc. Large semen-producing companies like ABS, Semex, CRV etc., are making inroads into the Indian market with such technology. The Government of AP which identified dairy farming as one of the key sectors to achieve double-digit-inclusive growth has proposed to subsidise sexed semen by 50 per cent, since each straw costs ₹1500 which is 40 times more than the conventional semen. The Government also proposes to pilot in selected areas with selected herds in an organised way under the supervision of veterinarians to document results.[6]

Different stakeholders in the Round Table emphasised on the need for a breeding policy with different breeds coming in and indiscriminate breeding practices by private players. Effective regulatory mechanism has to be put in place by the state governments.

Calf rearing programmes

Growth phase of the cows is confined to the first two years of their life. It is important that the calf is given nutritious feed in the form of concentrates or fodder right from its fourth month of birth. This will ensure a good milk yield when the calf becomes a cow. If the animal is introduced to the feeding schedule after six months of birth, the desired effect may not be to the full extent. The calf, depending upon its body weight/breed consumes around 1600 kgs of concentrate. This amount can be substantially reduced if good quality fodder is available. On an average, it is assumed that the calf comes to puberty at around 18th–20th month of birth and becomes a cow by calving for the first time around the 28th–29th month of birth, if managed properly.

---

[6] Achieving DoubleDigit Inclusive Growth: A Rolling Plan 2015–16. Government of Andhra Pradesh, 2015.

During the first 24 to 30 months of a calf's life, dairy farmers incur cost and get no cash inflows. Small farmers with very few animals find it difficult to rear calves and hence sell off the same after initial months. There are arrangements in rural areas where some households specialise in rearing calves but their financial capacity is limited to a few animals. There are schemes from banks for providing loans (refinanced by NABARD) to finance a calf's growth period. However, the banks do not provide adequate attention to this loan product. To ensure that the calves grow up as healthy and productive animals, calves programmes should be better organised with not just funds, but also supply of feed, fodder, concentrates and medicines.

Indigenous breeds have better adaptation characteristics, high production potential under low inputs and harsh environment and valuable genetic make-up. For the rural poor, they are easier to manage. Efforts for conservation of quality indigenous breeds also need to be strengthened. A number of quality indigenous breeds such as Sahiwal, Tharparkar, Gir, Rathi, Red Sindhi, etc., have higher milk yields than non-descript animals and are more adapted to the local conditions of the region where they are popular. The non-descript cattle should be upgraded by crossing with the elite indigenous breeds. There are some private initiatives undertaken in this regard. Last year, the GoI announced a national mission to conserve, develop and popularise indigenous breeds. The Rashtriya Gokul Mission worked on indigenous breeds comprehensively (Box 4.2) with private sector's participation. The first year's budget allocation was ₹1.5 billion.

3. Health care and extension services

Animal health and breeding services provision, veterinary infrastructure development and vaccinations are the responsibility of the state government. Extension activities in dairy management are falling far short of requirements. Farmers have not been able

---

Box 4.2: *Rashtriya Gokul Mission*

The Mission will be implemented with the objectives to development and conservation of indigenous breeds; undertake breed improvement programme for indigenous cattle breeds so as to improve the genetic makeup and increase the stock; enhance milk production and productivity; upgrade nondescript cattle using elite indigenous breeds like Gir, Sahiwal, Rathi, Deoni, Tharparkar, Red Sindhi and distribute disease free high genetic merit bulls for natural service.

Funds under the scheme will also be allocated for establishment of Integrated Indigenous Cattle Centres—'Gokul Gram'—and strengthening of bull mother farms to conserve high genetic merit indigenous breeds. The Gokul Grams will be established in the native breeding tracts and near metropolitan cities for housing the urban cattle. They will act as centres for development of indigenous breeds and a dependable source for supply of high genetic breeding stock to the farmers in the breeding tract. The Gokul Gram will be self- sustaining and will generate economic resources from sale of milk, organic manure, vermi-composting, urine distillates and production of electricity from biogas for in-house consumption and sale of animal products. It will also function as state-of-the-art in situ training centre for farmers and breeders.

Each Gokul Gram will be set up in a PPP mode. It will maintain milch and unproductive animals in the ratio of 60:40 and will have the capacity to maintain about 1,000 animals. Nutritional requirements of these animals will be provided for in the Gokul Gram through an in-house fodder production. Disease free status of Gokul Gram will be maintained through regular screening of animals for important diseases like brucellosis, TB and JD. An inbuilt dispensary and AI centre will be an integral part of the Gokul Gram. It will also be set up near to metropolitan cities for managing urban cattle. Metropolitan Gokul Gram will focus on genetic upgradation of urban cattle.

Source: Brochure on Rashtriya Gokul Mission, Department of Animal Husbandry, Ministry of Agriculture, GoI 2015.

to realise the full productive potential of their animals because they lack information on feeding and management practices. Extension services focused on women involved in livestock rearing would enhance milk production considerably.

Public extension services have played a major role in technology transfer in the Indian crop sector but in the livestock sector, public service delivery has remained weak. Consequently, only 5.1 per cent of the farm households were able to access any information on animal husbandry against 40.4 per cent for crop farming households.[7] The base line study of NDP shows that in the last one year (2012–13) only 0.84 per cent of the milch animal rearing households participated in any training and only 0.33 per cent participated in demonstrations. Though women spend more time in animal rearing, their participation in trainings and demonstrations was much lower than that of the men.

The veterinary and animal science services are a highly specialised area and need qualified and technical manpower. Extension activities by the State Animal Husbandry departments suffer from inadequate human[8] and also financial resources. The extension services are mainly run by veterinarians who operate from veterinary dispensaries to treat animals. Shortage of technical manpower for field services affects the timeliness of services and increase cost to the farmers.

Basic infrastructure and facilities for animal health care are also found to be inadequate. Working Group of the Planning Commission notes that "there are a total of 8,732 veterinary hospitals/polyclinics and 18,830 veterinary dispensaries in the country providing services for the large livestock population. Not only is their number grossly inadequate compared to the requirements, these also have poor infrastructure in terms of dilapidated buildings, lack of equipments, etc. The polyclinics, wherever established, lack the adequate infrastructure for surgical interventions and diagnostic imaging. There is acute shortage of manpower to manage these institutions and provide required services". During the Round Table on smallholder dairy, the stakeholders mentioned that diagnostic facilities at field levels in terms of good clinical laboratories, equipments, quick and quality diagnostics and the human resources having expertise in these areas are practically non-existent.

With improvements in the quality of livestock through cross-breeding programmes, the susceptibility of these livestock to various diseases including exotic diseases has increased. GoI has been providing 100 per cent funding for control of certain diseases such as the foot-and-mouth-disease (FMD), Brucellosis etc. Foot and Mouth Disease Control Programme (FMD-CP) is being implemented in 313 specified districts in 12 states and 6 union territories with 100 per cent central funding for cost of vaccine, maintenance of cold chain and other logistic support to undertake vaccination. However, from the current year, the central government has reduced funding to 50 per cent and expects the states to bear the rest. This can lead to inadequate vaccinations since some states may not give importance in view of the low budget provided for this.

Similarly, the National Control Programme on Brucellosis (NCPB)[9] initiated in 2010 envisages mass screening of cattle and buffaloes to ascertain incidences of disease and vaccination of all female calves. Experts mention that even adult animals should be vaccinated as against

---

[7] Planning Commission.2011.http://planningcommission.gov.in/aboutus/committee/wrkgrp12/agri/AHD_REPORT_Final_rev.pdf

[8] As per the Report of the Working Group on Animal Husbandry and Dairying, 12th Five-Year Plan, only 34,500 veterinarians are employed for field services as against the requirement of 67,000. Similarly, against the requirement of 7,500 veterinary scientists for teaching and research, only 3,050 are available. Availability of para-vets and other supporting staff is only 52,000 as against the requirement of 2,59,000.

[9] It causes abortions and infertility in animals. Prevention of abortions will add new calves to the animal population, thus leading to enhanced milk production.

only calves since the disease can spread to humans through consumption of milk. Two more diseases which are prevalent in cross-bred cows are Infectious Bovine Rhinotracheitis (IBR)[10] and Bovine Viral Diarrhoea (BVD)[11] which should be taken more seriously by the government; information about disease management needs to be propagated to farmers and vaccines should also be made available widely.

Other concern is the indiscriminate usage of antibiotics which has resulted in consumers getting milk having residues of antibiotics. There are no means of verifying antibiotic residues in milk at most societies and collection centres.

Veterinarians and other technicians require training in appropriate usage of medicines. There is also a demand from dairy farmers that mobile veterinary services should be introduced and treatment should be provided at low cost. Farmers are showing the willingness to pay for such services. Veterinary services, especially vaccination, AI etc., have traditionally been provided for free or at a very subsidised rate. Since the past few years, there has been an increasing awareness that states pay heavily to offer these services which are easily available to farmers. Consequently, many states have instituted partial or full-cost recovery of fees for providing these services.

There are also concerns about laymen acting as para veterinarians/artificial inseminators with limited training (who are often thought of as doctors by farmers). Since in some of the far-flung areas, veterinary doctors are not willing to be posted, at the grassroots, cadre of local youth paravets are being deployed. However, they need to

---

[10] It is a contagious, infectious respiratory disease that is caused by Bovine Herpesvirus-1 (BHV-1) and can affect both young and older cattle.

[11] It is a viral disease which primarily affects cows and can also affect other ruminants (sheep, goats, wild ruminants). The affected animals show an array of clinical signs like diarrhoea, fever, mucosal erosions etc. However, a majority of infected animals do not show any clinical signs at all. In some cases, the animals die because of the disease.

Box 4.3: *Farmers' education by government of Maharashtra*

in order to ensure the quality of veterinary services, Maharashtra Livestock Development Board, Government of Maharashtra, carried out farmers' awareness campaigns through mass media like radio and television. When farmers availed services from veterinary doctors or technicians, the aspects they should check were elaborated. For example, when AI is being carried out, a farmer needs to check whether the straw has been chosen by the service provider depending on the breed, production level of the cow, temperature etc. Similarly, for vaccines, disposable needles should be used. The campaign covers those aspects which farmers should look for while availing veterinary services.

Source: Dr Dhananjay Parkale, Deputy Commissioner of Animal Husbandry, Government of Maharashtra, Pune.

---

be well trained and deployed with appropriate supervision so that the community gets at least the basic services. Farmers also need to be educated about what to expect from such services (Box 4.3).

In field interactions, farmers mentioned that in spite of rearing animals for more than half a decade, they required more knowledge to address new issues. Mechanisation, where feasible, should be made available. Milking machines, chaff cutters were some of the requirements when herd size increased and farmers want some demonstrations to be done in villages so that they can check the utility of new equipments before buying. While farmers' school concept has been followed successfully in crops, the same has not been adopted well in livestock. Some progressive farmers in the villages can be intensively trained in dairy management to develop model farms which includes records to be kept, veterinary services and questions to be asked to service providers etc. These model farms and trained farmers can pass on their knowledge to other farmers.

With the extension services being inadequate in most parts of the country, some dairy units in the cooperatives and private sectors are arranging for such services at reasonable costs for the dairy farmers. They realise that the knowledge and skills to be imparted to farmers has to be continuous and it takes them time to adopt/change practices. As a thumb rule, 10 paise per litre of milk is spent on extension services.

Nestlé India established the first milk factory in India. The factory produces milk powders, infant products and condensed milk. Nestlé works with around 110,000 milk farmers and collects over 300 million kgs of milk every year from Punjab, Haryana and Rajasthan. The job of sourcing milk from farmers is done by private commission agents appointed by the company. Nestlé operates a network of 1,100 agents who receive 2.3 per cent commission on the value of the milk supplied to the dairy. Nestlé assists the farmers to increase milk productivity and expand their herds via financial assistance, technical assistance regarding feeding practices, breeding, mechanisation of dairy farms and making veterinary services available through a team of around 35 veterinarians and farmers' training and education.

Warana, a cooperative, procures on an average 3 lakh litres of milk from 70,000 members per day. Warana arranges for veterinary services at a nominal fees of ₹50/- per animal. Seeds for fodder are provided at 75 per cent subsidy. The cooperative partners with universities and also other government departments to transfer the latest knowledge to farmers. They also propagate the usage of machines like milking machines so that the drudgery of farmers is reduced.

4. Feed and fodder

India, with only 2.29 per cent of the world's land area, is maintaining about 10.71 per cent of global livestock population.[12] Feed largely determines good milk yield; the nutritive value of feed and fodder has a significant bearing on the productivity of livestock. For the farmers, the feed cost constitutes about 60 per cent to 70 per cent of the operating expenses.

The Working Group of Planning Commission estimated that for achieving the targeted milk production of 160 million tonnes by 2020, 494 metric tonnes (mt) dry fodders, 825mt green fodder and 54mt concentrates would be required annually. The current deficit of green fodder, dry fodder and concentrates is 63 per cent, 24 per cent and 76 per cent respectively.[13] The following table (Table 4.6) presents the fodder scenario in the country and the large gap that needs filling.

Table 4.6: Demand and supply of fodder: An estimate

(in million tonnes)

Year	Supply		Demand		Deficit as % of demand (as actual)	
	Green	Dry	Green	Dry	Green	Dry
1995	379.3	421	947	526	568 (59.95)	105 (19.95)
2000	384.5	428	988	549	604 (61.10)	121 (21.93)
2005	389.9	443	1,025	569	635 (61.96)	126 (22.08)
2010	395.2	451	1,061	589	666 (62.76)	138 (23.46)
2015	400.6	466	1,097	609	696 (63.50)	143 (23.56)
2020	405.9	473	1,134	630	728 (64.21)	157 (24.81)
2025	411.3	488	1,170	650	759 (64.87)	162 (24.92)

Source: Excerpted from the Handbook of Agriculture, Chapter 37, ICAR 2012. The estimates pertain to the livestock population and not just dairy animals.

[12] Annual Report of the Department of Animal Husbandry, Dairying & Fisheries, Ministry of Agriculture, Government of India, 2014.

[13] The World Bank. 2010. NDSP, Project appraisal document, http://documents.worldbank.org/curated/en/2010/04/12157650/india-national-dairy-support-project.

There is stagnation in the availability of green fodder and the deficit over the years is increasing. The major reasons for shortage of feed and fodder are increasing pressure on land for growing food grains, oil seeds and pulses and inadequate attention to the production of fodder crops. Crop residues are the largest single source of bulk feed material available to farmers for feeding livestock. These include coarse and fine straws, leguminous and pulses straws. Crop diversification, which has been seen in the recent years with commercial crops replacing the traditional cereal crops especially the coarse cereals, has an impact on the availability of crop residues. The area under cultivated fodder production is limited to only five per cent of the total cultivable land and has remained static since the last four decades. Owing to the importance of food crops, cash crops and their higher profitability, it is very unlikely that the area under fodder cultivation would increase substantially.

Fodder from common property resources is another major source of feed for animals. The dependence of marginal and small farmers on common lands around their villages to meet the demand of fodder for at least 4–5 months of the year is increasing as the quality of animals is improving. But lack of efficient management of common property resources is a major constraint in availability of these resources for fodder. The grazing lands are gradually diminishing. Majority of the grazing lands have either been degraded or encroached upon by restricting their availability for livestock grazing. In the states of Haryana, Punjab, Gujarat and some parts of Rajasthan, land use for green fodder production is estimated at 10 per cent or more. While Bihar, Rajasthan, UP, Haryana, J&K and Kerala have shown growth in land use for fodder cultivation, Maharashtra has registered the maximum decline in land usage.[14]

---

[14] Suruchi Consultants, Dairy Industry Vision 2030, 8th in series, 2014. http://www.suruchiconsultants.com/pageDownloads/report/63_Surchi_DIV_2030.pdf

Box 4.4: *Bran and wheat at the same price*

The cost of wheat bran, a by-product of wheat and used in cattle feed is ₹18 per kilo whereas the cost of wheat itself is only ₹19 per kilo. I read in newspapers that India is exporting wheat bran and hence the prices for domestic users have also increased. Government has to look into the pricing mechanism and ensure appropriate policies for exports so that farmers are not deprived on both sides.

Dairy Farmer, Pune.

Source: Round Table discussions with groups of dairy farmers and dairy experts in BAIF, Pune on 17 August 2015.

Manufacturing of compounded cattle feed is by and large with the private sector agencies and dairy federations. The usage of compounded cattle feed has not witnessed the desired level of growth over the years. The escalating price of feed ingredients (Box. 4 4) such as de-oiled bran and molasses which constitute 35 per cent and 12 per cent of the cattle feed respectively can render dairy farms unviable. The wholesale price index (WPI) of milk and cattle feed has kept the same pace in the last five years.

Awareness and adoption of improved fodder production and conservation technologies among farmers can significantly increase the production and availability of green fodder in term of quality and quantity. Institutions like BAIF, NDDB demonstrate cultivation of improved varieties of fodder crops. The Ration Balancing Programme (RBP) envisaged in the NDP will facilitate the dairy farmers in providing a nutritionally balanced feed which can be cost effective since it uses locally available ingredients with dairy farmers (Box 4.5).

Though the availability of feed and fodder has improved since the last decade, still a lot is required to be done to bridge the gap between the demand and availability of fodder; at today's demand level for milk production, there is a need to double the land for fodder growing/pasture land development. The National Livestock Mission (NLM) has an

> **Box 4.5:** *Ration balancing programme of NDDB*
>
> Balanced feed rations should be developed depending upon the crop/fodder cultivated in a particular region and optimally utilising locally available feed resources, thus reducing cost and increasing resource optimisation. Farmers feed their animals based on their traditional knowledge and information passed through generations and in most cases, the quantity of feed/fodder offered to animals is either more or less than the requirements. This leads to an imbalance of protein, energy and minerals in their ration. Animals on such an imbalanced ration produce milk sub-optimally, making the cost of milk production higher with adverse effects on health and fertility. Therefore, it is necessary to educate farmers on feeding of balanced ration. NDDB has developed a software that can be used on computers as well as phones. With the help of this software, balanced ration is formulated considering the animal's profile, i.e., cattle or buffalo, age, milk production, milk fat, feeding regime etc., and milk producers are advised to adjust the quantity of locally available feed ingredients offered to their animals along with area-specific mineral mixture.[15] Under the ration balancing programme introduced by NDDB, more than 70,000 milch animals have been covered in about 1,500 villages till March 2014. The result has shown that adoption of a balanced ration can significantly reduce the cost of feeding and increase the quality and quantity of milk produced by milch animals, thereby giving an economic benefit of ₹15 to ₹35 per animal/day to the farmers.[16] The National Dairy Plan proposes to reach 40,000 villages through the Ration Balancing Programme.
>
> *Source:* Annual Report, 2013–14, NDDB.

important component to promote availability of feed and fodder to substantially reduce the gap between availability and demand.

5. Reliable data and information

Availability of reliable and in-time information is crucial for livestock development planning but there is an acute scarcity of such information. Moreover, for meeting the challenges of globalisation, it is imperative to have comprehensive and reliable knowledge of the ground realities on all aspects of livestock production system.

Unlike crop sector where a number of schemes and surveys for collecting the information are made, there are only two mechanisms for compiling information on animal husbandry and dairying. These are the (a) Quinquennial (five yearly) Livestock Census and (b) Integrated Sample Survey. In addition, the NSSO also conducts a decennial survey on land and livestock holdings. Integrated Sample Survey generates information on production and yield of major livestock products like milk, eggs, meat and wool on an annual basis. Not all states carry out the Survey regularly and not all of them carry it out in any given periodicity. Therefore, the reliability of data is doubtful.

NDDB compiles useful information on the milk procurement, prices, value addition and other aspects of milk production and processing collected from the vast network of dairy cooperative structure in the country. However, the public access to this data base is limited. NDDB is now bringing out state-wise statistical profile for all major milk producing states; four states have been completed. This includes trends in human demographics, animal population and production, inputs for enhancement of productivity such as breeding, health and nutrition and government expenditure along with supporting resources. The objective of this publication is to provide a detailed presentation of various parameters, underlying factors and their inter-linkages so as to enable

---

[15] NDDB, Ration Balancing Programme, 2015, available at: http://www.nddb.org/services/animalnutrition/rationbalance.

[16] NDDB, Speech by Chairman at CII, Dairy Vision 2025, 2015, available at: http://www.nddb.org/about/speech/dairyvision.

effective planning and implementation of development interventions.

Participants in the Round Table on smallholder dairy farming recommended developing a database of each animal (like the way vehicles are registered) so that there was a continuing health and production record and any health interventions could be appropriate. With internet connectivity and computerisation being planned at the panchayat level, it should be possible to pool the data of animals for analysing the patterns and trends in a given geographical areas for planning suitable interventions. Hurdle can be the considerable investments required for MIS and also in training and awareness raising of farmers.

National Dairy Research Institute (NDRI) in its Vision 2020 document[17] recognises the following: "Strategic planning for dairy development of the country depends upon basic and precise availability of data, giving complete, spatial and temporal view of dairying and dairy-related linkages, whether vertical or horizontal". It proposes as part of its Vision, "establishing a strong database covering vital aspects of dairying in India viz., milk production, marketed surplus, procurement, processing and distribution across different agro-climatic regions." Information technology will be used for developing databases on a uniform platform, which can be shared by the potential users including planners, administrators, policy makers, economists and the scientific community at large. At the village level, the Institute will establish information banks that will provide the necessary information regarding not only dairying but also agriculture as a whole. Understanding the market and preparing itself to respond to the emerging market trends will be the prime instrument for enhancing the domestic livelihood opportunities in the dairy sector.

---

[17] Source: www.ndri.res.in

6. Financial services
Credit

Since good quality animals are expensive, dairy farmers require credit for the purchase of animals. Separate data on credit flow for dairy developments at national level are difficult to come by since many farmers prefer buying animals under the facilities of the Kisan Credit Card. The Round Table on smallholder dairy farming conducted at BAIF threw some light on field realities. Farmers are hesitant to borrow from the banks and increase their herd size since dairy is not considered a profitable venture and hence they might not be able to repay with interest. They prefer to increase the number of animals through breeding and rearing process. Shankar Rout, a farmer, has a herd size of 40 cows, out of which 30 were produced at farm and only 10 were procured from outside. He mentions, "The farmers were earlier getting loan from dairy cooperatives at zero interest. Since these dairies are not making adequate profits, they do not lend any more now. Banks, due to their bad experience in dairy portfolio, have turned conservative in lending for dairying. While farmers are producing calves and increasing the herd size, they need loans for constructing sheds, machinery etc., for which they are unable to get bank loans".

Private dairies engage milk collection agents who also double up as money lenders. They use the thumb rule of credit worthiness which is ₹10,000 as advance for per litre of milk poured in a day. The farmer is paid ₹1 or ₹2 less per litre for the milk price towards interest. The principal is repaid separately if the farmer wants to break this relationship. The lender is not interested in getting the loan repaid so that he can continue to get milk at a cheaper rate. Farmers have not calculated the rate of interest that they pay; they feel the pinch when another dairy collection centre pays ₹20 per litre and they get only ₹17 because of the loan that they have taken. However, small farmers lack the financial resources needed to get out of the present arrangement and move to another dairy which does not provide advance. Since majority of the farmers are in need of funds, such relationships continue.

Gokul and Warana dairy lent to farmers for purchase of feed and animals. The principal and interest were recovered from the milk price to be paid to the farmers. However, when the government announced loan waivers, the farmers expected the dairies also to waive off their loans. When loans were not waived off, they became disgruntled because they had borrowed from the dairy and hence incurred a 'loss'. Hence the dairies scaled down their loans and at present no lending is undertaken. Warana provides guarantees for bank loans for its long- standing farmer members.

It is perplexing that farmers hesitate to borrow from banks since they don't consider dairy as profitable enough to meet their regular repayment instalments. In SHGs, nearly 40 per cent to 60 per cent of the loans are taken for animal rearing, mostly for purchase of dairy animals. They borrow at 18 per cent to 24 per cent rate of interest per month and regularly repay loans within two years. Hand In Hand[18] which took a loan from Agriculture Development Fund–Tamil Nadu (ADFT) and lent on to 937 women for purchase of cross-bred cows has found repayment performance to be excellent.

Insurance: The Working Group of Planning Commission for the 12th Five-Year Plan estimated that only six per cent of the animal heads (excluding poultry) are provided insurance cover. Risk management and insurance as components of Sub-mission on Livestock Development of NLM are being implemented in all districts of the country (earlier it was only 300 districts) since May 2014 and all types of livestock are being covered. Benefit of subsidy is restricted to only five milch animals per beneficiary per household as against two animals earlier (female cattle/buffalo yielding at least 1,500 litre of milk per lactation are covered). As per the annual report of the Department of Animal Husbandry, 1 million animals have been insured during 2014–15, up to December, 2014. The offtake is very limited as compared to the cattle population of about 300 million.

Government-subsidised mandatory credit-linked insurance schemes are designed to enable the policyholder to repay the bank loan (Box 4.6). It is distributed to loanee farmers through the partner-agent model by the banks. Premiums are decided by insurers at the state level through a bidding process (subject to a cap of 4.5 per cent), the government subsidises at 50 per cent of it, while the farmers pay the remainder.

Box 4.6: *Milch cattle insurance by Karnataka government*

With foot-and mouth disease and road accidents claiming the lives of thousands of cattle in the past, the State government has decided to implement the livestock insurance scheme to encourage farmers to insure their milch cattle and buffaloes. Under the scheme, a maximum of five cattle/buffaloes would be covered by a farmers' family. The maximum insurance cover for an animal is ₹50,000. So far, milch cows and buffaloes purchased under bank loans covered under the insurance scheme. Now, it has been decided to provide insurance cover for all milch animals in the State. While the Government will bear 40 per cent, the Karnataka Milk Federation and other milk producers' societies would bear 30 per cent of the premium for the insurance cover to milch cows. The beneficiary farmer would have to bear rest of the amount.

Source: Nagesh Prabhu. 2015. 'Milch cattle, buffaloes to be covered under livestock insurance,' *The Hindu*, Published on 2 August 2015. Available at: http://www.thehindu.com/news/national/karnataka/milch-cattle-buffaloes-to-be-covered-under-livestock-insurance/article7492039.ece.

---

[18] An NGO headquartered in Chennai.

The product covers up to two animals per farmer for a maximum of three years. Only productive animals (largely cross-bred cows yielding more than 1,500 litres of milk) are eligible, thereby excluding many indigenous animals. The product only covers the death of the animal, although low yield, diseases, extended dry periods, price fluctuations and lack of inputs are other common risks faced by the farmers. As result of high incidences of fraud, insurance companies are forced to adopt measures of extreme caution at the time of policy issuance and claim settlement.

In recent times, some insurers are displaying interest in milch animals' insurance and loan-linked sales (outside government-subsidised schemes) is picking up, largely through individual agents. Forty per cent of TATA-AIG's livestock portfolio and 30 per cent of United India's cattle portfolio of INR 1.07 billion are outside the government schemes. Dairy farmers, overall, are still wary of insurance more because of the formalities to be fulfilled for death claims and uncertain benefits even after insuring at market rates. Apart from underwriting and issuing policies, insurers should train local resource persons such as the dairy cooperative staff, the milk collection agents or the paravets on filing of insurance claims as this is the most vexatious process in which customer dissatisfaction is high.

7. Milk marketing

About 50 per cent of the milk producing households are estimated to sell milk where as others use it for their own consumption.[19] Dairy farmers are highly dispersed and are located far away from consumer markets; and milk is highly perishable. Thus, they require efficient marketing and processing systems along their entire supply chain—from production to consumption—to reap optimal returns. Aggregated marketing and processing activities assume added criticality in India since most livestock producers are

small, resource-poor and often unable to establish their own linkages with the markets, processors and consumers.[20]

Milk cooperatives procure about 10 per cent of the total production which is around 18 per cent of the marketable surplus.[21] A similar quantity is reportedly procured by the private sector. Both these sectors together account for only about 35 per cent of the marketable surplus.[22] This means that a large quantity of milk remains unprocessed. The installed processing capacity of the cooperative sector is 43.3 million litres/day, while they actually process an average 33.5 million litres/day. As per the available data, the registered (as different from installed) capacity of private sector milk processors in India is 73.3 million litres/day.[23]

The base line study of NDP found that in the 14 milk producing states, more than 55 per cent of the milch-animal rearing households sold milk. A much larger per cent of population sold milk in Kerala (91 per cent), Tamil Nadu (86 per cent) and Andhra Pradesh (80 per cent). The study also found that the share of milk sold to organised sector was 45 per cent; out of the 14 states, Karnataka led with 89 per cent and the least being West Bengal where only 10 per cent of milk sold was to the organised sector. While cooperatives collected 32 per cent of the milk sold, private dairies (13 per cent), individual milkmen or *dudhias* (39 per cent) and farmers (15 per cent) also collected milk for marketing. Households preferred organised sector primarily for the price and timely payments, at least every fortnight. Dudhias were preferred for doorstep milk collection, especially where there was a lack of channel for milk collection.

For most of the private dairies, agents procure milk from farmers. Some private

[19] Making Indian Dairy Farming Competitive: The Small Farmer Perspective, A White Paper, Yes Bank, 2015.

[20] NABARD, 2015, Annual Report 2014–15.

[21] Production during the year 2013–14 was 137.69 metric tonnes.

[22] Nanda Kumar T. 2015. CII: Dairy Vision 2025 Delhi: Keynote Address Speech at CII, available at: http://www.nddb.org/about/speech/dairyvision

[23] Nanda Kumar T. 2015.

dairies have established village societies for milk collection that follow the cooperative model. It is common for private dairies especially the agents to make loans to farmers, which is a key reason for the large share of milk directed to this channel.[24] Private sector, large multinational companies (MNCs) and retail chains are rapidly expanding their dairy operations and in the last 15 years, have created capacities equal to the ones set up by cooperatives in more than 30 years. While the private sector grows, it is in the interests of livelihoods and inclusiveness that cooperatives and dairy-producer companies retain their existing share of milk handled by organised sectors so that competition-based set of checks and balances prevail in the market.

Of late, adulteration of milk has been highlighted as an issue in several states. Milk being made up of 87 per cent water is prone to adulteration. Moreover, its high nutritive value makes it an ideal medium for rapid multiplication of bacteria, particularly under unhygienic production and storage conditions. Milk's quality concerns go beyond the farm level and require assurance of safe milk at all stages. Cooperatives, private dairies or any other form of dairy farmers' organisations have to engage in assuring the quality through education, training and practice of clean milk production. It is also important to develop diagnostic facilities for milk testing including infrastructure and human resources that enable continuous monitoring for quality.

8. Price paid to dairy farmers

Milk procurement price is either on fat basis or on fat-and-SNF (solids-not-fat) basis. A dudhia traditionally measures the fat content by dipping his fingers into the milk and sets a price based on his perception of the customer. Many collection centres use basic centrifugal machines for fat measurement which do not generate any individual data or receipt for the farmer. The farmers are paid not on the basis of an individual's record but on the basis of the average of fat and SNF. The data is calculated at the central level and not at the collection centre. These collection centres do not promote transparency and farmers supplying good quality milk are also penalised due to others' bad practices.

The digital testing machines capable of generating individual data are expensive but are meant for measuring cow's milk. Since buffalo's milk has high fat content, the machine has to be often recalibrated with centrifugal machines which adds to the workload of centre operators. Testing of milk for safety and quality parameters at the collection centres is almost non-existent. Quality of milk procured is an important element in the supply chain and calls for quality testing at the local level itself. Quality control is possible only through well-equipped laboratories and trained technical manpower. Some of the companies interested in clean milk production are investing in adequate milk testing that also tracks milk of individual pourer so that the whole collection centre is not penalised due to a few individuals (see case study 4.2 on Sahayog clean milk at the end of the chapter).

Milk's price is set by the cooperatives in many states. This price is used by all other players to set their prices. In the organised sector, the Gujarat Co-operative Milk Marketing Federation (GCMMF) reportedly pays the highest prices in the country. It is evident that where dairy farmers' organisations are strong, the prices that the farmers get are higher. Successful milk cooperatives have shown that through a process of efficient procurement, transparent pricing, product development and marketing, at least 75 per cent to 80 per cent of the consumers' rupee can be transferred to the farmers.

During the year, prices fell in states like Karnataka where milk unions cut the procurement prices due to excess milk

---

[24] Round Table on Smallholder Dairy Convened by BAIF and Access Development Services for This Report on 17 August 2015 at Pune.

production. Milk prices fell in Tamil Nadu when Government of Kerala banned milk[25] from the state citing adulteration. Farmers in some states like Maharashtra and UP faced reduction in price reportedly due to fall in prices of skimmed milk powder (SMP). Private dairies in North India which primarily manufacture SMP, ghee etc., are reportedly paying farmers ₹30–31 per litre for buffalo's milk against ₹39–40 a year ago. In Maharashtra, dairies are getting cow's milk delivered to the plants at ₹20–21 per litre. They procure it from the farms at ₹17–19. A year ago, these prices stood at ₹29–30 and ₹26–27 per litre, respectively.[26] Considering the woes of dairy farmers, Government of Maharashtra is considering declaring a minimum support price for procuring milk.[27]

However, this minimum support price is mandatory only for cooperatives and private sector is not governed by this. Cooperatives cannot procure all milk produced in the state as their capacity to handle milk is limited.

Farmers also found that the market for milk is national and not just within a state. Farmers in Telangana mentioned that the recent initiative of the state government to invite Nandini (Karnataka), GCMMF (Amul) and two other private companies from Tamil Nadu to sell milk in the twin cities of Hyderabad and Secunderabad made them face some uncertainty. These large dairies brought in milk from other states for marketing in Telangana which caused local dairies to temporarily stop buying milk from the farmers (Box 4.7).

Box 4.7: *Global downturn in SMP prices and small farmers*

The industry attributes the downturn in prices paid to dairy farmers to world prices of skimmed milk powder. Skim milk powder rates at Global Dairy Trade averaged $2,467 a tonne on April 1, 2014 down from $4,126 a year ago and the peak of $5,142 two years ago. In 2013–14, India exported nearly 1.3 lakh tonnes of SMP whereas during 2014–15, hardly 30,000 tonnes got shipped out. India produces an estimated 6 lakh tonnes of SMP annually, equivalent to about 70 lakh tonnes of milk (about 50 per cent of milk produced in the country). Of the total 6 lakh tonnes of SMP, roughly 4.5 lakh tonnes is produced by private dairies in North India and Maharashtra. The balance is by cooperatives and South-based firms like Hatsun Agro and Heritage Foods. Low global prices, apart from rendering exports difficult, have impacted domestic market.

There are dairy units that only trade or convert milk to milk powder having little touch with consumers. Many milk processing plants were set up in the boom period. With the change in fortunes, they are unable to switch their marketing strategy and start selling to consumers directly. Dairies are selling SMP at around ₹180 per kg at present, against ₹270 a year ago. Ex-factory prices of ghee have similarly dropped from ₹310 to ₹260 a kg. At ₹180/kg SMP and ₹260/kg fat price, dairies would realise slightly over ₹3,300 from processing 100 litres (103 kg) of buffalo milk containing 6.5 per cent fat and 8.5 per cent SNF. After excluding ₹200–₹250 of processing and packaging costs, they can barely pay ₹3,100 or ₹31 per litre for milk delivered. SMP exports falling from 1.3 lakh tonnes to 30,000 tonnes would leave a surplus of 1 lakh tonnes. Without any outlet for this powder, either through exports or a government-mediated commodity grant aid programme for South Asian neighbours, there will be a glut. The farmer will pay dearly for the global price fluctuations.

Source: (a) Round Table on smallholder dairy farming held at BAIF on 17 August 2015 (b) Crashing milk prices worldwide is latest farmer worry at home by Harish Damodaran, *Indian Express*, published on 5 April 2015.

---

[25] Kerala bans milk from Tamil Nadu, *Deccan Herald*, published on 12 June, 2015.

[26] Crashing milk prices worldwide is latest farmer worry at home by Harish Damodaran, *Indian Express*, published on 5 April 2015. Available at: http://indianexpress.com/article/business/commodities/crashing-milk-prices-worldwide-is-latest-farmer-worry-at-home/#sthash.DEVurtfC.dpuf.

[27] Brace for milk price hike as government plans to fix MSP at ₹20 by Sujit Mahamulkar and Bella Jaisinghani, *Times of India*, published on 20 May 2015.

However, these large dairies quickly set up a local procurement network and some of them offered a higher price than the local dairies to build a local supply base in order to save on transportation costs from neighbouring states. Some stakeholders mention that the lower price offered for milk in Tamil Nadu and Maharashtra was partially to procure low and transport to Telangana. Farmers in Telangana are also not sure of how long they will get such a price for.

Even with falling milk procurement prices in some of the states, the retail price of milk for consumers has been increasing, thus improving the margins for different players in value chain (Figure 4.2). Indian milk industry's claim of passing on 80 per cent of consumers' rupee to the farmers does not hold true in most cases. Experts mention that transportation, chilling, pasteurising, packaging and distribution, at best cost ₹10 to ₹12 per litre when dairies operate at scale. When the consumer is charged ₹40 per litre on an average and the dairy farmer gets ₹23 on an average, there is a need to study who benefits. Stakeholders in the Round Table on smallholder dairy farming advocated strong governance measures for the industry for ensuring quality and appropriate pricing, keeping in mind the well-being of both producers and consumers.

9. Viability of dairy farming

Milk production has been witnessing a steady increase over the years. The price of milk also registered a steady increase till 2005–06. Since 2006, the wholesale prices of milk showed a markedly sharp increase. Production's response to the sharp increase in prices has been muted and not proportional. The average price increase per annum in the twenty-one year period from 1992–93 and from 2013–14 was about 15.3 per cent whereas production registered an increase of only 6.6 per cent. In the ten year period between 2004 to 2014, milk prices increased at an average of 16.1 per cent

Figure 4.2: Trends in milk production and prices

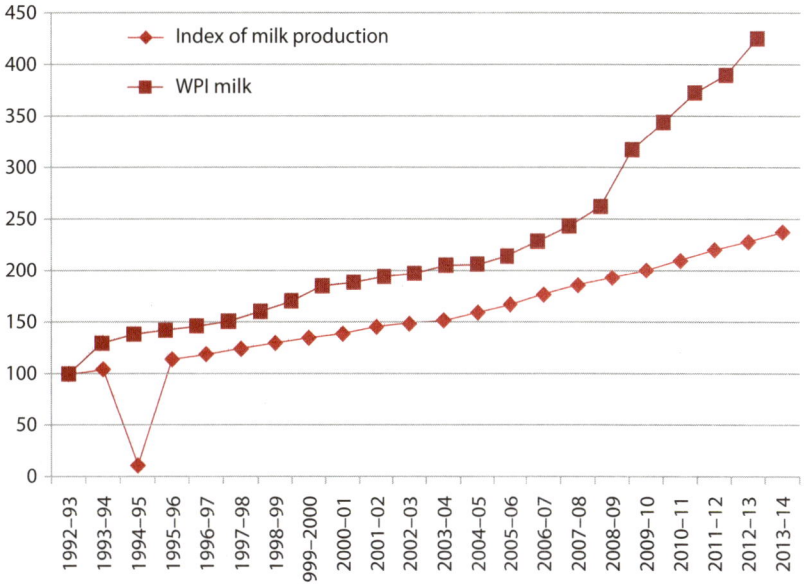

Source: Index of milk production based on Department of Animal Husbandry statistics. Whole sale price index of milk based on WPI data of CSO.

per annum whereas production increased by only 6.1 per cent. The lack of production to increasing milk prices is perhaps on account of uncertain viability of dairy farming at farmers' level, even at higher prices of milk. Interactions at different levels from individual farmers to small dairies and financing institutions reveal that unless well- managed and supported with linkages of all kinds, dairy farming may not be remunerative enough on a stand-alone basis.

Many dairy farmers find the prices being paid for milk currently, to be unviable. Feed cost which constitutes 60 per cent to 70 per cent of the cost of milk production has been increasing. Labour cost also has been increasing. Procurement prices have been falling in some of the large milk-producing states. With export-oriented milk processing, the dairy farmers also experience the vagaries of international trade. However, reducing the herd size by culling less productive animals is also not an easy option due to the ban on beef and beef products.

Many farmers calculate the viability of dairying on the basis of milk procurement prices. If the value of manure and other wastage utilised in farms is calculated, then return on investment (ROI) appears better. However, many farmers do not keep a detailed account of costs and benefits arising out of dairy farming. They mention that such calculations are a proof of the unviable prices that they get and will force them to consider winding down the business. One trend which is clear is that the younger generation of farmers is not keen to continue this business.

Ashok More, a small farmer in Pune taluka who had a few indigenous cows since the 1970s, commenced cross-breeding of his animals when it was introduced in the mid-seventies. He benefitted from the increased milk production of cross-bred cows at 10 litres a day and hence increased his herd size gradually. In the early 1990s, he had as many as 15 cross-bred cows. However, during 1993–95, there was a business downturn since the local cooperative was not able to procure all the milk due to glut in production in Maharashtra. Since milk marketing became an issue, he decided to decrease the herd size. When in 2000s, milk was again in demand and he wanted to increase the herd size, his sons did calculations of income and expenditure of the dairy business and refused to join saying, "it was not profitable." At present, he has only five animals and he and his wife carry out dairy farming. He engages one labourer for milking. He sells raw milk locally at ₹26 per litre and meets the demand for pure milk from consumers who want to buy from him directly instead of buying packaged milk. At this price, according to him, he is not making any profit. However, he is using dung for farm manure and cow urine is collected and sold to a trader for Ayurvedic preparations. If the value of these is calculated, then profitability improves. He feels that unless farmer gets a minimum of ₹30 for cow's milk, the dairy business is not profitable.

Incomes from dairy farming are a significant source in smallholder farms. At the lowest class of landholdings, incomes from livestock form almost 25 per cent of total revenues (Table 4.7). Across all farm households, income from livestock formed about 12 per cent of the total income. Viability of dairy farming is critical to most farm households and critically so for small farms.

The question of cost and incomes from animal farming was addressed by the NSSO in its 70th round national survey. The survey results indicate that there is a cash surplus when income and expenditure is compared in all the major states (Table 4.8). The non-cash expenditure in the form of own labour and captive sources of feed and fodder are perhaps not part of the reckoning. Dairy farmers in some states such as AP, Haryana, Gujarat, Orissa and Tamil Nadu seem to produce higher surpluses per rupee spent compared to other states.

Table 4.7: Average monthly income of farm households from different sources 2012–13

Size class of land possessed (ha)	Income from wages/salary (₹)	Net receipt from cultivation (₹)	Net receipt from farming of animals (₹)	Net receipt from non-farm business (₹)	Total income (₹)
(1)	(2)	(3)	(4)	(5)	(6)
< 0.01	2,902	30	1,181	447	4,561
0.01–0.40	2,386	687	621	459	4,152
0.41–1.00	2,011	2,145	629	462	5,247
1.01–2.00	1,728	4,209	818	593	7,348
2.01–4.00	1,657	7,359	1,161	554	10,730
4.01–10.00	2,031	15,243	1,501	861	19,637
10.00 +	1,311	35,685	2,622	1,770	41,388
All sizes	**2,071**	**3,081**	**763**	**512**	**6,426**

Source: Key Indicators of Land and Livestock Holdings in India, NSSO 70th round, December 2014, NSSO, MOSPI; GoI.

Table 4.8: Economics of dairy across the supply chain

S. No	Particular	Milk price
1.	Procurement from farmer	24
2.	Quality testing & transportation	1.2
3.	Royalty to milk aggregators	0.6
4.	Transportation to BMCU	1
5.	Chilling cost	0.4
6.	Processing, packaging and admin	3.1
7.	Packaged milk distribution	0.45
8.	Retailer commission	1.2
9.	Marketing	0.2
10.	Margins	1.85
11.	Consumer price	34

Source: Livelihood Mapping of Shrawasti District, UP. Commissioned by GIZ-NABARD, Access Livelihood Consulting India, Hyderabad, 2012.

The economics of procurement and sale of milk at a local area was worked out as part of a livelihood mapping strategy in Shrawasti district of UP for NABARD by Access Livelihoods Consulting India (ALC). The workings show that at a small dairy cooperative level, it is possible to pay ₹24 for a litre of milk to the farmer and sell at ₹34 to the customer, with all the supply chain costs factored.

V. Institutions of dairy farmers

Cooperatives are the key institutions in a formal dairy sector. Cooperatives have played a phenomenal role in organising the disbursed dairy farmers and providing them inputs for dairying and ensuring marketing of a highly perishable commodity. Of late, producer companies of dairy farmers are also being promoted.

1. Cooperatives

About 15.46 million farmers have been brought under the ambit of 1,62,600 village level dairy corporative societies up till March, 2014.[28] The cooperatives have a three-tier structure: (a) primary societies at the village level (b) unions at the district level and (c) federations at the state level.

The success of the GCMMF, known for its Amul brand and its Amul model of cooperative, is acclaimed. Amul, founded in1946 in the town of Kheda in Gujarat, has a three-tiered institutional structure with village-level dairy cooperatives at the village level, federated into a milk union at the district level and a federation of milk unions at the state level. More than 15 million milk producers bring their milk to 144,500 dairy cooperative societies across the country. This is processed at 184 district cooperative unions and marketed by 25 state marketing federations. Over the last four years, Amul has ensured 59 per cent increase in the milk procurement price to its farmer–members which resulted in 46 per cent growth in its total milk procurement.[29] Amongst the various drivers of its success, the integration of financial products and services has been an important factor.

However, there is a perception that cooperative organisations have not been equally successful in many states. Cooperatives in other states are organised differently than the GCMMF cooperatives. The GCMMF cooperatives operate like a true representative of the farmers and are run by professionally qualified managers. In most states, the cooperatives are managed by civil servants and function more as government bodies. Also, they are weak representatives of dairy farmers.

Of the 14 major milk state cooperatives in the country, 10 have state government equity, of which six have government equity in excess of 51 per cent. Twelve of the 14 cooperatives have government officers as Managing Directors (MDs) appointed by the state government. It is not uncommon for these officials to be changed very frequently. Cooperatives are mere parastatals and do not work in the true spirit of cooperatives with elected farmer representatives

---

[28] Annual Report 2014–15, GoI, 2015. Available at: http://dahd.nic.in/dahd/WriteReadData/Animal%20Husbandry%20English%202014-15%20(1).pdf

[29] Annual Report 2014–15, 2015, NABARD, Mumbai.

and professionals who run the organisation. This governance structure influences the functioning of the entire chain from the state federation to the village societies and thus significantly impacts farmers' involvement and benefits. The government influences the decisions of the board members of a federation. For instance, if the government feels that increase in milk prices may affect consumers, the board does not hike the price, which affects dairy farmers. Moreover, several cooperatives are reportedly defunct; no stock taking or studies have been done by the State.[30]

The primary differences between the GCMMF cooperatives and other state cooperatives are price and services. In Gujarat, the price paid to farmers is based on fat content; there is regular testing of each farmer's milk supply. In most of the other states, there is hardly any testing of milk. In other state cooperatives, the village society president wields a lot of power and typically decides the prices paid to farmers. Reportedly, farmers with some degree of influence receive higher prices than others. Being the lead organisations, the cooperatives also set a benchmark for prices paid by other buyers. Thus, if the farm gate price paid by the cooperative is low, other players also pay a low price.

2. Producer companies

To insulate dairy farmers from political interference and to counter the increasing competition from private players, new forms of organisations such as producer companies are being considered. This form provides the same legal and regulatory framework as enjoyed by other companies but protects the members' interest as per the basic principles of cooperation: voluntary and open membership, democratic member control, member economic participation, autonomy and independence (Box 4.8).

---

[30] New Milky Way by Jyotika Sood, published on 15 February, 2015. Available at: http://www.downtoearth.org.in

> **Box 4.8:** *Dairy producer companies are the new generation co-operatives*
>
> Till the economic liberalisation in 1991, cooperatives grew in a protective environment without any competition. And this phase made India one of the largest milk producers in the world. Now these cooperatives that we had set up in the last 50 years are failing us because politics is overtaking them. Barely 15 per cent of our villages have cooperatives. The private sector is entering only where cooperatives were established to exploit the existing infrastructure. They are not taping the potential of other villages and promoting milk production there. This will lead to a milk crisis. The private sector has got more processing capacity than cooperatives today and they have done it in much shorter time than cooperatives. The private sector is going to grow; the cooperatives will also grow but at a slower pace. So, NDDB is trying to introduce the producer company model in villages that are not covered by cooperatives or where cooperatives are defunct. So in coming years, cooperatives and producer companies can together compete with the private players.
>
> Amrita Patel, Ex Chairperson, NDDB
> *Source:* New Milky Way by Jyotika Sood.

Since 2005, NDDB has been promoting dairy producer companies and this model is extended to eight states. Due to frequent changes in cooperative laws in AP affecting the autonomy of cooperatives, many of the dairies registered under the Mutually Aided Cooperative Societies Act are now transforming to producer companies. Apart from NDDB, NGOs and technical-service providers have also promoted dairy producer companies that are operational in AP, Bihar, Gujarat, Haryana, Maharashtra, Punjab, Rajasthan and Uttar Pradesh.

However, unless these producer companies are linked to a well-established marketing network such as NDDB or a private dairy company, they will face serious problems in marketing milk. Indur Milk Producer Company is functioning in Nizamabad district of Telangana and has been promoted by Indur Intideepam Mutually

Aided Cooperative Society (IMACS), a federation of SHGs. The company has been functional since past 5 years and the peak level procurement of milk was 12,000 litres per day. It showcased that dairying can be profitable for both the producers and the company in an area which had deficit in milk. The company has been selling milk to bulk buyers. Seeing the pressures on margins, the company started selling milk in pouches. However, last year the Telangana government invited other state dairies such as Amul, Nandini and so on to sell milk in the twin cities. This led to some turbulence in the dairy sector. The bulk buyers were not able to lift milk. Due to competition from established players, the producer company saw its procurement and also market share in milk business going down. The producers are now bracing to tackle this competition. Similar situation was also experienced by other milk producer companies in AP, Madhya Pradesh and Rajasthan. Some of them sold off the bulk milk coolers already established to repay loans.

3. SHGs and dairying initiatives

Women SHGs have gained prominence with major livelihood initiatives for poverty reduction in the country, utilising this institutional form to mobilise women and enable them to access financial and livelihood services. While women have been borrowing for the purchase of milch animals, integrated support systems for dairy management have been few.

Society for Elimination of Rural Poverty (SERP) in AP, which has the largest network of SHGs and federations (VOs and *mandala samkhyas*) in the country, took up a dairy initiative. Andhra Pradesh Dairy Development Cooperative Federation (APDDCF) had bulk milk coolers and other infrastructure which were not well utilised due to poor mobilisation of dairy farmers, low volumes of milk supply and high overhead costs. Mandala Samkhyas where potential for dairy exists are entrusted with the milk procurement from VOs

and chilling. Thereafter they transport the milk to milk union's processing plant.

Dairy producer groups were formed out of interested SHG members. They had to manage the animals in a common shed for which the government provided subsidies for shed and machinery such as chaff cutters. Other services such AI, feed, veterinary support were organised through institutional linkages. The milk procured has not seen dramatic changes and the utilisation of the infrastructure has also not improved much. However, 70 per cent of the dairy farmers are benefitting from the purchase of animals, inputs and marketing services that they are availing locally. As per SERP, under the Rural Inclusive Growth Project of World Bank, dairy value chain will be focused with comprehensive and integrated services reaching the dairy farmers.

There are several NGOs that work with dairy farmers, especially in extension services through bare-foot technicians. There are also a few NGOs that are promoting dairy value chain, trying to address the needs of dairy farmers comprehensively. SRIJAN has been working with dairy farmers in Rajasthan and MP (see case study 4.3). DHAN foundation has set up a milk processing plant and carries out value addition in Tamil Nadu, though profitability issues arise now and then. Hand in Hand—an NGO for promoting the SHGs of women with the goal of job creation—found that in spite of taking large numbers of loans, asset creation was limited. While women reared dairy animals in a traditional way, the income was limited due to lack of integrated and comprehensive support. Hence Hand in Hand initiated dairy related activities.

Four case studies at the end of the chapter look at how NGOs and private sector entities created an impact through dairy-based interventions in a comprehensive manner throughout the dairy value chain. BAIF, a large NGO of international repute, led the breed improvement programme in the country successfully. Hand in Hand set up a producer company for dairy farmers after linking them with credit and all production and marketing linkages. Sahayog, a micro-finance company and private enterprise group, set up a clean-milk-producing-dairy-producer company in Madhya Pradesh with considerable benefit to farmers. SRIJAN, a Rajasthan-based NGO has worked hard to bring together very poor dairy farming women to set up a fledgling producer company that caters to all the needs of dairy farming. Each entity in its own way has faced challenges and dealt with them, in the process earning the support and the respect of the communities where they worked at.

Dairy-based livelihoods are a critical part of rural households, especially the poor and the landless. There has been tremendous progress made by the dairy sector in terms of improved productivity, better quality, organised marketing and aggregation of milk from smallholders to an extent not witnessed in any other rural produce. There are a number of good models and ongoing projects to improve the ground conditions further in favour of smallholders. Challenges however remain as technical, commercial and financial problems continue to dog the sector. In a globally linked market for milk and derivatives, farmers suffer the most in case of falling milk prices; processors and marketers gain in case of an increase in prices. Environmental issues and equitable use of natural resources require to be closely looked at in expanding the dairy sector. At a small farmer's level, it is not clear if dairy-ing is a remunerative enterprise. When all linkages are available and a fair marketing organisation provides the outlet for milk, there is likelihood that farmers will make profit. Mostly, the cooperative milk chain is able to provide a realistic price to farmers. Others continue in dairying despite its not being profitable as it is an easy way of converting their labour into cash (and that too at regular intervals) instead of looking for wage employment. The entry of socially oriented institutions in order to organise the local dairy farmers into producer collectives with comprehensive end-to-end

solutions is a laudable initiative. Such interventions should be supported by an appropriate policy framework and easy partnerships with government-driven extension services. Despite its obvious employment potential for vulnerable people, public funding for this sector seems to be much lower than warranted. Public investments in animal health care and extension services go a long way to reduce risks of the vulnerable smallholders in dairy sector.

VI. Case studies

The following four case studies are of four different institutions taking unique initiatives to address the needs of dairy farmers.

Case study 4.1: BAIF model of dairy development

BAIF—which was established in 1967 to generate gainful self-employment for rural poor—found that the best option for resource-poor farmers was strengthening the existing mixed crop–livestock farming system. Cattle, being widely accepted by all sections of community and because of an increasing demand for milk in India, motivated the BAIF to promote cattle development as an important tool for poverty alleviation.

Cross-breeding to improve productivity

The concept of cross-breeding of cattle has been tested and upscaled by BAIF nation-wide. Initially, Gir and other non-descript cows were used to produce cross-bred cows with policy support from the Government of India. Technical and funding support from donors such as Danida, Scottish and British Milk marketing boards enabled the BAIF to set up the required research facilities such as the bull mother farm, semen freezing units etc.

The initial strategies used by BAIF included doorstep delivery of insemination services, involvement of farmer organisations, use of semen of selected bulls, ensuring the quality of semen and implementation of activities through trained AI technicians in order to win the confidence of animal owners. All these were backed by the research support of a team of specialists. Based on the success of BAIF in breed improvement, a number of farmers' cooperatives invited it to take up dairy cattle development in their area of operation, thus expanding the programme in several states. In the 1980s, cattle cross-breeding programme by BAIF was recognised as a part of IRDP and invitation from several states helped in establishing cattle-breeding centres. Technical soundness of the programme, use of state-of-the-art technology for producing frozen semen, effective and efficient doorstep delivery services, follow-up of inseminated cows for pregnancy and calving, rapport of the team with the famers and production performance of cross-breds contributed to such recognition. BAIF also developed breeding services for buffaloes and indigenous breeds of cattle. This initiative enabled the BAIF to contribute towards conservation and development of indigenous breeds of livestock, thereby maintaining biodiversity.

Transition to integrated cattle development programme

BAIF, over a period of time, transitioned the cattle breeding programme to cattle development programme since the resource poor could not fully benefit from single intervention. Thus, production support activities included fodder development, supply of subsidised calf feed and farmers' training to ensure suitable growth and management of heifers till they attained maturity which takes around two to three years.

Animal health support activities such as diagnostics, vaccination, deworming, first aid etc., were also developed. BAIF also commenced integrating livestock development into its natural resource management programmes since in rain-fed-semi-arid areas, improvement of livestock cannot be sustained unless it is supported by natural resource management such as watershed and silvopasture development projects to ensure availability of water, feed and fodder.

Milk-marketing initiatives have largely not been taken up by the BAIF and cattle owners are linked to dairy cooperatives for milk marketing.

The central research station at Uruli Kanchan plays a key role in the success of the livestock development programme by providing critical technical inputs throughout the country. Multi-disciplinary expert teams plan crucial aspects of the programme like breeding, reproduction, nutrition, health, fodder production etc. Technologies were either generated or tested and suitably modified for these crucial aspects of the programme. Suitable recommendations for field staff and farmers were also provided based on these.

Some key numbers as on 31 March 2015 were:

- **No. of centres:** 3,749 in12 states, covering 5.26 million families in 88,272 villages cumulatively.
- **No. of AI carried out:** 2.5 million/year.
- **Cows/Buffaloes in production:** 1.0 million.
- **Value of milk produced:** ₹4000 crores/year.

Coverage of a centre

The cattle breeding centre typically carries out the following:

- Coverage of 12–15 villages; 1,000–1,500 families
- Coverage of 1,500–2,000 breedable cattle and buffaloes
- AI at doorsteps
- Conservation of native breeds
- Close follow up and monitoring
- Support services: vaccination, health care etc.
- Advice on nutrition and forage production
- Focus on poor beneficiaries
- Development of local organisations
- Community paravets to be well-trained and supervised to carry out the activities.

The Programme is self-sustainable after initial support for about 5–7 years.

Ensuring sustainability

To sustain livestock development after the project funding is over and to ensure that rural families continue to reap the benefits, livestock service providers are developed using trained individuals selected by the community. These service providers offer services under the supervision of a qualified veterinary surgeon. Another initiative is the formation of self-help, farmer interest groups (FIGs) to take up support activities such as livestock health services, marketing and feed preparation and so on.

A system of collecting service charge for breeding services has been put in place since free services are not valued and payment for services makes the service provider accountable for quality. During the project period, the system of collecting charges enabled a corpus fund to be created in SHG/interest groups which manages these funds and partly uses to procure services.

Key impacts[31]

BAIF has developed an in-built mechanism to periodically compile data on conception rates and to examine the trend. The data analysed from four states for ten years uptil 2008 showed that AI per conception was 1.9 to 2.6. Buffalo conception rate, though, was low in the initial years. Over five to seven years, it was almost comparable to that of a cow's.

Change in herd size and composition

Small sample studies in Maharashtra, UP and Rajasthan showed an increase in herd size, especially an increase in the number of cross-bred cows and a decrease in the number of non-descript cows.

Change in milk production

Approximate calculations show that cows that produce 2,000 litres in a lactation period are profitable. Observations from recorded data on milk production from three states were analysed by the BAIF.

In Maharashtra, data on milk production for over 20 years among different economic strata showed that there was a three-fold increase in milk production of cows belonging to landless and small farmers, whereas for large farmers, the increase was about 30 per cent. Milk production for all categories was above 2,000 litres per lactation. The average increase in milk production per cow per farmer was more for landless and small farmers which could be due to better personal attention paid by them. A study in UP indicates that though the Programme increased the milk production per family, it was not as high as in Maharashtra due to lack of market linkages, low level awareness among producers and also due to being a newer initiative. In Karnataka, milk yield of crossbreds increased substantially and reached an average of 2,464 litres per lactation.

Another significant aspect was an improvement in milk consumption per day per farming family by 1 to 2 litres due to improvement in the availability of milk.

Change in share of family income from livestock

Sample-based studies in three states showed encouraging results. In Maharashtra, the increase in share of livestock was the highest for landless families (41 per cent to 93 per cent) while for small farmers the increase was 30 per cent to 49 per cent. A major contributor to the income was milk (60 per cent to 67 per cent), followed by sale of animals (30 per cent to 35 per cent) and manure (3 per cent to 5 per cent).

During 2013–14, BAIF directly spent ₹0.7 billion for its various programmes. Out of this, 72 per cent was spent on livestock, 6 per cent on wadi, 1 per cent on watershed development and 21 per cent on other activities related to training etc. Out of the above mentioned amount, 60 per cent was received from government, 15 per cent from international donor agencies, 10 per cent from corporate houses, 11 per cent was contributed by the communities and 4 per cent was mobilised from BAIF also.[32]

---

[31] The Milky Way: BAIF Way of Dairy Development, BAIF Development Research Foundation, 2012.

[32] Annual Report 2013–14, BAIF, 2014; BAIF, Pune.

The livestock development programme implimented by the BAIF is unique. It is the largest programme implemented by an NGO in India in terms of geographical spread, number of families involved, integration of development, extension and applied research and also a duration spanning four decades. Increasing demand for milk and a large number of low productive bovine population owned by the weaker sections of the society have been the compelling factors for expansion of BAIF's dairy development programme while demonstrating its feasibility to policy makers. Analysis of field data shows achieving the goal of creation of livelihood asset that can generate self-employment and increase income of the rural poor. Changes were gradually made into the programme by taking up indigenous cows and buffaloes to extend the benefits to a larger numbers of households, particularly those living in fragile areas. Linking livestock development with development of natural resources improves feed resources. Facilitating the involvement of people and empowering them to manage the activities on their own has ensured sustainability.

Case study 4.2: Hand in Hand, Tamil Nadu

Hand in Hand took grant support from Nederlandse Financierings-Maatschappij voor Ontwikkelingslanden N.V. (FMO) and NABARD for developing the value chain. The following support services were designed for the dairy livelihoods of members in Tamil Nadu so that there was positive impact on incomes and asset base of the households (Figure 4.3).

- **Credit facilitation**: Women were keen to buy cross-bred animals but since these were expensive and loans from SHGs were insufficient, they often borrowed money from moneylenders-cum-milk-traders who normally charged exorbitant rates of interest. Interested women formed activity- based groups and provided credit support.
- **Insurance cover**: Women had or heard about others having bad experiences in dealing with insurance companies. However, looking at the high cost of animals, it was desirous of procuring insurance cover. Hand in

Figure 4.3: Sequencing of activities

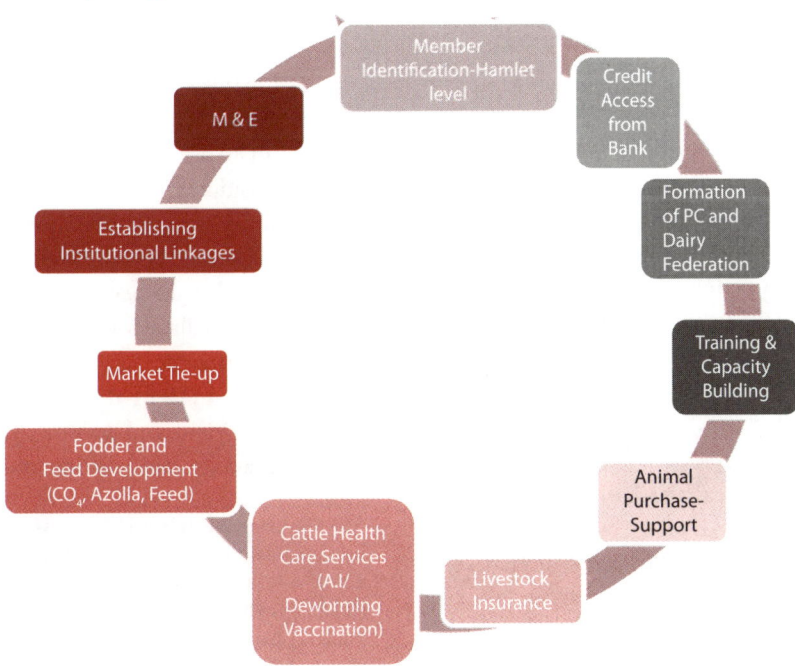

Source: Hand in Hand.

Hand negotiated with two nationalised companies for an insurance cover of three years with a premium of ₹1200 for an average value of ₹40,000 i.e., ₹3 per ₹1000.

- **Developing an institutional support system:** Hand in Hand facilitated additional institutions such as federations (for mobilisation and support services) and producer companies (for forward and backward linkage business) for supporting dairy farmers sustainably.
- **Intensive training**: Hand in Hand developed a 15 day training module with hands-on practical training for women since managing cross-bred animals required intensive management. The training was spread over six months for absorption of good practices.
- **Developing integrated service model:** To address the need for veterinary service, breeding (artificial insemination) service, feed and fodder availability and marketing tie-up with companies.
- **Incentive approach** to encourage the organisers to retain and mobilise members to consider it a business enterprise.
- **Hand in Hand** has also deployed a highly qualified professional team to work on the project.

Progress made till March 2015 is:

- Training: About 1,000 members had received basic training.
- Credit for animal purchase: 2,128 animal loans (1,902 loans by Agricultural Development Finance Company, Tamil Nadu and 226 loans by different banks) given.
- Membership: 923 members have been enrolled.
- Total milk procured: 598,039 litres.
- Amount realised from sales: ₹13.56 million.
- Feed arranged: 25 tonnes of feed sold with a small margin.

The key challenges faced in organising dairy farmers are (a) high fluctuation in milk price paid by the companies is making producers wary (b) retention of members (c) ensuring quality and clean milk production in light of age old practices is difficult to be overcome (d) with government distributing free cows, availability of cows at reasonable rates (e) Women prefer to have limited number of animals due to intensive work involved and expansion of herd to bring in business outlook is difficult.

Case study 4.3: Maitree dairy–A women's initiative in dairy[33] (Rajasthan)

When one meets the Board of Directors of Maitree Dairy and hears their journey in setting up an all-women dairy producer company, the tenacity and grit of these women is palpable. SRIJAN's hard work in some of the difficult areas, capability to turn a near-failure-like-grant-based programme to a sustainable initiative needs appreciation.

SRIJAN has been working in the Tonk district since 2002, mobilising women into SHGs and also into livelihood groups. The World Bank funded District Poverty Initiatives Project (DPIP-I) was implemented in the seven poorest districts of Rajasthan including Tonk from 2000 till 2007. The project inducted graded 'murrah' buffaloes from Haryana into beneficiary families organised into Common Interest Groups (CIGs). The government provided a subsidy of 80 per cent when the recipients were in a position to invest 20 per cent of the cost from own savings. The murrah breed was chosen over local breeds for its high milk yield and for longer period of productive life to provide villagers with a good breed to improve the yield.

While the idea of induction was to improve the yield and income, the local conditions and existing rearing practices in

---

[33] This case study is based on discussions with the board and staff of the producer company. The informative and elaborate case study 'The establishment of Maitree, a producer company of women' a case study by Stutilina Pal and Debasish Pradhan under the guidance of Sankar Datta and Ved Arya has provided valuable insights and inputs.

Rajasthan and the needs of the introduced murrah breed brought rearers and animals under heavy stress. The attention given to various aspects of rearing by rearers in Haryana such as shelter for the animal, nutrients in feed, drinking water, bathing and veterinary services, had resulted in high yield. In Rajasthan, murrah faced great difficulty in acclimatising to the rocky land and dry weather. The buffaloes were left in the fields for grazing and they stopped eating due to the extreme weather change. Some animals also died due to snake bites. People lost their hard-earned saving that was spent to supplement the DPIP grant to buy murrah buffaloes.

At the same time, cost of rearing went up for the rearers due to the introduction of various measures to improve rearing practices. The major cost factor was nutrition feed. Unlike in the past where cattle used to graze on their own, for murrah, rearers were required to buy animal feed and mineral mixture from the market. The rearers found it difficult to recover the cost by selling milk in the local market. For NDDB or SARAS (a brand of Rajasthan Cooperative Dairy Federation Limited) to open collection centres at a particular location, availability of certain assured quantity of milk was imperative. Individually rearers were unable to give that assurance.

This clearly indicates the need of going beyond just providing milch animals to poor households. The cost of rearing murrah was far more than the return they got by selling milk. It was strongly felt in the group meetings as well as in the cluster meetings that sale of milk by individuals would not yield the potential of the rearing activity. The milk has to be aggregated and marketed for better price realisation.

Gradually, the need for collective action brought two structures into being. One was the Maitree Federation that promotes SHGs and addresses the needs of these groups in their linkages with banks, internal savings and credit, and promotes dairy operations under Maitree Dairy. Maitree Dairy initiative got its membership from the Federation membership. Many poor women also joined the Federation once they entered the system through the Dairy. Thus, the two peoples' collectives are mutually reinforcing.

Maitree Dairy has been functional since 2006 but was registered as a producer company in 2013. As of 31 March 2015, it is operational in 40 villages in two blocks with five milk routes. 1,440 shareholders who are pouring milk to the company have contributed a capital of ₹14 lakhs. There are 56 milk collection centres (at flush season the centres will be 83). Three thousand and five hundred are registered milk pourers. Since the company is owned by producers, its governance is in the hands of the people who own it. The company has a 10-member-elected board. The Board of Directors has selected a chief executive officer [CEO (a professional from SRIJAN)] to help them run the company and oversee the day-to-day business.

Pushing the frontier

Dairy requires scale-of-milk production and committed pouring, needs attention to both quality and quantity of milk and requires a strong institutional framework to ensure linkages with viable market channels in order to reap the potentials of the initiative. This requires training and perspective building of the members and the elected leaders of the federation on dairy management. SRIJAN arranged for a few leaders to visit the Mulukanoor Dairy in Andhra Pradesh to give them an exposure. This visit changed the world view of many potential leaders who now felt motivated to build their 'own' dairy enterprise.

Federation leaders have to play different roles at home, in the field, rearing of animals and also entering into male's domain of milk marketing. Social stigma of entering the men's domain was the most challenging. The success of the institution was linked to the confidence and trust that the members have in their institution and in its office bearers. The Federation leaders worked hard and improvised systems such as milk payment once in five days to build trust.

Attention given to animal rearing practices

(a) Professionals from SRIJAN organised regular training to train women on improved rearing practices, importance of the fat content and how to measure and enhance it.

(b) Being conscious of the challenges that the members were facing with murrah bufaloes brought in from Haryana, members were asked to buy murrah from nearby villages to achieve scale-in-milk collection with acceptable fat content. They were also encouraged to induct indigenous breed. Since people had traditional knowledge of rearing local breeds, it could easily get adjusted to the environment.

(c) Efforts were made to find a balance between the need to procure quality feed and the need to control costs. Women learnt to prepare low-cost nutritious feed for the animals to improve their fat content and quantity of milk production. SRIJAN introduced the Federation to the concept of bulk purchase of minerals and feed instead of individual purchase. Feed shop was one of the initial steps taken by the Federation in the direction of setting up necessary infrastructure.

(d) With the help of SRIJAN, AI was experimented with to improve the local breed. With the support of Sri Ratan Tata Trust (SRTT) and tie up with BAIF, two AI centers were set up and success rate of 42 per cent was achieved with 598 inseminations. As the government had started AI services at Panchayat level, this was discontinued. Since semen quality is not good and the conception rate is about 25 per cent, the dairy is considering recommencing the captive AI services once again.

(e) In 2010–11 after exposure to IBTADA (urdu word meaning 'the beginning'), community resource persons called *Pashusakhi*s (animal friend) were developed for providing backward linkages to the dairy women. About 105 pashu-sakhis are providing deworming and vaccination services at village level and facilitating connection with veterinary department for AI. They provide timely knowledge for preventive measures and training to the rearers. Each household pays ₹50 per month for these services which is in turn paid to the Federation. Pashusakhis also link the rearers with the government's scheme of veterinary services from the veterinary department. These services are provided at panchayat level where the rearers can access mineral mixture, calcium and also AI services.

(f) Pashusakhis are working with about 2,000 farmers and follow up with them on adoption practices. They also propagate fodder growing, urea-treated green fodder, Napier grass, Lucerne grass, azolla etc. To meet fodder scarcity during January to June, a variety of Bajri has been introduced which provides fodder with low water.

(g) SRIJAN carried out a small sample study in seven villages and found that the average milking days had increased from 120 days to 180 days per animal due to the work of pashusakhis who ensured good feeding practices, timely deworming, vaccination and AI.

(h) Pashu Rahat Sewa—a mutual insurance—has been operational. Each woman contributes ₹1000 out of which ₹500 are for insurance premium and ₹500 for health which includes two times vaccinations, four times deworming, two consultations from doctors and one time provision of mineral mixtures and calcium.

Milk marketing

SRIJAN helped the Federation to set up milk marketing infrastructure. In 2007–08, a bulk milk cooler (BMC) of 2,000 litre capacity was installed with ₹7 lakhs grant support from the American India Foundation. In 2008, Dewan Foundation gave a grant to SRIJAN with which another BMC of 5,000 litres was set up. In 2012, a third BMC of 5,000 litres was added and at present the installed storage capacity is 13,000 litres. The peak procurement is 12,000 litres during the winter months and comes down to 40 per cent during the summer months. Average procurement has been 4,800 litres per day.

It was crucial to open the supply lines with different bulk purchasers of milk to get a good price for the milk collected at the diary. When Maitree started its operations in Tonk, there were no other comparable institutional players. As a result, Maitree was able to get a good supply of milk from its members and a good price from the local vendors. However, to organise the milk collection centres, milk routes and also to ensure payments based on fat content as per individual pourer, were the major challenges faced and tackled by the federation leaders with the support of SRIJAN professionals. Apart from the capacity to handle management issues, women also had to find time from their other regular tasks to make the new systems and processes work. The women have now learnt to balance their different roles and responsibility towards the dairy and the Federation.

Maitree, since the last 6 years, has been selling to bulk buyers and to a few institutional buyers as well. While the total milk volume increased, losses also increased as in flush season, prices paid by the institutional buyers were uneconomical. Maitree received ₹35 per litre from the buyers but had to pay ₹33 to ₹34 to the pourers.

Since November 2014, the company commenced retail marketing at the suggestion of dairy consultants. The milk is procured within 2.5 hours, chilled, pouched and packed in ice boxes and sold. Testing for bacterial counting is also done. Necessary government clearances and licenses such as the Food Safety and Standards Authority of India (FSSAI) license have been procured for selling the milk. Two outlets were opened where unpasteurised raw milk is pouched and sold. The taste of unpasteurised milk is appreciated by the consumers. Sixty per cent of the milk is sold as raw milk with no standardisation or mixing of powder. The rest of the milk is processed as curd, butter milk, cream, ghee and skimmed milk for marketing.

The company is using mobile technology —WhatsApp—to communicate with dealers and also with secretaries of milk collection centres. Another group is being established with pashusakhis. The company has a contact person in each area who helps resolve local issues. Saras is the major competitor, followed by Payas and in some pockets, Amul. However, the demand for milk is high according to the company, especially in villages where the animal population is low.

Staffing

At present, the dairy engages 4 route supervisors, 2 lab in-charges, 1 doctor, 1 accountant, 4 cleaners and 2 drivers. The company's CEO is a professional from SRIJAN and is on the payroll of SRIJAN.

Financials

The total investment required to get the company on its feet were over ₹10.5 million. The producers' company did not have enough capital to establish even the minimum infrastructure required for managing a dairy business involving so many members. Assets such as bulk milk chilling units (BMCUs), fat-testing machines, lacto scans, milk van and other dairy equipments had to be acquired. Expenses also had to be incurred on winning the trust of the community members, thus slowly weaning them away from the traditional practices of production, building community groups, developing leadership and organising exposure visits. As the company's balance sheet was not strong enough to negotiate loans from banks, SRIJAN had to supplement its funds with support from donors such as the Axis Bank Foundation (ABF), American India Foundation (AIF), Government of Rajasthan, Rajasthan Mission on Skill and Livelihoods (RMoL) and Sir Ratan Tata Trust (SRTT). Till 2013–14, the company received grants.

At present, all expenditures except the salary of the CEO are borne by the company. The company had to face losses during the last two years but in the current year (2015–16), due to retail marketing, the company is in profits.

Key challenges being faced

Milk marketing

The company would like to ensure that the unpasteurised milk is 100 per cent pure and clean. This is a challenge due to limited resources to invest in technology. Financing for new technology (pasteurisers, packing machinery, quality control laboratory, MIS with computer back-up) to scale up operations further with quality, remains a challenge for Maitree.

Limited resources

Maitree has limited financial and technical capacity to invest in infrastructure. Finding resources including loans is not easy. The company also needs professionals in marketing, quality control and finance. It also needs to have adequate working capital to pay the milk pourers on time.

Services to dairy farmers

Livestock assistants are on government payroll. While some are trained and perform well, others do not. Moreover, there are certified paravets who are not supervised well and indulge in lot of malpractices. Hygiene factors in vet care centres need improvement. Moreover, government workers do not provide timely vaccinations. SRIJAN covers only 40 per cent to 50 per cent of the animals in a village. Partial vaccination cannot contain disease spread. There is limited benefit out of AI since non-graded animals still roam in the villages and need to be castrated.

Feeding practices

In spite of training and awareness raising, farmers do not use balanced feed. Cash-in-hand is an issue for many smallholders. Since they want immediate benefits out of expenditure, during the dry period, feeding practices are poor and they leave the animals to fend for themselves.

Maitree is the product of grit and determination of women and appropriate professional support from SRIJAN. While it has managed to survive and service the poor dairy farmers, it continues to face several challenges. The biggest challenge faced by Maitree was that of getting organised. Acquiring both financial and non-financial inputs at the right time has been a continuing challenge. With women as the target groups, gender dimensions had to be addressed and concerted efforts had to be taken up to groom women into leadership, especially in market access. Substantial investments need to be made over a prolonged period to promote such a producer company. The current thinking among development institutions that by supporting producer collectives for three years it will be possible to stabilise the PCs' operations is incorrect. A producer company can take five to eight years to stabilise. Support and linkage organisations need patience and perseverance to ensure that the collectives provide sustainable services to members' livelihoods.

Case study 4.4: Sahayog clean milk initiative (Madhya Pradesh)

Sahayog Clean Milk Private Limited (SCMPL) is a private limited company engaged in setting up comprehensive milk collection and processing with an eventual collection and chilling capacity of 200,000 litres per day in and around Harda district of Madhya Pradesh. The company commenced its operations in 2013 after the preparatory work of surveys and farmers' consultations for about a year. The SCMPL has the objective of linking the dairy farmers to a reliable, transparent and fair market in a business-like and sustainable manner. Currently, SCMPL collects about 50,000 litres of milk per day from about 15,000 farmers through more than 275 primary milk collection centers (PMCs) covering about 300 villages.

The company has organised 275 PMC at village level in the district of Harda and in some parts of the surrounding districts like Sehore, Dewas and Khandwa. PMC operator is a local youth, well-trained by the company and is paid partially on fixed amount and the rest based on the business generated. Every village that supplies milk has a PMC located within a distance of 5–10 kilometers. At each PMC, 50–200 farmers pour milk daily. The PMCs typically operate throughout the year and serve the dual purpose of milk collection and distribution of dairy inputs like feed and mineral supplements, fodder seed etc. The milk collection and supply chain comprises of daily milk collections at the village level, transportation of collected milk to chilling centre/s and then eventually to the main dairy or processing plant for pasteurisation/packaging and distribution.

The company invests in capacity development of the field staff and dairy farmers. Thirty-two paravet workers on the company's payroll are local youth from the farming community and holding their first job. They have been trained intensively for two months which includes practical training, periodic visits to butchery for analysing each and every part of the animal, demonstration farms in other states for improved practices in dairying and so on.

Working with dairy farmers

The company works with the farmers existing animals which have low productivity. Most of the farmers have two to three animals, mostly buffaloes. Traditionally, cattle has been a part of crop husbandry but due to lack of milk- marketing arrangements and limited cash flows, the care of animals and investments in animals has been low. Earlier, milk was for home consumption only. Since farmers had to manage all productive and non-productive animals with the existing cash flows, feeding and other care was not optimal. The company is encouraging farmers to adopt better rearing practices to invest more in the existing animals to enhance their productivity.

The emphasis of company's services is on improving the yield of all existing animals

rather than introducing high breed cattle from other states/areas. If a small farmer buys a high yielding cross-bred animal/ buffalo, they face problems in managing the animals and even in handling and marketing of milk. The company expects sustainable livelihoods for farmers over a five-year time frame.

Farmer services

Training to farmers

- In partnership with the NSDC, SCMPL provides skill-based training to farmers for upgrading their skills related to dairy farming. A sister company— Sahayog micromanagement, a section 25 company—has taken soft loan from NSDC which is repayable in 10 years. This capacity building training is also not subsidised but built into the business model and repayment comes from the milk company on the basis of the milk handled.
- Since the start of the programme, over 13,000 farmers have been trained.
- While men have been targeted for trainings, so far the company is planning to impart training to women from the current year.
- An extensive three-day training programme for farmers is conducted wherein knowledge and information is passed down to farmers about clean milk production in addition to cattle management, breeding and feeding. The company spends about ₹1,000 on training one farmer.
- Within the next three years, SCMPL intends to train more than 75,000 farmers. SCMPL also strives to build the capacity of the existing PMCs through training programmes and veterinary services.

AI services

- SCMPL's paravet team serves more than 400 villages across Harda, Dewas, Hoshangabad, Khandwa and Sehore districts. The emphasis is on improving the existing breeds. AI facilities are managed by the company, professionally. Farmers are advised to shorten the gap between two lactations. The acceptance of AI is increasing. Though credit is being made available for purchase of animals, the long term objective of the company is breed improvement.

- These paravets were previously the unskilled and the unemployed youth of Harda and Dewas districts who were later trained to provide veterinary services.
- Best quality semen is procured from different parts of the country and administered for breed improvement.
- From May 2013 to September 2014, the Sahayog team has conducted a total of 9,100 AIs. The AI service is available at the doorsteps of the farmers at a nominal fee of ₹200 which also includes pregnancy diagnosis within the first three months.
- Success rate of AI has been more than 50 per cent while the national average is reportedly at 18 per cent.

Veterinary services

- Through paravets and empanelled veterinary doctors, 24-hour veterinary support is provided to farmers for nominal fee. Medicines are also provided on cost basis.
- Regular veterinary camps are organised where oral deworming is done and infertility treatment through intra-uterine therapy is also carried out at nominal charges of ₹30 and ₹50 respectively.

Input services

- SCMPL provides high-quality fodder, mineral mixtures, calf starters and other supplements through PMCs.
- The company is planning to establish a cattle feed plant to ensure good quality feed at reasonable prices.
- The company is training farmers in silage making and fodder cultivation such as the African tall maize, MP jowari

etc. Initially, these have been undertaken with progressive farmers.

Financial services

- Credit facility is available to farmers from the Sahayog Microfinance company, a sister organisation. Lending has commenced recently and the repayment amount is deducted from the price payable to them for milk. The company is negotiating with local banks for financing the farmers directly but the procedures are cumbersome. Banks like the IDBI Bank, The Ratnakar Bank Ltd (RBL) are coming forward for business correspondent (BC) arrangement with the microfinance institutions (MFIs).
- The track record of milk pouring, consistent milk pouring, cashflow analysis are considered before financing is done.
- Due to monitoring and cattle health cover, the company has been able to negotiate good premium rates with insurance companies. Cattle insurance for death of the animal is available for a premium of ₹3 per ₹1,000. Infertility cover is covered at an extra payment of ₹1 per ₹1,000.

Farmer helpline

The company operates farmers' helpline through telephone and on an average five calls per day are received. While about 45 per cent calls are about payments, the rest are regarding cattle care, loan availability etc. Farmers getting low rates for the milk get upset and the team has to visit and provide counseling and solutions to them.

Transparent dealings with farmers

The company accepts even very small quantities of milk (as small as 250 ml from a farmer) but the maximum quantity that s/he can pour is not capped. PMC Operators takes a sample of the milk and evaluate it in an Electronic Milk Analyzer which displays the fat percentage, SNF percentage, quantity of milk and the payable amount to the farmer. Unlike other companies that take

100 ml of milk for sampling, Sahayog's PMC utilises only 20 ml for testing. The milk is then finally weighed on an electronic weighing machine and a slip is given to the farmer which is a record of his/her outstanding payment and is updated in his/her account electronically. Since each PMC is connected to a central server, Sahayog can trace each can and each PMC through MIS. In case of any issue of bad quality of milk, the farmers are not penalised. The company has been analysing milk for adulteration and the farmers have been counselled to provide clean milk. Over a period of time, adulteration practices have been curbed.

Payments are made every fortnight which ensure regular flow of income and financial stability. In 28 centres, payments are made directly in the bank accounts of the farmers and in other centres, account opening processes are on. The accounts are opened in the names of women, though it is a challenge to open bank accounts. Thus, the entire process is designed to be fair, transparent and farmer-friendly.

Milk chilling and processing to ensure clean milk

The milk routes are designed in such a way that within four hours of production, the milk reaches the chilling centers to ensure low bacterial growth. Stainless cans are used at farmers' level and also at the collection centres.

SCMPL has created a state-of-the-art processing plant for pasteurisation of milk and production of value-added products like ghee, paneer, *dahi*, *mawa* and lassi. This plant is located in Sandalpur and Dewas with a handling capacity of 1.5 lakh litres per day. The structure of the plant is designed in such a manner that it reduces heat emissions, thereby promoting energy conservation.

Utmost care about hygiene is taken in this plant and an automatic clean-in-process system has been installed that maintains hygiene in the plant by cleaning even the most hard-to-reach areas, twice a day. The milk is pouched using advanced machines which can pouch 40,000 litres of milk in a day. The machines ensure consistent quality, minimum leakages and less maintenance charges. The milk is pouched in a five-layer pouching film pack which reduces chances of contamination and leakages while providing the pouches better tensile strength.

The workforce of the entire plant is comprised of local residents and youth. This generates livelihood opportunities for the local populace.

SCMPL takes pride in the fact that 100 per cent of the milk procured is through its own milk collection centers. However at times, the company faces severe competition in certain pockets. Once a PMC is found successful, other dairies enter the village. In some villages, the business is divided among four to five dairies. In order to attract farmers, other dairies initially mention higher fat content and make a larger payment. In due course, farmers understand the issue and return back. This affects the viability of a PMC. Since the company has long-term plans for improving the dairy business, it manages these downturns.

Previously, SCMPL sold the entire milk procured to bulk consumers which included reputed firms like Haldiram's (Nagpur), ANIK Industries Limited (Dewas) and Modern Dairy. In business-to-business (B2B) the company found very little margins and had to move into value addition in order to earn better margins, eventually to be passed on to farmers.

From April 2015, SCMPL has started selling packaged milk under its brand Pure-1. In the near future, SCMPL plans to launch value-added milk products under its own brand name which will be sold in bulk and later developed into packaged products. SCMPL plans to launch its products in a phased manner in major towns across the routes to Bhopal and Indore.

Key outcomes

The outcomes achieved by the company within a short time are impressive. Eighty per cent of the villagers are loyal though farmers are price-sensitive. The company found that poorer farmers are more reliable, loyal to the company and keen to invest more in their capacity development.

Educating farmers to change age-old rearing practices are resulting in improved yield and fat content. Farmers are now understanding that clean milk production is beneficial to everyone in the value chain. Earlier, farmers had to be educated to avoid adulteration and produce clean milk.

Farmers have mentioned that with transparent systems, they are now able to understand the pricing aspects. With holistic services, some farmers are able to earn a profit margin of 30 per cent in dairy.

However, this does not include depreciation for the value of the animal and other investments. Some farmers mention that with an increase in rates of fodder, oil cakes and labour, they find profit margins decreasing. Farmers would like the margin to be higher at 40 per cent.

Now, farmers are keen to invest more in animals since assured milk marketing facilities are available.

SCMPL is unique since being a private company, it is investing in the capacity of farmers to manage their cattle better and also to improve their incomes. At the same time, it is also ensuring clean milk to consumers (Annexure 4.1).

ANNEXURE 4.1
Milk cooperatives (2013–14): Some numbers

State	No. of milk cooperatives	Milk procurement (000 litres per day)
Haryana	7,216	400
Himachal Pradesh	813	61
Punjab	7,385	1,154
Rajasthan	16,953	2,245
Uttar Pradesh	23,378	371
Assam	249	23
Bihar	16,675	1,484
Jharkhand	58	9
Nagaland	48	2
Odisha	5,155	390
Sikkim	357	15
Tripura	99	4
West Bengal	3,284	161
Andhra Pradesh	5,332	1,729
Karnataka	13,772	5,161
Kerala	3,789	963
Tamil Nadu	11,066	2,378
Puducherry	102	36
Chhattisgarh	998	43
Goa	180	63
Gujarat	17,025	13,738
Madhya Pradesh	7,376	825
Maharashtra	21,481	3,085
India	1,62,791	34,340

Source: Department of Animal Husbandry, Dairying & Fisheries, Ministry of Agriculture, GoI.

Producer Companies: Aggregation and Value Creation for Farmer– Where Is the Goalpost?

Chapter 5

Last year's report carried the conceptual and systemic underpinnings of producer companies in the Indian context. In the current year the effort has been to dialogue with producer companies, their boards, members and other stakeholders, especially the promoting institutions in different states including some of the resource agencies. Many POPI, such as Access Development Services, Access Livelihoods Consulting, AFARM, AKRSP, Action for Social Advancement (ASA), BASIX, Catalyst Management Services/Vrutti, CCD, BAIF, Ambuja Foundation, Srijan etc., were met and consulted to understand the ground-level developments. The narrative is based on field information, observations and experiences of stakeholders.

Formation of producer companies[1] during 2014–15 saw a fillip with policy and funding support from central and state governments which has led to manifold increase in their numbers. 2014 was declared as the year of FPOs by the Department of Agriculture, Government of India and a year-long drive was undertaken to increase awareness about the importance of FPOs among a diverse range of stakeholders: the farming community, state governments, banks and other financial institutions, private sector companies, civil society organisations and elected representatives of the people. According to SFAC data, 570 FPOs exist and about 300 are in different stages of mobilisation.[2] Four hundred thirty-two of the producer organisation in SFAC database are in company form and 138 in other forms. A number of organisations in cooperative form are in the process of transforming into producer companies. The statewise position of producer organisations is given in Annexure 5.1. Uttar Pradesh, Madhya Pradesh and Tamil Nadu are the top three states by number of producer organisations.

Some state governments have been pro-active in policy and budgetary support to producer companies. The state of Madhya Pradesh (MP) which has registered 24 per cent growth in agriculture sees FPOs as key for inclusive growth in agriculture. Several measures have been announced by the government for promotion of FPCs, viz., treatment of FPCs on par with cooperatives for issue of licenses for inputs supply, fertiliser supply on credit basis, ₹25 crores infrastructure support to FPCs every year under RKVY. Interest subvention on the lines of farm

---

[1] In 2002, through an amendment in the Indian Companies Act, 1956, the Government of India (GoI) enacted the Producer Companies Act by incorporating a new section IXA in the Indian Companies Act,1956 based on the recommendations of the Y.K. Alagh Committee set up for this purpose.

[2] Statewise FPO registered in the country as on date 7 May 2015. http://sfacindia.com/PDFs/Statewise-FPO-registered-in-Country07-05-2015.pdf

credit is also being considered. Similarly, the Government of Andhra Pradesh aiming at double digit inclusive growth, has identified promotion of FPCs as one of the high growth opportunities and plans to provide budgetary support for formation of FPCs.

Formation of FPCs is seen as a key strategy to address the issues being faced by small and marginal farmers. Due to increased fragmentation and sub-division of land, farmers with marginal landholdings have limited choices in technology adoption, investments and markets. FPC members have the potential to leverage collective strength to access financial and non-financial inputs and services and appropriate technologies, reduce transaction costs, tap high value markets and enter into partnerships with private entities on more equitable terms. With fragmentation of holdings making large-scale economies impractical, FPOs offer a form of aggregation which leaves land titles with individual producers and uses the strength of collective planning for production, procurement, value addition and marketing to enhance income realisation from members' produce.[3]

The major support for FPCs has been from SFAC and NABARD. SFAC was mandated to lead a project to promote FPOs in close collaboration with state governments, civil society and technical organisations as well as private sector companies. Working across 25 states, the project has helped to mobilise approximately 10 lakh farmers in over 800 FPOs (both registered and under formation) by April 2015. While presenting the Union Budget for 2014–15, the Union Finance Minister announced that a Producers Organisation Development and Upliftment Corpus Fund of ₹200 crore to be utilised for building of 2000 FPOs in the next two years to supplement NABARD's Producer Organisation Development Fund

(PODF). The fund has become operational and 835 FPOs have been approved during the financial year 2014–15. A grant assistance of ₹6.55 million has been sanctioned for the promotion and capacity-building/nurturing of these FPOs.

Structure of farmer producer companies

Producer companies are usually mobilised and nurtured by civil society organisations. Most of them are farmer producer organisations that promote Farmer Interest Groups (FIGs) at village level for productivity enhancement measures and also for aggregation of outputs. FIGs are aligned crop/product/craft wise. The producer company functions usually at a cluster level of 5 to 15 villages depending on density of population and interest shown by farmers. Where necessary a cluster of FIGs are also formed which is an informal structure for exchange of ideas and communicating with farmers. A few producer companies (PCs) have a block as a catchment area but ownership and member connect are seen as issues. Last year's report carries a detailed discussion on this and has recommendations on area coverage. Few PCs are formed as the apex of federations as in the case of BAIF[4] and CCD[5] which has a multi-district operational area with a large membership base. Such multi-district, multi-state structures require strong senior management and good field monitoring systems.

A more recent initiative especially by SFAC is to form a state-level apex PC of producer companies functioning in the state (Figure 5.1). State-level apexes are nurtured by a POPI.

Formation of state apex of PCs has been taking shape since the past two years in states like MP, Karnataka, Maharashtra, Rajasthan, Uttar Pradesh and West Bengal, which have

[3] Pravesh Sharma, 2014, Transforming Agricultural Markets and Value Chains in the 21st Century: Farmer Producer Organisations and Policy Challenges, http://www.ggkirma.in/discussionforum/blogdetail.php?id=15&catid=2

[4] Bhartiya Agro Industries Foundation, Pune–a leading NGO.

[5] Covenant Center for Development is a Madurai based NGO working in several agricultural value chains.

Figure 5.1: Emerging model of producer companies

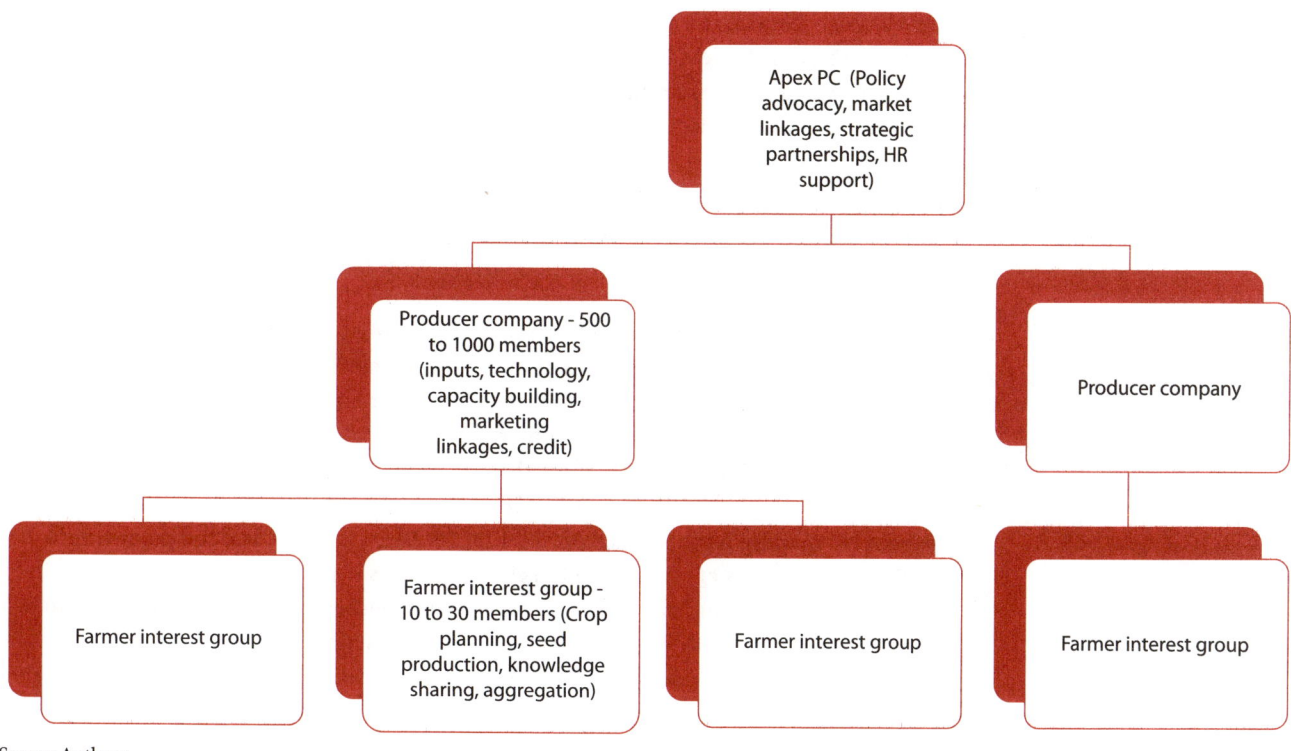

Source: Authors.

shown good progress in the promotion of FPOs. Apex federations can arrange finance, deal with input suppliers and look after marketing on behalf of their constituents. Madhya Bharat Consortium of Farmers Producer company limited has 43 member PCs with 56,000 member farmers. PCs with poultry and livestock farmers have not been taken as members since the apex wants to concentrate on crops and vegetables. The main role being played by the apex is market linkages. The apex also has plans to act as a wholesale lender to new PCs whose growth is hampered by lack of loan funds.

Gujarat apex producer company has an informal membership of 27 PCs with 15 being shareholders. The apex is facilitating corporate tie-ups especially aimed at national and international markets. Similarly for inputs, especially supply of quality seeds to the farmers, the apex will be consolidating demand from all PCs and negotiating with companies and large dealers. The apex will take up policy issues

with relevant authorities. Many producer organisation promoting institutions see the apex institution as their withdrawal strategy from PCs. They have a plan for nurturing the PCs for five to seven years and gradually withdraw their direct support to the PCs as apex PC strengthens. Since most of the apex institutions are facilitating business linkages they are expected to earn a commission and cover their costs in a period of two to three years.

Data on producer companies

While the national data base of SFAC shows 570 FPOs including cooperatives, key stakeholders mention that more than 1000 PCs are functional in the country, out of which 400 have been formed during 2014–15. The year has seen many FPCs getting promoted. However, there are also reports that some of the PCs promoted in the earlier years have dissolved or have become defunct due to inability of the promoter to support beyond three years.

One of the initiatives taken by Access Development Services for this year's report was collection of basic data on membership, governance, staff, business and key financials. In spite of close follow up, data was received from only 64 PCs, from 7 states (Jharkhand, MP, Maharashtra, Odisha, Rajasthan, Tamil Nadu and Telangana) and 17 districts[6] covering 62 blocks.

Only 10 of these responses are complete in all aspects. While one can understand the reluctance of promoting organisations to share detailed data on business specific to individual FPO, inability to share other basic data raises serious questions about the existence and actual functioning of PCs and also the monitoring reports being called for by POPIs. Since PCs are promoted largely through government funds and apex PCs are operational in states with larger concentration of PCs, it should be possible to track the performance of PCs. Future policy initiatives and modification of existing strategies for support and nurturance of FPOs cannot be designed in a data vacuum. Information on membership, active users, business volumes, market access, impact of the FPO on incomes of members etc., should be gathered so that the fledgling organisations can be provided the right direction through appropriate incentives. SFAC and NABARD need to invest in a web-based monitoring mechanism, which can facilitate monitoring at different levels—PC themselves, by POPIs, by apexes, by funders; this will also build confidence of financial institutions in lending to PCs.

Member mobilisation and ownership

Access was able to collect membership data from 47 FPOs for 2014–15. The minimum and maximum numbers of total shareholders are 11 and 5637, respectively, with

the average number being 922. Six PCs, especially focusing on dairy, have exclusive women membership, the other companies have mixed membership. Many PCs are being promoted under SFAC funding or NABARD funding. The data available with SFAC (May 2015) shows that the average membership per FPO was marginally more than 1000. The PCs interacted with during the mission mention that there is a potential to increase the membership four fold to 4000.

Access Livelihoods Consulting Company, Hyderabad promotes larger mobilisation. ALC aims to promote PCs of 10,000 households in 20 to 25 villages over a eight year time frame. The company believes that unless a producer to consumer model is established, benefit may not accrue to producers; hence ALC works on shorter value chains where connection with end consumer has very few intermediaries. While production is carried out in villages within 30 to 35 kilometer radius, sales to end consumers is also aimed in a radius of 100 kilometers. Thus, commodities with local markets are targeted in the FPCs promoted by ALC.

Though membership on the basis of shareholders is larger at 750 to 1000, true ownership in terms of patronage and availing of services is yet to stabilise. Fund release by funding agencies is based on the membership targets to be achieved. SFAC requires 1,000 members whereas NABARD has an understanding with promoting organisations that at least 750 members will be mobilised under each PC. Some of the state government schemes for promotion have lower membership targets, of 500 to 750, to be achieved. The funders require these performance benchmarks to be achieved in 12 to 18 months. At present many of the POPIs are working in new geographic zones where they are commencing work for the first time; rural populace, especially farmers are used to receiving subsidies and other freebies. Mobilising them to manage their own institution sustainably and convincing them to subscribe to share capital

---

[6] Badwani, Chhatarpur, Cuttack, Jhabua, Mehboobnagar, Mandya, Mayurbhanj, Nagapattinam, Nanded, Nizamabad, Nuapara, Pune, Ratlam, Singbhum, Tiruvannamalai, Kanchipuram and Tonk.

after making them understand the concept, principles and business of a producer company is time consuming. At present the local leaders who form the initial interest group/ governing body convince others to pay the share money and thus become a member.

Producer companies are reluctant to increase membership beyond the mandatory minimum since they raise the expectations of members, but may be unable to fulfill them in the short term due to lack of funds. While initial mobilisation brings in membership, converting the shareholders into active members has been a problem. During the field interactions with a number of PCs, the active membership was much less. This is on account of the limited services and products offered by the PCs. Where PC arranged input supply, especially urea, active membership increased and there was also interest from households in the area to become shareholders. On output marketing very few PCs met had taken steps on aggregation. Where aggregation and marketing was done, active membership was high in the crops chosen for marketing.

POPIs and also some PC board members mention that the understanding of the functions of the company and ownership among members is low. Active members range between 20 per cent to 50 per cent. Active is defined as availing the services of the company. Attrition rates are not tracked by many POPIs as of now. Indicators for member ownership and norms of member patronage are yet to evolve. These are likely to vary based on sector/commodity and also for each type of service. AKRSP mentions that in FPC, package of practices should be adopted by 100 per cent, input supply by 60 per cent and marketing by 20 per cent to 30 per cent at the end of three years. Providing market linkages for more members requires tremendous efforts in supply chain management, which FPCs and POPIs find it hard to manage.

Interactions with PCs also revealed that they deal with non-member producers as well, especially in marketing of produce; this

From promoting institutions, the communication with shareholders has been limited; business has been confined to a few farmers. Shareholder buy-in has not been given importance. In today's ground reality, PCs with 200 active members are called good working ones. Even with this small number of members, business break even can be achieved. However, sustainability of PC and impact of PC in a farmer's livelihood is likely to be very limited.

Source: POPI, MP.

trend is seen more in dairy PCs. In some of the PCs there are more non-members than members that are marketing their produce. The input supply services are restricted to members in some PCs, but extended to non-members in others. However, there is no clear strategy as to how these non-members can be made members to increase the strength of the PC. Member ownership in PCs is ranked as the topmost issue by both the boards of PC as well as the POPIs. The pace of initial mobilisation, communication to shareholders, activities to build company visibility and availability of funds to take up business activities have a bearing on the bond between members and the PC. Even five-year-old companies interviewed mention that member loyalty is a major area of concern.

The issue of member acquisition and member loyalty has to be dealt with by the promoters right from the design stage. The PC should be able to articulate the benefits to those who choose to become shareholders. Typically the PC would like to raise its business volumes by dealing with not just members but also non-members. But the PC should provide preferential treatment to members in terms of making available scarce inputs, offering a lower price to members on items sold to them, higher price for produce bought from members compared to non-members and build in patronage bonuses linked to the volume of business done by the member with the PC. Field interactions showed that non-members are also able to buy urea from the PC outlet at the same price as the members do.

Urea is in short supply and restricting its sale to members first and then giving them to non-members at a higher price would have been a clear winning strategy. The quality of other inputs sold by several PCs was good and they were sold below the market price. In such cases it should have been possible to make the non-members pay a higher price than members so that the non-members choose to become members thereby strengthening the PC. In case of output marketing, the PC can either charge a service fee from non-members or offer a slightly lower price than offered to members. When such preferential treatment is afforded to members it has two fallouts; the first is that the members understand the benefits of membership in an economic sense and second, the non-members are motivated to become members looking at benefits foregone. Patronage bonuses tend to increase the volume of business that members do with the PC and counters competition from external buyers of member outputs.

A further issue is that PCs have been trying to make profits to show that they have turned the corner, and higher profits are assumed to reflect greater strength. Being a farmers company, the PCs should part with the maximum benefits to active members through higher prices for produce purchased and lower prices for inputs and other services. By so doing the PC will keep its profits to the minimum and avoid paying out shareholders surpluses as income tax. When needed the members can be requested to invest additional equity in the company. Since there is no open market for the producer company shares, issues relating to share values do not arise. The focus of PCs' governance should rightly be on benefits to active shareholders and not on value of shares.

Sector experts mention that just because farmers are shareholders in a company for five to seven years doesn't mean they will remain loyal. Even established companies with good market linkages find that member loyalty can be an issue. Producers decide from a trading point of view to sell their produce to whoever offers a higher price. Producer companies should communicate with members as to the reason for their being part of the company, the services provided and the reasons for members' continued use of the company's services. Most PCs are yet to build strong relations with the members. There is little advice on production, and package of practices especially for farmers; little do companies realise that farmers are loyal to the input dealer cum trader since he gives advice along with sale of inputs.

Major activities undertaken by producer companies

The basic purpose of the PC is to collectivise small producers for backward linkage for inputs like seeds, fertilisers, knowledge and extension services and forward linkages such as collective marketing, processing, market led production etc. to gain collective bargaining power for small farmers or producers. Financial services especially credit and insurance are other needs of the producers that the PCs can facilitate.

The activities being taken up by PCs can be grouped into three (Figure 5.2). (a) Technical and skill services and input supply for productivity enhancement, (b) Marketing linkages and (c) Financial services. Most PCs begin operation with aggregation of input requirements and try to organise input supply. Some of them on account of the POPIs expertise have commenced providing advice of cultivation with advisories on varieties and package of practices for productivity improvement. Most dairy PCs have been formed for addressing the marketing constraints and thus the initial activities involve marketing. Financial services provision, especially credit for individual member of PC, is rare. Producer companies find finance for their own operations scarce and it is even more difficult to find funds for onlending to members. Some PCs especially in Rajasthan were able to tie-up bank loans for their

Figure 5.2: Services offered by PCs

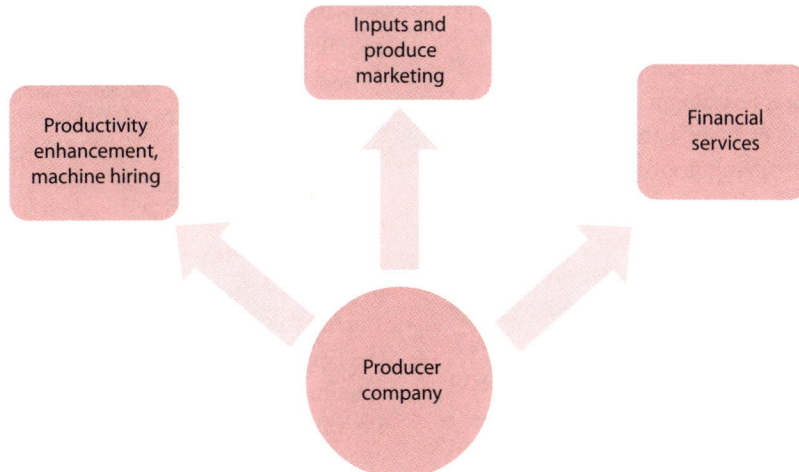

Source: Authors.

members and thus played a critical role in credit facilitation. Some PCs offer insurance related to the livelihood (cattle insurance, crop insurance etc.), usually in collaboration with insurance companies. A few PCs mentioned that they supplied inputs on credit to the members but discontinued the same on account of bad debts. Leasing of machinery is also being undertaken in some PCs. In Madhya Pradesh the apex PC is arranging for leasing of high-quality farm machinery and implements from EM3, a private company, at negotiated rates to be made available to the PC members.

In Access database, out of 65 PCs, 6 PCs reported input supplies to their members, and 9 PCs reported marketing of the produce. Their average turnover is ₹19.30 million and if the data of two large PCs (one, ₹47.50 million and the other ₹83.70 million) are left out, then the average comes down to ₹6.10 million for a sample of 9 FPOs. Turnover of ₹4.5 to ₹6 million has been mentioned by three- to five-year old PCs met during the field visits.

Most of the PCs work on multiple commodities; though there had been a thinking that dealing with multiple commodities will stretch the capacity of PCs especially in forging market linkages, the model that is evolving is that of dealing with three to four commodities. Farmers rarely restrict themselves to one crop. In any given geographical area, a significant proportion of farmers grow more than one crop. A PC focusing on just one crop will find it difficult to acquire members. A PC thus needs to focus on a handful of major crops in the area in order to gain a decent member base. Moreover, FPCs dealing with a single commodity can remain inactive for four to six months in a year and the interest of the board and farmers in the PC wanes. In areas with changing cropping pattern the PC might find itself without business in some years as members do not grow the concerned crop.

Moreover, many FPCs are in rainfed areas where there is higher risk of crop failure and have small farmers as members; the PC has to work with the farmers on multiple crops so that farm risk is managed better. Moreover lenders are also not comfortable with a single commodity/crop approach. Some FPCs are in niche crops, such as seed production; they collaborate with State Seeds Corporation as in the case of Rajasthan and District Poverty Initiative Project (DPIP), MP.

Unique Selling Proposition (USP) of PC is to work on production enhancement; neither trader nor broker can do this.

Source: POPI, Gujarat.

Input supply

Most of the FPCs commence their business with inputs supply including skills and technical services on crop/animal husbandry and health care. Dairy PCs are also arranging for quality cattle feed, fodder demonstrations, veterinary support etc. Quality inputs delivered on time at the doorstep keeps farmers bound to the PC as otherwise they have to deal with issues of spurious quality, high prices etc. FPCs bring economies of bulk purchases and the assurance of quality in inputs like fertiliser, seeds and chemicals. FPCs in many states are involved in input supply. Lack of credit is one issue which is constraining input supply business.

Producer companies are able to arrange the supply of seeds and fertilisers of established brands and required quality. A number of challenges are faced by FPOs in this business. (a) First and foremost is that getting necessary licences from agriculture department to stock and sell inputs have not been easy. The private traders whose business is under threat and who have influence over state departments prevent the issue of necessary permits and licences to PCs. (b) The next level of issues have been from the members who find it difficult to break the traditional ties with traders where inputs are bought on credit. The traders also have a variety of seeds, pesticides and fertilisers to choose from. Facing funds constraints, the FPCs demand cash from members before purchase, they have limited products because of limited tie-ups with dealers etc., (c) FPCs are also unable to match the traders' tactics; to get inputs at reasonable rates, tie-up with dealers are done for a fixed price three months in advance. Seed/input marketing companies ask PCs to observe retail prices. However, traders indulge in unfair practices of selling below the fixed price of the dealer. They are even willing to incur losses in the short term in order to wean away members from FPCs and hurt the FPCs business. While members become disgruntled with high prices of FPC, the trader makes profits in other products he

sells. FPC thus has to face several issues in input supply business. State apexes of PCs are taking up these issues at higher levels.

Aga Khan Rural Support Programme is forming a FPC of farmers to promote drip irrigation. Since 2011 the NGO has been promoting drip irrigation and finds that a farmer is able to irrigate upto three acres of land under drip irrigation with the same quantity of water which was earlier used in 1 acre of flood irrigation. The NGO avails the benefit of the Government of Gujarat scheme implemented by Gujarat Green Revolution Company (GGRC), wherein GGRC has tied up with suppliers for installation and after sales service. For one hectare, GGRC provides ₹20,000 as subsidy, farmer own contribution is ₹7,500 and AKRSP provides a loan of ₹17,500 to the farmer, which has to be repaid to their PC. GGRC transfers these funds to the supplier and also monitors their functioning. AKRSP's funds are grants to PC and loans to farmers, and this revolving fund is later used to increase the area under drip irrigation and also used for working capital in the PC for inputs supply.

Very few FPCs are managing agri-service centers offering comprehensive solutions to the farmers in crop management including soil testing, inputs supply, leasing of machinery, other common facilities such as moisture meter, weighing, stitching machines etc. Since modern agriculture needs to be run as a business, where technology and good agronomic practices play a key role, FPCs need to evolve into competent providers of productivity and marketing solutions.

Marketing of output

Getting a fair price for their produce is the key need of small producers. Among FPCs, vegetable growers are seen as more progressive in market dealings and are also more used to price fluctuation. Farmers raising single crops in rainfed conditions are not seen to be market savvy. POPIs mention that the capacity of the PC boards to understand the market dynamics thus plays a crucial role in their readiness to take up this business.

Some PCs only facilitate linkages with the markets but do not procure from farmer members and market themselves. Some have initiated collective marketing of produce with varied levels of success. SFAC has tied up with RML Information Services, formerly known as Reuters Market Light, to connect 380 FPOs with dealers and buyers. A few have managed to get agricultural produce market committee (APMC) licence to trade and have entered into partnership with institutional buyers to procure for them from the *mandis* for which they earn a commission. Some POPIs like Vrutti, find that trading in commodities requires specialised skills and should not be undertaken by FPOs.

State level apexes of PCs are developing their skills in forging market linkages. Madhya Pradesh state apex PC mentions, "We find the PCs are able to market the produce of only 20 per cent to 25 per cent of their members. Capacity and availability of funds are major constraints. We identify buyers, match the need of buyers with what the farmers produce, work with PCs in improving quality since mismatch in quality is high and also negotiate for better deals. Role specification is important. Like Amul we want PCs to market what they can at their level and come to us where they need support; we don't want to force PCs to market only through us. Brand development is the key role of Apex."

FPCs mention that marketing of farm produce is not an issue but finding reliable long-term buyers has been a challenge. Marketing of seeds produced by the farmers has not been smooth—where the seeds fail to meet the quality parameters, farmers are not paid and this affects not only the existing farmers but also hampers the enrolment of more members. Dairy PCs have usually tied up for marketing with larger dairies but there have been issues in such market linkages forcing them to enter retail marketing. (See Chapter 4 on dairy initiatives).

Some FPCs participated in SFAC's scheme of procurement under MSP last year. Since the price offered by SFAC was higher than the market rate, producers were willing to wait even for three days near the

FPCs with small farmers as members, limited staff capacity and funds constraints have to plan their business very carefully. While running the marketing business in PC, high level of precaution is needed; if the farmer loses, he will lose trust in the institution.

Source: POPI, Gujarat.

office of FPC to sell their produce. However, this year though MSP was offered, since the rate was less than the market price farmers were not keen to sell. Access Livelihood Consulting mentions that during 2013–14, under MSP, FPCs in Telengana did business worth ₹180 million and during 2014–15 since MSP was lower than market rate, business was substantially lower at ₹30 million. PCs were linked with private sector companies like TATA, Mahindra and Mahindra with working capital support from FWWB.

AFARM, in Maharashtra participated in SFAC scheme of supplying vegetables to urban centers in Pune by tying up with housing colonies, hotels, malls, and the initiative worked for three to four months. Agency tie-up requires continuous supply of adequate quantity at specified quality. AFARM worked with growers in five villages but found that crop planning for required supply requires professionals to work with them for a longer term. Short-term support of even two cycles is not sufficient to sustain supply under such tie-ups.

However, one key aspect that has to be borne in mind is that farmers also borrow from traders and money lenders for inputs. These lenders have the first call on the produce. Unless FPCs offer production inputs, advise and extension services along with credit, the traditional market linkages may remain unbroken.

Corporate tie-ups

Some FPCs are also forging corporate tie-ups. For vegetables and fruits marketing, corporate tie-ups have been popular. The other commodity is soya where companies like ITC and Hindustan Lever have shown interest. Shresta and 24 Mantra who market organic produce are keen to provide staff support to ensure production that can be certified as organic.

POPIs mention that marketing tie-up with companies have generally not been very encouraging.

1. Knowledge of NGOs in marketing is negligible and through trial and error they are developing their skills to deal with corporates. POPIs mention that the biggest challenge is finding professional staff who can negotiate with corporates.

2. Companies have reliable tie-ups with large traders who assure year round supply of commodities and goods of the required quantity and quality; PCs, in their initial days, are unable to offer this. Corporates will only deal with PCs if they offer better quality at cheaper price.

3. Companies do not offer right value to the producers. While procuring directly from the PCs, they offer the same or even lower price than what farmers get from markets even though the company may be saving on procurement costs. A number of cases were cited where corporates initially contracted a certain price but later lowered the rates to match *mandi* rates. FPOs needs to network, have storage systems and develop more capacity to supply larger volumes for major part of the year.

4. Producers expect premium price at doorstep marketing. Boards of some FPCs were expecting 25 per cent to 30 per cent premium to market rate and expected the POPIs to negotiate on their behalf. POPIs find that the producers are usually not aware of the quality of their produce; while their produce is C grade they presume it to be A grade and expect high premiums. Education on quality parameters should precede any corporate tie-ups.

5. Some POPIs mention that many times farmers also play truant. For centuries farmers have been cheated while marketing their produce. Expecting to be treated in an unfair manner, they don't play fair as well. Adulteration, mixing poor quality with good quality goods, delayed delivery and last minute pull out from contractual obligations to supply are some problems expected from the farmers. Such unfair practices do not go well with companies and they withdraw from the scene after a bad experience.

6. POPIs who have promoted corporate tie-ups with PCs with vegetables growing farmers mention that the experience has not been found remunerative by the farmers. Corporates follow strict norms in grading but offer only market prices. In peak seasons, the staff have to physically exert to sort out vegetables, working for 18 hours a day. While staff reject about 10 per cent to 15 per cent at their level, corporates like Reliance, Heritage etc., carry out another round of grading at their level and reject another 10 per cent to 15 per cent. Overall rejection can be as high as 30 per cent and these corporates only pay market price. Farmers find it difficult to market the rejected vegetables which are perishable in nature. Some of the PCs are evaluating whether they should go for local marketing rather than corporate tie-ups.

Corporates should prefer direct procurement from FPCs over traditional supply chains knowing fully well the exploitative nature of traditional supply chain. Corporates should make some efforts to manage the value chain. Agents are in main mandi; we are requesting that corporates should send the agent to FPC to determine quality and procure offering market price at farm gate. We are not asking for premium price. We are willing to bear the transportation cost till *mandi*. It appears to us that some of the corporates do not want transparent procurement. In front of government officials they promise but don't follow. We are disappointed with corporates; they should behave more responsibly.

Source: POPI.

Some of the private sector companies are also trying to address the issues faced by farmers and build better relations with them. Vippy Industries, a private sector company in MP, initiated a market linkage facility for farmers and established three soya procurement centres,[7] out of which two were managed by FPCs. These procurement centres were established with the objective to ensure transparent practices and fair prices to farmers and on the other hand, for the company, provide quality soya and build better relations with farmers. While promoting market linkage initiative, the company has experienced challenges like poor quality soya from farmers, transportation issues with small farmers, limited working capital availability with FPCs and legal formalities like getting APMC licences etc (Box 5.1).

Box 5.1: *The CCD experience: Dealing with corporate partners is not easy, but doable*

Experience of institutions like Covenant Center for Development (CCD), Madurai also corroborates that it requires special skills for doing business with corporate partners. CCD formed Aharam, a PC in 2005, with membership of six farmer federations and three SHG federations functioning in six districts of Tamil Nadu. These federations largely consist of small farmers in rain-fed areas. CCD, through the company, provided the farmers advise on crop production and took measures to decrease costs of production. With ICRISAT's technical support, the company worked with farmers in own seed production and propagation among farmers. Organic inputs and integrated pest management practices encouraged farmers to take up multiple cropping. While some products like cotton, chilli, coriander are undertaken in organic conditions and duly certified, others are near organic.

CCD has been facilitating corporate linkages from 2006. Based on suggestions from the corporates, the company has been initially hiring processing units and then investing in value adding facilities. The organic cotton value chain initially started with ginned cotton to be supplied to an institution in Pondicherry. The company set up a ginning mill and then moved to fabric making on the basis of direct orders from international organisations. A special purpose vehicle (SPV) was created for investment in the cotton value chain with co-investments from private sector/social investors and PC.

Similarly, for mango grown under rainfed conditions, initially they were aggregated and supplied to corporates who in turn arranged for pulping through local facilities. The company worked with the farmers in tree management through bio-pesticide management, organic inputs which decreased costs of production. Parle Agro, one of the major procurers, asked PC to invest in processing to supply high-quality pulp. With investments from a Canadian organisation, a SPV, Kalasam Sacred Foods, now manages the mango pulping and marketing. About 2,000 tonnes of mango are pulped and marketed each year.

CCD mentions that PC needs deeper pockets for initial investment in social mobilisation, engaging professional staff and also for initial investments in land etc., AVT McCormick, a company exporting spices and condiments has forged partnership with PC for supply of condiments, such as chilli, coriander etc., For the primary level cleaning, drying and grading, the export company is ready to invest in machinery worth ₹20 million to handle large volumes which will be in the company's books; however, PC will have to invest in land, drying yard and godowns for the machinery to be installed, which will cost ₹5 million. CCD finds that the primary cleaning and selling can increase the price by 20 per cent and is trying to find ways of investing in the infrastructure.

CCD has been having corporate linkages for 17 years and shares detailed information about the purchase orders, zero rejections and financial transactions to build new linkages for co-investments.

Source: Discussions with CCD.

---

[7] Mr. Praneet Mutha, Director, Vippy Industries Ltd. Dewas, Madhya Pradesh. India, as mentioned in Sustainable Soy newsletter, February 2015.

Volume: 2 Issue: 1, February 2015, a quarterly newsletter of National Platform of Sustainable Soy.

Since most PCs do not have godowns or warehouses to store, they are unable to hold the produce and respond to enquiries from bulk buyers. Moreover, producers want cash immediately on harvest or production and they do not want to delay marketing. Warehousing options are being tried by some POPIs. Institutions like AKRSP mention that creating infrastructure and machinery can be done once business has scaled up and initially the operations can be through hired facilities.

POPIs also find that FPCs of small farmers (holding 1 to three acres) has limitations; they are averse to taking risks. There are several growers' federations especially of export oriented cash crops or horticulture crops in Maharashtra that are successful because larger farmers are members and small farmers benefit from the risk taking ability and business acumen of the larger farmers in doing business.

> We are farmers; we are not business people. Input supply and also collective marketing business requires acumen and intelligence. After two years of funding support we are now on our own; we do not have staff. Board has to manage the affairs of the company.
>
> *Source:* FPC, Rajasthan.

Overall, POPIs find that collective marketing with grading, sorting and linking with local markets and larger traders (either individually or collectively) is easier to manage for PCs than working on corporate linkages or struggling with APMC licenses. Individual producers benefit from savings on transportation costs and price difference due to grading and thus are keen to deal through PCs. Bringing transparency in dealings—weighment, pricing etc.—with producers, has benefitted the producers. POPIs mention that it is difficult to follow all the laws and rules, pay taxes and still pay the market price to farmers.

Warehouse financing

Farmers, especially small and marginal, normally do not get the benefit of the upside in price for produce. They are almost always forced to sell the produce soon after harvest when the prices are at the lowest in order to repay formal or informal debts and on the preparation of the next crop. Delayed marketing to ensure higher price realisation for the farmers has been facilitated by a few FPCs through warehouse receipt financing.

SRIJAN has promoted the women farmer's producer company, Samridhi Mahila Crop Producer Company Ltd. which is providing various services to its members like agri-inputs, quality seeds, crop advisory services and marketing facilities. In 2013 the PC did a pilot on warehouse receipt system (WRS) to increase incomes of small-scale farmers by enabling them to get better prices for their produce and gain access to get credit through a WRS.

Post-harvest, farmers have an option to either sell the soya at a collection centre at best price at that time (PC provides daily prices to farmers every evening) or hold the commodity in approved warehouses till they realize a better price. The sale would happen through a partner spot exchange like NCDEX or directly to an agri-corporate. In case the farmer decides to store the commodity, finance is arranged from ICICI Bank at reasonable rates of interest against the security of produce. The presence of the spot exchange and the corporate ensures better price discovery for the farmer. When the farmer decides to sell the produce subsequently, the loan is liquidated and the upside is available to the farmer as gain after adjusting applicable costs.

During 2014–15, 78 farmers stored 1,286 quintals (average price was ₹3,317 at the time of storage and ₹3,951 at the time of sale). After meeting costs of storage and interest costs, an average ₹300 per quintal was the net gain from marketing after storing soya for six months. However, the women farmers have to convince their family to store at warehouse. Market fluctuations in price of guar gum, another popular produce of Rajasthan has made farmers wary of storing and selling.

Value addition has been tried by very few PCs in farm produce. Milling of grams and converting spices to powders have been attempted by a few. POPIs find that a very high level of preparedness and understanding of markets is needed for entering such value addition. To move up the value chain may take five to seven years after formation of PC. However, lack of working capital restricts the scale of procurement from farmers and such value addition. Moreover, taxes eat into profits and affect viability. While other private players may be indulging in tax evasion practices, FPCs pay the taxes and find the margins squeezed.

Sorting, grading and packaging for selling in local markets are the minimalist value addition that many FPCs do. This activity requires investment of ₹1 to 3 lakhs that FPCs usually get as grants through government or donor schemes. FPCs are realising the need for godowns but are concerned about year-round utilisation and over-capitalisation. For seed producers more sophisticated facilities are needed. MP state apex PC plans to create such common infrastructure with government and private sector funding at a regional level where a cluster of PCs can utilise such facilities. PCs also mention that the land for construction of common facilities should be provided by the local panchayat since lot of wasteland is available. This will save PCs from setting aside large sums for purchase of land. PCs working among tribals have an additional issue of inability to purchase land since land owned by tribals is not available for purchase. Government has to allocate the land.

Lenders like Ananya Finance mention that for marketing and processing facilities PCs should seek private sector partnerships and investments through a special purpose vehicle based on co-investment principles, which will be managed professionally. Choice of technology plays a key role in determining efficiency, profitability and market acceptance. Especially value addition investments near the high end of the value chain are often beyond the capacity of POPI and thus PCs require private sector partnerships.

Staffing in PCs

Producer companies initially require at least three staff; Chief Executive Officer (CEO), accounts and a community facilitator/business promoter. Additionally, four to five local resource persons are engaged to work with producers and farmers. However, except a few, most of the FPCs interacted with, had no CEO and the post is largely lying vacant. Hiring and retaining qualified staff has been difficult. PCs do not have staff who can grow their business. Local resource persons are usually employed in all PCs especially FPCs. These are mostly progressive farmers who are also on the board of the PC. However, there is limited oversight on their work; there have been reports that with inadequate knowledge they have misguided producers in some instances.

Managing inputs and produce marketing business, requires a competent person and this involves payment of fair salary. Many

> Staff salaries being provided are very low, ₹15,000 to 20,000 per month for a CEO. Staff with education from a good institute ask for ₹30,000 to ₹40,000. If the staff selection and capacity is good then time taken for achieving sustainability of PC will be less.
>
> *Source:* POPI, MP.
>
> By law the staff is a CEO, but by qualification and salary he is a clerk. It is difficult to find qualitative persons who will bolster business and improve the trust levels of farmers—chicken or egg, which comes first kind of situation.
>
> *Source:* POPI, Gujarat.

PCs are not able to afford one. There are instances where CEOs are appointed after lengthy selection processes but never trained.

During the project funding support phase of SFAC/NABARD/donors, the professional staff of the POPI have been working with the PCs. Usually such technical staff work with four to five PCs. However, some of the promoting organisations of FPCs do not have the technical expertise on commodities, or crop husbandry. Thus, the staff capacity of POPIs to work with FPCs, especially in the chosen crops, requires a review.

Few of the POPIs are able to provide similar support after the project funding is exhausted for which they mobilise separate funding. FPCs promoted by ASA, ALC and Vrutti follow a three to four staff model. They mention that CEO salary should be supported for the initial three to four business cycles till business stabilises. They are planning to support PCs for a longer time frame (7 to 10 years), which also involves bridging operational costs including salaries where found necessary. However, most POPIs are neither able to provide professional expertise after the funding is over nor able to raise resources for operational costs of the PCs, which can pay for salaries.

When qualified staff are not on roll, members are also not keen to expand business especially by taking loans. PCs are caught in a vicious cycle of lack of business, lack of staff, lack of funds and lack of ownership of members. The Board of directors carry out the functions of staff in many PCs. Banks naturally feel uncomfortable with this situation and often query "who is the face of the company?" Poor staff resources and capacity is often cited as one of the reasons for lack of loan funding by banks.

Governance in PCs

Boards of PCs are playing a crucial role in keeping the operations going since many PCs face staff constraints and fund constraints. As per the data gathered by Access from PCs, the average number of directors is nine (based on data for 45 FPOs). In ten companies, the number is less than nine. The number of male directors reported for 42 FPOs, ranges from 1 to 15, and for women, these numbers from 19 FPOs are 1 to 12. Twenty-four PCs had exclusive male boards with no woman member and 11 PCs had exclusive women boards.

In some of the boards, the representatives of the POPIs take most positions. POPIs identify professionals as independent directors or advisors to PCs. POPIs however are finding it difficult to completely hand over the management and reduce dependency since there is a concern that freedom can be misused. There needs to be a balance between the POPI, board and management roles in the PC.

Most of the board members also act as LRPs either on paid basis or draw an honorarium. In the absence of staff, board members carry out the staff functions often without adequate remuneration. Thus, boards play a dual role of governance and execution, which is not a healthy practice in the long run.

AFARM finds that instead of only small farmers if the board of directors consists of a few better off farmers, the FPC is managed well. The large farmers are well integrated with government and banks and thus manage to mobilise more resources. The ever-present threat perception of elite capture prevents most POPIs from bringing affluent farmers on boards.

POPIs lay emphasis on board capacity development. Some of them have developed different modules for training. But much of the training to the board is given on the job by POPI staff who attend the board meetings. State apex PCs are also planning to undertake extensive board training. Boards of PCs mention that they require training on business aspects; business planning, legal compliances, financial management and resource mobilisation.

At present most boards are not compensated for their work. Like corporates, PCs also need to pay a share of profits to directors.

Instead of activity based incentives the board has to decide yardsticks of good performance, work to achieve multiple targets and offer a share in profits to directors. This will motivate other competent members to come forward to take board positions and improve overall governance.

Benefits seen by farmers in FPCs

During the interactions with boards and members of 22 PCs, the PCs are reported to offer the following benefits:

1. Savings of 15 per cent to 20 per cent of input costs.
2. Fair practices in price fixation, weighment, timely procurement and prompt payment.
3. Bargaining ability increased as a collective.
4. Input advisory.
5. Convergence with government schemes.

While the reduction in input costs is quantified and experienced by the members, the others are yet to be quantified at the member level. But if the listed benefits are perceived, it is a good augury for the PCs.

Funding promotion of PCs

SFAC and NABARD are the two major agencies funding the promotional costs of PCs. All major centrally sponsored schemes of Department of Agriculture and Cooperation, Ministry of Agriculture, GoI have incorporated special provisions for promotion and development of FPOs during the 12th Five-year Plan. Some of the externally aided projects by the World Bank and IFAD also provide for formation of and funding for PCs. Some of the state governments like Andhra Pradesh, Rajasthan etc., are also pushing this forward with specific allocations and targets. Irrespective of the source of funding, the quantum of funding and attached conditions largely determine the quality and sustainability of PCs.

POPIs mention that for carrying out agribusiness, a professional team of four staff who can handle marketing, procurement, advisory services, finance and compliances, need to be funded for a minimum of five-year period; and this team will support 20 to 25 PCs depending on the geographical area. After this term the PCs should be able to pay for the costs of the team. In the initial period of promotion of a PC, three PC staff and four LRPs are required. Their costs and partial staff salary of POPI require about ₹1 million per year. SFAC's funding norms are widely perceived to be more realistic, with financial assistance ranging between ₹3 to ₹4.5 million over a three-year period. NABARD at present provides ₹1 million as promotional cost per PC for three years and POPIs mention that the fund allocated by GoI, ₹2,000 million, is divided among the target 2,000 PCs to be formed. POPIs mention that the present funding support from all these agencies is geared towards basic mobilisation but not towards agribusiness stabilisation at PC level.

NABARD has forged partnerships with NGOs to form producer groups, especially in watershed development project areas. As a strategy this is appreciable since the target group would have been mobilised for carrying land- and water-related activities, and building on such mobilisation for strengthening the agriculture and allied activities of farmers through an appropriate institutional structure is the logical next step in improving the livelihoods of farmers. NABARD expects that from the first year the PCs will undertake business and start earning incomes. However, most of the partners mention that the quantum of funding is not adequate to place qualified staff who can handle complex inputs and outputs marketing functions and meet their salary requirements.

Many state government programmes, especially externally aided programmes, have provisions for seed capital and revolving fund for the PCs ranging between ₹0.5 million to ₹2.5 million, apart from promotional costs. However, POPIs mention that in spite of PCs fulfilling the laid down norms, the release of funds is delayed even beyond a year. This apart from delaying the business plans of PCs, also affects the morale and trust of members in PC mechanism. Timely release of funds even for capacity building trainings has been a major problem. To make the government release funds requires continuous follow up and rapport building, which many POPIs find as tiresome. POPIs opine that project financing of PCs is increasingly becoming a number game. A POPI working in Uttar Pradesh mentions "In the initial set of PCs six months were spent in mobilisation and PCs are strong; then government asked us to speed up to form 90 more. This speed undermines the quality".

Overall, POPIs indicate that there is little funding for capacity building of POPI staff and for undertaking field visits for monitoring of PCs. POPIs also find that the funders assume that the organisation works with captive farmers, which is not always the case and mobilisation time varies; strict timelines for registering PC is leading to compromises being made on mobilisation. PCs need a longer term support than the three-year time frame being considered by funders. Due to lack of funding some of the POPIs withdraw after three years with half the job done.

SFAC, NABARD and other funders need to carry out a field-based evaluation on results achieved by the second year; if the results are satisfactory then they should extend flexible need-based support to POPIs for a longer term to ensure sustainability of PCs. If SFAC has funded for three years and the initiative is showing results, then NABARD should provide further support to stabilise the agribusiness of PCs. Funding institutions can specialise in early stage, post start-up stage and mature stage PCs so that the differing needs of PCs in these different stages are adequately and appropriately addressed. There is a need for better co-ordination between funders to ensure whatever has been initiated is consolidated and PCs reach their full potential so that the producers reap substantial benefits.

Financial position of PCs

Overall availability of share capital and reserves with PCs are limited. On account of their infancy and low profitability, PCs are unable to raise their net worth. Raising share capital from members who are poor is a problem and other options need to be explored. Mobilising grants from international agencies, corporates and foundations is one option. Some of them like CCD float special purpose vehicle in which social investors and PC co-invest for value addition.

Some POPIs have mobilised grants for purchase of machinery and equipment used by PCs; POPIs intend to transfer these assets in the name of the PC once they are mature. For the present PCs remain dependent on donors for grants not only for investments, but also for their operational expenditure. Unless concerted efforts are taken to mobilise equity, enhance membership, introduce easier business lines, such as input supply that can earn a surplus, the PCs will take a long time to become financially strong. The state/donor support should require a significant equity mobilisation effort from members as otherwise member ownership might weaken. Financial position of the PCs will determine access to loan funds and the ability to expand, outreach and turnover. Despite the potential for business having been established through member mobilisation, the further steps for realising the potential are not forthcoming. A critical shortcoming is that the POPIs also struggle with the institutional form where non-producers cannot invest in equity of the PC. Alternative means of non-producer contribution to capital funds such as special class of quasi-equity instruments can also be issued though this option doesn't find favour with PCs and POPIs.

Loan fund mobilisation

Banks are not warming up to financing of PCs and much of POPIs time and efforts are spent in mobilising working capital. This is also corroborated by the Access data which shows that out of 64 FPOs, only 11 FPOs have reported to have taken loan from some source, with a minimum loan outstanding of ₹0.35 million and maximum of ₹1.52 million and average being ₹0.41 million. POPIs mention that the major lenders are (a) FWWB, (b) Ananya Finance, (c) Caspian, (d) NABKISAN, (e) Manaveeya, (f) BASIX (LMP fund) and (g) NABFINS. IDBI bank and Punjab National Bank are reportedly showing some interest. Canara Bank and SBI, have framed a policy and scheme for financing producer companies.

Friends of Women's World Banking (FWWB) has played the role of a first lender to the PCs. FWWB loans are collateral free and at reasonable rates of interest (6 per cent to 13 per cent depending on the source of the funding and terms agreed with the FWWB's lender/donor). PCs and POPIs are highly appreciative of the role played by FWWB in building the confidence of the PCs in undertaking business since the loans were often accompanied by capacity building as well. FWWB carries out in-depth assessment and lends to PCs on the basis of business plan, member strength and patronage and management capacity rather than balance sheet alone.

LAMP fund, set up by BASIX group for lending to PCs, has also come in for appreciation. With the initial loan from FWWB and LAMP, PCs are able to demonstrate a credit track record which should enable them to access loans from banks. FWWB has, in the last five years, cumulatively disbursed ₹223 million to 35 PCs. As of 30 June 2015, ₹41.76 million is outstanding to 21 companies. Seventy per cent of companies take repeat finance either from FWWB or from Ananya Finance Inclusive Growth (a sister company). FWWB mentions that the repayment rate in general is very good; except in one case there have not been any write off in the last four years. Ananya Finance, a recent entrant in the market has commenced lending from January 2015.

FWWB is of the view that unless POPIs support PCs for five years, the institutional and business strength of PCs will not be adequate to carry out business profitably.

Since margins are thin in most of the businesses, building the business volumes are key to achieve cost coverage. Systematically building such volumes of business require capacity to plan and execute in the PCs for which POPIs continued support is critical.

While FWWB largely lends for working capital and small machinery, Ananya Finance is developing longer term loan products for warehouse financing, processing machinery and equipment aimed at post-harvest financing. While funding working capital requirements, Ananya evaluates marketing tie-ups. Ananya is also forging partnership with IDBI bank for acting as business correspondent for financing to PCs wherein Ananya carries out the due diligence and also monitors PCs.

While NABARD has been keen on promotion of PCs, their lending norms to PCs is stringent and loan portfolio to PCs is limited. NABARD sanctioned financial assistance of ₹1,577 million (₹1,536 million as loan and ₹42 million as grant) to 65 new producers' organisations during 2014–15. The disbursements amounted to ₹1,019.8 million (₹1,004.4 million as loan and ₹15.4 million as grant). The assistance has been largely for setting up marketing and processing infrastructure in a wide variety of crops and commodities. PCs mention that compliance with the norms of NABARD (a) two to three years audited balance sheets and (b) Collateral requirements, are very tough to meet unless POPI is willing to borrow on its balance sheet and on lend to PCs. Two large POPIs mention that NABARD has shown more keenness to lend through the promoters than to the PCs directly.

Though some of the commercial banks have issued instructions and guidelines for lending to PCs, branch managers are yet to appreciate the concept and get enthused. Bankers find that based on the balance sheet strength and asset position, 90 per cent of PCs are not bankable. Not having adequate capital is the major impediment as per bankers.

To address this problem, SFAC is implementing the Equity Grant and Credit

Guarantee Fund Scheme with an outlay of ₹1500 million for FPCs since 2013–14. This scheme enables registered FPCs to access equity grant to double member equity upto a maximum limit of ₹1 million. The scheme also provides a credit guarantee to financial institutions which extend loans to producer companies without collateral upto ₹10 million. During the financial year 2014–15, SFAC has sanctioned seven projects amounting to ₹4.26 million under Equity Grant Fund. The scheme has been slow to pick up due to some procedural issues and stringent eligibility criteria set for equity support under which many PCs do not qualify. Moreover, information on the scheme has not reached many PCs. The PCs require the support of POPIs to file the applications. SFAC is reportedly simplifying the processes to improve off take of the equity fund grants.

Bankers are yet to fully appreciate the credit guarantee being offered by SFAC and have not shown much interest. POPIs find the loan limit of ₹10 million for credit guarantee to be insufficient and want the limit to be increased to ₹50 million. The credit guarantee cover is not available to non-banking institutions which are actually empathetic to the PCs, have a deeper engagement and provide loans on a clear understanding of the potential. SFAC should consider extending credit guarantee to institutions like FWWB, NABFINS, Ananya, Manaveeya etc., that are keen to expand their portfolio with PCs and can effectively use the guarantees.

The branch managers of banks have not shown much interest in either the PCs or marketing loans (Box 5.2). In fact, lot of bankers haven't heard about PCs. POPIs mention that RBI's policy support and NABARD's developmental role are needed for financing PCs wherein branch managers need to be trained in assessment and appraisal of PCs as was done in spreading SHG bank linkage in the first 10 years of SHG programme.

According to some of the POPIs, board members of PCs being small producers also hesitate to take responsibility for borrowing large sums. Training to board of PCs on developing a large future vision, business planning and loan management needs to be

---

Box 5.2:   *Working capital woes*

CCD mentions that due to lack of working capital, PC is unable to meet the large volumes of produce demand by the corporates. Companies are willing to advance ₹0.5 million for procurement. However, procurement is done in a narrow window of opportunity when the produce is harvested. For example, though the mango season is of three months, procurement for pulping is done in 30 days since in the initial and last month the cost is high. To procure 3,000 tonnes the company requires ₹30 million. Similarly, for procurement of chillies, the first to third harvest are the best; the fourth and fifth harvest are not suitable for international trade. To procure 2,000 tonnes of chillies in 20 days, the company requires ₹200 million. The company is able to procure only 15 per cent of demand due to scarcity of working capital. In spite of established track record, books of accounts and evidence of good working relationship with corporates, banks especially branch staff are not keen and insist on collateral and personal guarantees.

CCD then approached the companies to finance the farmers for initial ploughing and seeds costing ₹5,000 per acre. If these costs are met farmers are willing to wait for upto 20 days after harvest for their payment. But companies that had bitter experience of financing farmers earlier through traders were unwilling to provide input loans to farmers.

CCD now is endeavouring for linking NABARD financed godowns and warehouses to be compliant with warehousing legislation so that farmers can store produce closeby instead of travelling 40 to 60 kilometers, which increases transportation costs. Moreover, farmers have faith only in local warehouses. If warehouse receipt financing system is made available, then PC can procure non-perishable commodities over a longer period and manage with a lower amount of working capital.

Source: Discussions with CCD.

carried out. Exposure visit to other PCs with good loan repayment performance will have to be arranged. The boards of PCs have to be involved in business planning so that the confidence to borrow from the bank is developed.

When farmers borrow individually from a bank they get concessional credit but at the same time their collectives get loans at commercial rates. If the PCs act as pass through intermediaries for production loans, the farmers will not be able to benefit from the subsidies available under direct bank loans. Since support to farmers is the objective, a policy reset is warranted to remove the distinction in interest rates between direct loans and indirect loans, especially when the intermediary is a farmers' collective.

The business plans facilitated by POPIs are robust and range from ₹10 million to ₹50 million of turnover. However, the attained turnover is hardly 30 per cent to 50 per cent in many of the PCs for which lack of funds is cited as the most important cause. As Vijayalakshmi Das, MD, Ananya Finance points out that unless finance flows, businesses and member patronage will be low, and if producers are not availing services from their organisation, the whole investment made in creating a producer organisation will fail to fructify.

Access to finance for PCs should be improved vastly, looking at their potential to impact value addition and income at the farm level. The current scenario points to inadequate equity, scarcity of funds for long-term development, very limited working capital for business operations in input and output marketing and no arrangements to mitigate liquidity risks (Box 5.3). While attempts at providing small equity contributions to a limited number of PCs are ongoing, the schemes are not designed to help PCs realise their potential and take up strategic long-term investments. No facile market options exist for contributing to equity of PCs on account of restrictions on shareholding. Some feasible options are:

- A subordinated debt capital fund should be set up which can offer long-term loans that charge higher interest rates at the later end of maturities. The size of debt can be determined as multiples of member contributed equity so that PCs continue to mobilise additional equity. The debt fund should be tradable as units in the stock exchange.
- Recognise loans given to PCs for onlending to farmers for production purposes as direct agricultural loans. Such loans

---

Box 5.3: *Old problem and a new solution*

A federation of SHGs in the hills of Uttarakhand was awarded a contract by the Integrated Child Development Scheme to provide nutritious home rations for rural households in one block. The federation had to buy local millets and pulses from members and some other goods, such as jaggery and dates from the market. The federation was in a position to do a business of about ₹50 lakhs per annum, providing employment for 20 to 40 women in sorting, packing and delivery of the rations throughout the year. But the federation required working capital of about ₹25 lakhs as payment from ICDS was not expected to be regular, but lumpy. The federations found it difficult to borrow from banks, which required collateral. The federation then requested the constituent SHGs to bor-

row from banks and relend to the federation. The federation was prepared to pay 1 per cent more to SHGs than the rate of interest at which SHGs borrowed from the bank. The federation was able to access more than ₹20 lakhs by way of working capital through this mechanism. The business fetched a handsome profit to the federation after paying interest on the loan. More importantly the price of Madua, a local millet and Kali Bhat, black soya, increased in the market benefiting small farmers.

Source: Based on discussions with officials of Integrated Livelihood Support Project, Uttarakhand, implemented by the Government of Uttarakhand with a loan from International Fund for Agricultural Development.

should also enjoy the low interest rates available under direct bank loans so that farmer willingness to avail the loan from PCs is not diminished.

- Set up a marketing loan facility under which PCs can directly borrow from banks or NABARD up to a specified threshold against hypothecation of inputs, crops and commodities in trade. To increase bankers' comfort the guarantee scheme operated by SFAC can be extended to these loans.
- NABARD should also operate a refinance line for intermediary institutions, such as FWWB, Ananya, Manaveeya and any other willing NBFC for onlending to smaller PCs. This will ensure that NABARD supports the PCs either directly or indirectly, consistent with its capacity to take-in small loans in its books.
- The PCs should also design equity contributions from members from out of incremental benefits produced. Particularly when patronage bonuses are declared, the members can be persuaded to invest a portion of the payments into equity. While the easier option is to transfer a part of the profits into reserves and shore up net worth, it would be a tax inefficient way of building capital funds. By making due payments to members, the PC can collect the tax part of the payments, which would otherwise have been lost to both the members and the company.

Challenges in sustainability of PCs

The challenges identified by POPIs and boards of PCs are indicated in Table 5.1.

Table 5.1: Key issues and needs identified

POPIs/Apex of PCs	Boards of PCs
Finance for PCs' operations	Member ownership
Member ownership	Lack of qualified staff
Lack of qualified staff	Finance
Funds to POPIs to accompany PCs for a longer term	Training for board on legal issues, business planning, marketing

Source: Discussions with POPIs and Boards of PCs.

Legal form: Stakeholders question the benefit of mobilising small producers under a company form. A company form has lot of regulations to comply with, and compliance has a cost. PCs despite being farmer organisations do not get preferential treatment in taxation. These companies face additional issues in attracting and retaining professional staff, governance capacity and ability to raise capital. Tax issues are severe—32.05 per cent of tax has to be paid on income, which cooperatives do not have to pay. Company form has not attracted adequate bank financing so far.

Business mix: POPIs and PCs mention that PCs cannot be sustainable on inputs supply alone since the margins are low. Output marketing has to be the backbone of PCs. Trust between the PC and the producers has to be built for sustaining output marketing. Unless production advice and input services are provided to the satisfaction of the producers, they will find it difficult to break the members' traditional links. The key driver in sustaining member links is availability of funds for production operations of members in the form of banks loans.

Appropriate funding

As discussed earlier, lack of funds is affecting the implementation of business plans, outreach, visibility, ability to attract and retain professional staff and ultimately financial viability of PCs. Banks need to step in early in the evolution cycle of PCs. Other instruments to suit the needs of start-ups should also need to be devised. Mulkanoor women's dairy a success story had patient capital finance for seven years, which enabled it to stabilise its operations. Some of the donors and governments can establish patient capital mechanism with institutions like FWWB and Manaveeya who have a proven track record of financing start-ups. With a significant number of PCs having been formed already, it makes little sense to form even more without first facilitating financial and business linkages. If banks and financial institutions continue to be reluctant to engage with PCs, then it is a clear indication that they do not trust this form and structure. This lack of awareness and trust on the part of banks and financial institutions has to be dealt with. Financial linkages for PCs as an institutional class should be established and strengthened before committing additional funds for new PCs.

Advisory and mentoring support to PCs

Under the present funding arrangement that usually lasts three years, POPIs are unable to nurture the PCs. Institutional and financial sustainability of the PCs is fragile unless the POPIs have the means of providing technical and handholding support for another three to four years. Many POPIs mention that in three years' time, at best two business cycles are carried out. Business volumes adequate to meet the salary costs of the CEO and other staff cannot be built within three years. Vijay Mahajan in last year's SOIL report[8] had diagrammatically shown stagewise capacity and capital growth for the sustainability of PCs and had concluded that seven- to eight-year time frame is needed for a PC to be sustainable and provide meaningful services to producers.

Some POPIs are developing their strategies for supporting PCs beyond the initial three years. ALC signs contract with each PC by the third year of operation when the business has commenced. Annual plan discussions are jointly held, yearly targets set, services to be provided by ALC are specified and achievement of plan jointly monitored through specific indicators. In all large PCs (4,000 to 5,000 members), ALC places technical staff to help the CEO and other staff in their business. The contract specifies payment to ALC for its services, which is partially fixed and partially variable, based on achievement of outcomes.

Vrutti encourages farmers to pay for services from first year onwards. Cost of incubation and retainer costs are charged to FPO to be paid later. Transaction cost based on turnover in business and financial access costs are also collected. Thus, both FPOs and Vrutti are bound by deliverables and payment for services. Vrutti has established Farm Enterprise Facilitation Centers at district level which are staffed by professionals. BASIX group of institutions plan to grade the FPOs and give holistic support beyond the project/government support to those with A grade, for which they are sourcing separate funding.

The pool of resources to offer technical advice to PCs to expand their business and finances should be made available. While SFAC provides consultant support, they are largely from NGO background. State apexes have to create a resource base of identifying key experts with business experience who can offer advice.

While POPIs are contemplating and designing longer term support, SFAC and NABARD should extend support for five years in stages based on achievement of key results. When it is a well-established fact that PCs require about six years to attain maturity and financial strength to procure services, funding for a lesser term is not result oriented; and it might be sub-optimal use of resources to leave community based organisations incomplete.

Policy support

State governments need to play a major role in propagating the concept. Almost in every state visited, except in the case of MP the POPIs, members and office bearers in PCs and other stakeholders narrated countless experiences of how they had to deal with ignorance of PC form in government and bank officials. In some states the higher officials in the state and district are unaware of PCs. In Uttar Pradesh, the Agriculture Commissioner had issued instructions to district officials to support PCs through convergence of some of the state schemes.

[8] Access Development Services, 2014, State of the Sector report on livelihoods, 2014.

This has created awareness though results are reportedly uneven. In some states the awareness of PCs is very low as per POPIs.

By suitable amendments in the APMC Act governments can allow direct sale of farm produce by FPCs at the farmgate, through FPO owned procurement and marketing centres. State governments need to make provisions for easy issue of licenses to FPOs to trade in inputs (seed, fertiliser, farm machinery, pesticides etc.) for use of their members as well as routing the supply of agricultural inputs through FPOs as in the case of cooperatives. State governments need to consider PCs at par with cooperatives and self-help groups or federations for all schemes and benefits that are extended to these member-owned institutions. PCs need to be considered as key implementing agencies for various government schemes in the relevant sectors—agriculture, fisheries, dairy, handloom, handicraft etc.

Benefits to members

With patronage ranging from 20 per cent to 50 per cent members, there are questions raised on the effectiveness and efficiency of mobilising producers as PCs. This form is seen as costly vis-à-vis the benefits arising there from. However, some of the POPIs mention that establishing AMUL involved lot of grants. Similarly, oil seeds federation and other commodity federations have also attracted lot of subsidies and grants. Comparatively the investment in PCs has been limited. However, a study to evaluate the investments made in the last 10 years and net benefits to producers will be useful to determine the way forward.

Producer companies promoted under the World Bank funded DPIP have shown good performance and success rates in the view of several stakeholders. This has been due to a host of factors. The project support unit and specialised NGOs provided hand-holding and helped PCs progress through the preparation, start-up, and incubation phase, and several have achieved partial autonomy and maturity. They also helped

> Though organising producers into producer companies and promoting collective action are often recommended as the solutions to most of their problems, in practice, the pace of progress and level of performance leave much to be desired, in spite of the best efforts of all concerned …. Collective action remains a distant dream.
>
> *Source:* NABARD Annual Report, 2014–15.

catalyse convergence with government programmes. Grant support for go downs and machinery enabled PCs to store process and to grade the produce, achieving better prices for farmers. Monitoring by the World Bank helped overcome hurdles. Such a model of promotion and nurturance is no doubt expensive and resource intensive, but it has a better chance of achieving results.

To conclude, FPCs seemed such an obvious solution to several problems of the governments and large organisations in engaging farmers in meaningful ways with significant cost efficiencies and benefits on both the sides—the members and the other business entities. But the concept has taken a very long time to take roots. Even after 12 years there are very few examples of successful producer companies. The last two years have seen a positive bent towards PCs, judging from the number of PCs getting registered and the number of schemes designed to support PCs. But the emphasis seems to be on establishing more PCs rather than making PCs work for meeting members' interests and build them as sustainable, long-term institutions (Annexure 5.1).

In the policy front, a clearer articulation of the objectives with which PCs' promotion is taken up by public sector is a dire necessity. Public funds should not be spent on creating a number of institutions on the ground unless they are designed to actually deliver benefits to people at large. The schemes of support should focus on what kind of results should be achieved and quantify the different types of support required to achieve the results. The producers and the farming community in particular were not asking for new institutional types to better their livelihoods. They would have been happy if the rural cooperatives were made to work effectively. The new institutional form—the PC—is typically supply side thinking. Having brought in PCs as feasible solutions to several problems in producers' livelihoods, the onus is on the state and public sector to prove it to be so.

The cooperation and participation of producers in their companies is a necessary, but not sufficient condition for the success of this institutional form. The schemes of government and public sector institutions should address other problems—beyond

mobilisation of members—of the PCs in a comprehensive manner. These issues, as described in the preceding parts of the chapter, relate to adequacy of quantum of support in the initial stages, adequacy of the period of support, availability of patient capital, readiness of financial institutions to invest time in understanding this new institutional form and design loan products and lending processes, developing of pool of professionals at the district level to offer guidance, fair and transparent rules for market access, protection from unfair conduct by contracting parties that sell or buy goods from PCs and an incentivising tax regime. Before the novelty of the new institutional form wears off, the stakeholders should find the PCs a firm footing.

ANNEXURE 5.1
State-wise FPOs

		State-wise FPO registered in the country as on date (07.05.2015)					
		No. of farmers			No. of FPOs		
S. No.	State	Mobilised	Under Mobilisation	Total	Registered	Under the process of registration	Total
1.	Andhra Pradesh	5,976	6,024	12,000	5	7	12
2.	Arunachal Pradesh	1,750	0	1,750	2	0	2
3.	Assam	25,000	0	25,000	25	0	25
4.	Bihar	14,148	3,852	18,000	8	11	19
5.	Chhattisgarh	13,293	12,707	26,000	5	20	25
6.	Delhi	3,535	0	3,535	4	0	4
7.	Goa	1,810	0	1,810	1	1	2
8.	Gujarat	31,047	953	32,000	22	11	33
9.	Haryana	8,408	0	8,408	16	9	25
10.	Himachal Pradesh	3,698	1,152	4,850	0	4	4
11.	Jammu	3,694	287	3,981	1	2	3
12.	Srinagar	3,120	960	4,080	1	3	4
13.	Jharkhand	10,009	0	10,009	8	0	8
14.	Karnataka	25,904	58,596	84,500	14	68	82
15.	Madhya Pradesh	83,277	61,723	145,000	54	90	144
16.	Maharashtra	63,052	28,448	91,500	46	43	89
17.	Manipur	2,650	300	2,950	2	1	3
18.	Meghalaya	1,970	3,105	5,075	2	2	4
19.	Mizoram	1,700	1,000	2,700	0	3	3
20.	Nagaland	1,750	0	1,750	2	0	2

(Continued)

(Continued)

		No. of farmers			No. of FPOs		
			Under			Under the process of	
S. No.	State	Mobilised	Mobilisation	Total	Registered	registration	Total
21.	Odisha	26,097	12,803	38,900	6	35	41
22.	Punjab	6,288	0	6,288	7	0	7
23.	Rajasthan	51,277	6,223	57,500	42	7	49
24.	Sikkim	1,876	0	1,876	2	0	2
25.	Tamil Nadu	60,366	0	60,366	53	7	60
26.	Telangana	58,354	0	58,354	44	10	54
27.	Tripura	2,850	0	2,850	3	1	4
28.	Uttarakhand	44,004	0	44,004	7	0	7
29.	Uttar Pradesh	55,444	7,447	62,891	84	11	95
30.	West Bengal	58,599	10,901	69,500	17	50	67
	Total	**670,946**	**216,481**	**887,427**	**483**	**396**	**879**

The table header title: State-wise FPO registered in the country as on date (07.05.2015)

Note: The data includes producer companies and cooperatives.

Skilling India: An Aspirational Challenge

Chapter 6

Introduction

The years 2014 and 2015 saw several policy announcements by the Government on skill development to achieve its vision of a 'Skill India'. Recognising the need and urgency of quickly coordinating the efforts of all concerned stakeholders, the Department of Skill Development and Entrepreneurship which was created in July, 2014 was upgraded into a full-fledged Ministry of Skill Development and Entrepreneurship in November 2014. Major departments that provide skill development are transferred to the Ministry. The National Policy on Skill Development has been revised and the new policy addresses the key challenges in the skilling landscape, including low aspirational value, non-integration with formal education, lack of focus on outcomes and quality of training infrastructure and trainers. Pradhan Mantri Kaushal Vikas Yojana (PMKVY) a flagship scheme was launched in 2015. Since vocational training is a state subject, a subgroup of Chief Ministers on Skill Development have been constituted by National Institute for Transforming India (NITI) Aayog to suggest measures for strengthening State Skill Development Missions to enhance capacity and improve standards of skilling at the state level. Central government is even considering a proposal to make skill training a fundamental right guaranteed by the constitution to boost employability of the work force.[1] The attention and urgency being shown to skilling is due to the following factors.

Demographic dividend—A cliché but...

India's population projections show that the average age of India's population is expected to be around 29 years in 2020 as against 37 years in China and the United States of America, 45 years in West Europe and 48 years in Japan. As the developed countries have a larger proportion of ageing population,[2] the global economy is expected to witness a shortage of young population of around 56 million by 2020. India would by then have a surplus of 47 million youth. The increase in GDP growth in India has been partly driven by an increase in the share of working-age population. This demographic dividend is derived from a rise in the ratio of working age (usually 15–59) to that of dependent or non-working population (usually under 15 and over 60 year old).

---

[1] Sanjib Kumar Baruah, 2015, Skill Training can be Next Fundamental Right; Rudy, *Hindustan Times*, 20 July 2015. Available at http://www.hindustantimes.com/india-news/skill-training-could-be-the-next-fundamental-right/article1-1371060.aspx

[2] When the share of population above 60 years goes over 10% of the total population, the UN defines that society as aging.

China's demographic dividend will be over by 2015; India's is expected to continue till about 2040. During this phase most of the population contributes to the country's GDP and thus the lower dependency ratio[3] can result in high economic growth. India has to provide quality education and develop the skills of its large young population to fully reap the benefits of the demographic dividend.

The challenges for India get enlarged, as it needs to provide skills to the millions of workforce ready population, while facing an ever increasing migration of labour from agriculture to manufacturing and services. The country, however, has a big challenge ahead as it is estimated that only 2.3 per cent[4] of the total workforce in India has undergone formal skill training as compared to 68 per cent in UK, 75 per cent in Germany, 52 per cent in USA, 80 per cent in Japan and 96 per cent in South Korea.

The poor skill levels among India's workforce are attributed to dearth of a formal vocational education framework with wide variation in quality, high school dropout rates, inadequate skills training capacity and negative perception towards skilling and lack of 'industry-ready' skills, even in professional courses (Ernst & Young LLP and FICCI, 2013).[5]

Countries with higher and better levels of skills adjust more effectively to the challenges and opportunities of world of work. Potentially, the target group for skill development comprises all those in the labour force, including those entering the labour market for the first time (12.8 million annually), those employed in the organised sector (26.0 million) and those working in the unorganised sector (433 million). The current capacity of the skill development programmes for jobs is 3.1 million[6] per annum as against 12.8 million joining the workforce.

Figure 6.1:   Twenty-four high growth sector and state level district-wise studies in 2013

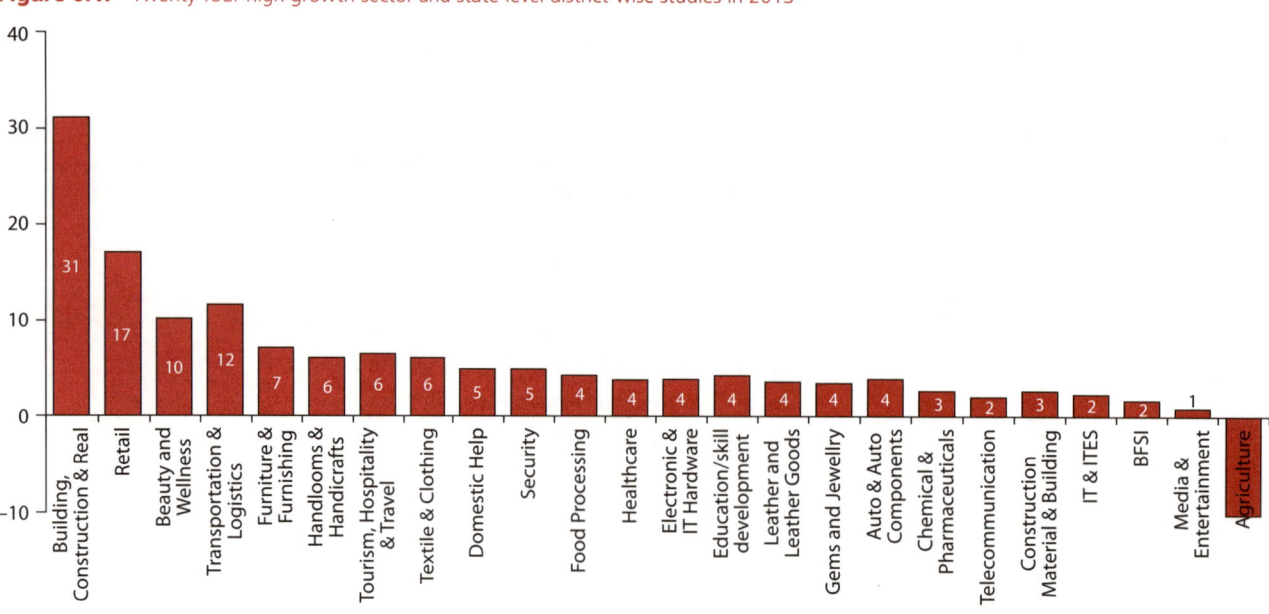

Source: NSDC (2015).[7]

[3] Refers to the number of children or elderly dependent on each earning person.

[4] GoI, 2015, Draft National Policy for Skill Development. Available at https://mygov.in/sites/default/files/master_image/Draft_National_Policy_for_Skill_Development_and_Entrepreneurship_2015.pdf

[5] Ernst & Young LLP and FICCI, 2013, Reaping India's Promised Demographic Dividend—Industry in Driving Seat.

[6] GoI, 2015, Annual Report 2014–15, Ministry of Labour and Employment, GoI.

[7] NSDC, 2015, National Workshop with States, Vigyan Bhawan, New Delhi, 9 May 2015, Skilling with Scale at Speed, a presentation.

As per the sector-wise studies done by NSDC, employment opportunities in India would increase from 461.1 million in 2013 to 581.9 million in 2022, across the 24 growth sectors, pointing at an incremental human resource requirement of approximately 120 million (Figure 6.1). Considering the overlap in the human resource requirement across a number of sectors, the unique number for incremental demand is estimated to be 109.7 million by 2022.[8] Whether it be skilled workers for an increasingly automated manufacturing sector or entry-level white collar jobs for the services sector, substantial gaps in human resources hold back the transformation of India from an agrarian and informal services-based economy to one focused on manufacturing and value-added services.

Figure 6.2: State-wise skill gap

Source: NSDC (2015).[9]

Disclaimer: This map does not claim to represent the authentic domestic or international boundaries of India. This map is not to scale and is provided for illustrative purposes only.

---

[8] Unstarred question 1339 answered on 7 May 2015 in Rajya Sabha.

[9] NSDC, 2015, National Workshop with States, Vigyan Bhawan.

Figure 6.3: Academic, technical and vocational parallel training structure/system in India: A flow chart

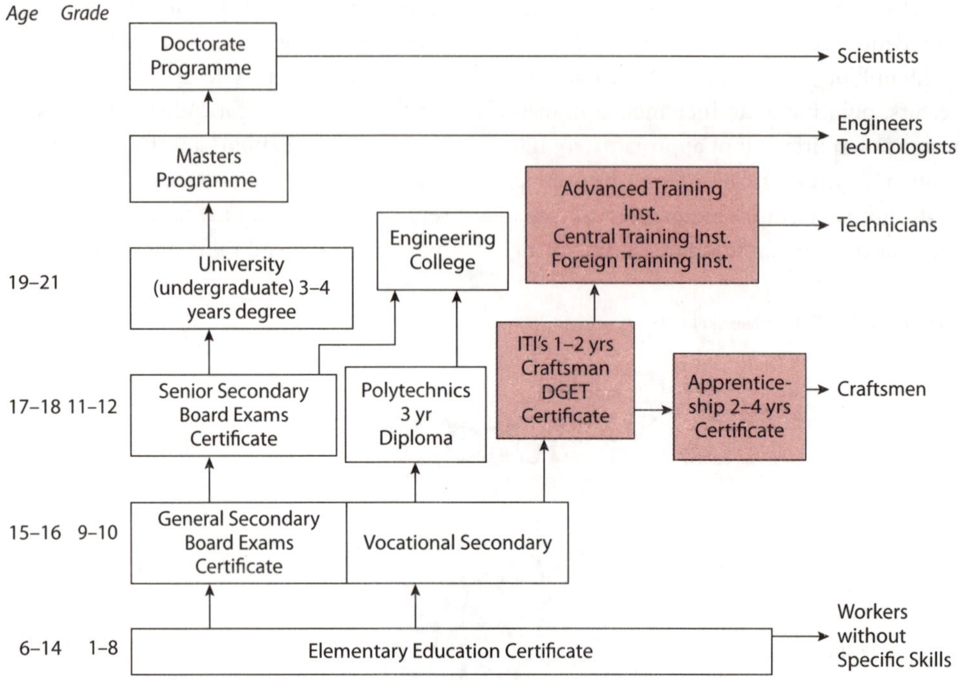

Age Grade

```
                    Doctorate
                    Programme ──────────────────────────────→ Scientists

                    Masters
                    Programme ──────────────────────────────→ Engineers
                                                               Technologists

                                    Engineering        Advanced Training
                                    College             Inst.               → Technicians
          University                                   Central Training Inst.
19–21     (undergraduate) 3–4                           Foreign Training Inst.
          years degree

                                                    ITI's 1–2 yrs
                                                    Craftsman        Apprentice-
          Senior Secondary    Polytechnics          DGET            ship 2–4 yrs    → Craftsmen
17–18 11–12  Board Exams       3 yr                 Certificate      Certificate
          Certificate          Diploma

          General Secondary
15–16 9–10   Board Exams        Vocational Secondary
          Certificate

                                                                      Workers
6–14  1–8          Elementary Education Certificate    ──────────→    without
                                                                      Specific Skills
```

Source: Indranil Biswas (2008).

More importantly, if the skill challenge is not met within the next decade, there is a risk that India may be unable to sustain growth in non-agricultural output and non-availability of skilled manpower may result in machines replacing labour on a large scale. This in turn will result in declining employment leaving large numbers among the increasingly youthful labour force unemployed.[10]

Present education and employment scenario

Given the scale of the challenge posed by the rapid economic growth and the rising share of working age population, the first dimension of the skill challenge is that the general education level of India's labour

---

[10] Santosh Mehrotra, Ankita Gandhi, Bimal K. Sahoo, 2013, Estimating the Skill Gap on a Realistic Basis for 2022, IAMR Occasional Paper No. 1/2013, Institute of Applied Manpower Research, Planning Commission, Government of India, February 2013.

Figure 6.4: Education level of workforce (per 1000)

Legend:
- Not literate
- Primary
- Middle
- Secondary
- Higher secondary
- Diploma/Certificate
- Graduate
- Post graduate+

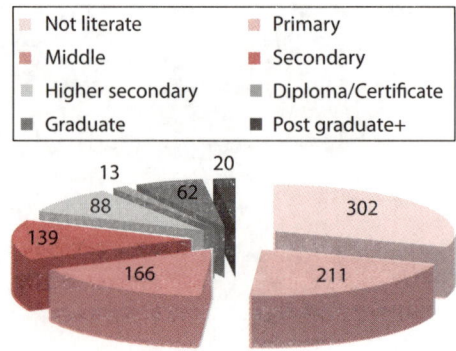

Source: Employment and Unemployment Situation among Social Groups in India, NSS 68th Round (July 2011–June 2012).
Note: The figure refers to population 15 years and above.

force in the age group 15–59 remains extremely low (Figure 6.4).

Of the labour force of 431 million between the ages 15–59 in 2009–10 nearly 126 million or 29 per cent of the labour force, are not even literate. An additional 102 million, or nearly 24 per cent, of the labour force either has below primary or only primary level of education, that is, over half of the labour force between 15–59 years of age has extremely low levels of education or none at all.[11] Low levels of education in the labour force, especially among those engaged in agriculture, makes it more difficult for the latter to move into activities in urban areas, except as labourers in the construction industry. The low level of general education also makes it more difficult to provide vocational training to youth who have not even completed elementary education (that is, until class 8).

The second challenge is to ensure that all children between the ages of 6 and 14 are completing elementary education by the end of the Twelfth Plan, as required by the Right to Education Act, 2009. It is difficult to prepare a teenager for a vocation if he/she has not completed at least eight years of schooling. School dropout rates now are high and if they continue to be so, it would be difficult to skill such youth into competent tradesmen or craftsmen.

The National Sample Surveys find that the labour force participation rate and work force participation rates are declining. The decline is on account of falling participation rates of women in labour and work force since 2004–05 (Table 6.1). The falling participation of women when the economy is growing and greater opportunities for mainstreaming women empowerment programmes are provided in the country is a matter of concern. Rural women participation in labour force has declined sharply, despite the opportunities created by MNREGS and NRLM. A study by the ILO[12] concluded that

> policy-makers should be more concerned about whether women are able to access better jobs or start a business, and take advantage of new labour market opportunities as a country grows (and hence contribute to the development process itself). For this reason, policy

interventions should tackle a range of issues, including improving access to and relevance of education and training programmes, promoting childcare and other institutional/legal measures to ease the burden of domestic duties, enhancing safety for women and encouraging private sector development in industries and regions that would increase job opportunities for women in developing countries.

According to the usual status (UPSS), at the all-India level, number of persons in the labour force as on 1 January 2010 was about 468.8 million which increased to 483.7 million as on 1 January 2012. This indicates an increase of 14.9 million of labour force at the all-India level between 1 January 2010 and 1 January 2012.

Categories of employment: Majority of the work force is self-employed followed by casual labour (Table 6.2). While regular

Table 6.1: Employment indicators by UPSS[13] basis (in percentage)

Years	Labour force participation rate			Work force participation rate		
	2004–05	2009–10	2011–12	2004–05	2009–10	2011–12
Rural	44.6	41.4	41	41.7	40.8	40
Male	56	56	55	55	56	54
Female	33	27	25	33	33	25
Urban	38.2	36.2	37	36.5	35	36
Male	33	56	56	55	33	55
Female	18	15	16	17	18	15
Total	43	40	40	42	39.2	39

Source: NSS 61st, 66th and 68th rounds on key indicators of employment and unemployment in India.

Table 6.2: Employment by different categories

Category of worker	2004–05	2009–10	2011–12
Self-employed	56.40%	50.70%	52%
Regular and salaried	15.20%	16.40%	18%
Casual labour	28.30%	33%	30%

Source: NSS 61st, 66th and 68th rounds on key indicators of employment and unemployment in India.

[11] Mehrotra, Gandhi, Sahoo, 2013, Estimating the Skill Gap.

[12] Female labour force participation in India and beyond, Ruchika Chaudhary and Sher Verick, ILO Asia Pacific Working paper, 2014.

[13] Usual Principal Subsidiary Status (UPSS) is the usual status of an individual determined on the basis of his usual principal status and usual subsidiary status taken together.

and salaried employment is increasing and has registered 3 per cent increase over 7 years but still it is low at 18 per cent in 2011–12.

During 2011–12, for both males (51 per cent of workers) and females (56 per cent of workers), majority of the workers were engaged in self-employment. The share of casual labour employment in the total workforce of both males and females was significant—29 per cent among male workers and 31 per cent among female workers. In the rural areas, the share of casual labour in the total workforce of males and females was almost the same (36 per cent for males and 35 per cent for females); self-employment was higher for females (55 per cent for males and 59 per cent for females) and regular wage/salaried employment was higher for males (10 per cent for males and 6 per cent for females).

Sectoral engagement: Among the workers, about 49 per cent, 24 per cent and 27 per cent were engaged in agricultural sector, secondary sector and tertiary sector respectively. Among the female workers, about 63 per cent were engaged in agricultural sector while about 56 per cent of the male workers were engaged either in secondary sector and tertiary sector. In rural areas, nearly 59 per cent of the male workers and nearly 75 per cent of the female workers were engaged in the agricultural sector. A more recent report, 'Education, Skill Development and Labour Force' is based on the Fourth Annual Employment–Unemployment Survey[14] 2013–14 conducted by Labour Bureau.[15] The survey results have been derived separately for persons receiving/received formal[16] and informal vocational training.[17] Population aged 15 years and

above who received/are receiving vocational training is estimated at 6.8 per cent at All India level. In rural and urban areas, it is 6.2 and 8.2 per cent respectively.

Out of the 6.8 per cent vocationally trained persons, 2.8 per cent received formal training and remaining 4 per cent were informally trained. About 76 per cent of the persons aged 15 years and above have reported to be employed at All India level who have received/receiving vocational training during the reference period. A significant proportion of females, about 39 per cent, have not joined the labour force after receiving vocational training in different fields. Among vocationally trained employed persons, 45.2 per cent are in self-employed category followed by 30 per cent under wage/salaried employee.

Among formally trained employed persons, about 60 per cent are reported in wage/salaried category followed by 26 per cent under the self-employed category. In case of informally trained employed persons, a majority of about 55 per cent are self-employed followed by 24 per cent under casual category and 15 per cent as wage/salaried earners. The survey results reveal that with increase in education level, the unemployment rate, among persons aged 15 years and above, has also increased. In case of 'graduates' and 'post graduates' the unemployment rate is about 14 per cent and 12 per cent respectively. Whereas, in case of 'not literate' and 'below primary' persons, the unemployment rate is less than 2 per cent each.

Higher levels of education do not improve employment prospects as seen in Figure 6.5. Inexplicably, unemployment levels are highest amongst those with a diploma or a certificate level education which includes a variety of technical trades and vocations (ITIs too award diplomas and certificates). With higher education, expectations of better jobs increase and a mismatch between available opportunities and aspirations develops. The link between education and employability needs strengthening. People pursuing higher education also need to be

---

[14] The survey has been conducted in all the States/UTs by covering all the districts covering 1,36,395 households and the field work executed from January 2014 to July 2014.

[15] GoI, 2014, Education, Skill Development and Labour Force, Vol. 3, 2013–14, GoI, Ministry of Labour & Employment, Labour Bureau, Chandigarh.

[16] Formal vocational training is a training which is acquired through institutions under structural training programme and led to recognised certificate or diploma.

[17] Informal training is defined as the process of acquiring the expertise in a vocation through ancestors over generations.

Figure 6.5: Educational attainment and unemployment levels

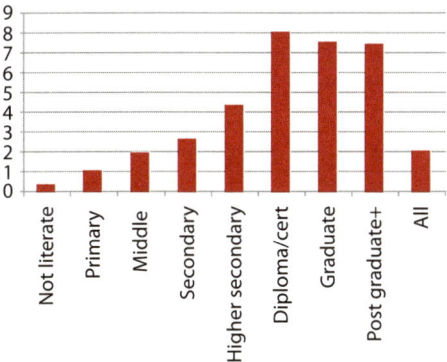

Source: Based on data from Employment and Unemployment Situation Among Social Groups in India, NSS 68th Round (July 2011–June 2012).
Note: The table refers to population 15 years and above.

counselled to develop realistic expectations of employment opportunities.

Labour productivity: Comparison of labour productivity growth[18] across Asian Productivity Organisation (APO) member countries during the year 2000–2012 shows that labour productivity growth has been the highest in China (9.1 per cent) followed by Mangolia (5.3 per cent), India (5.1 per cent), Lao PDR (4.6 per cent), Vietnam (4.4 per cent), Cambodia (4.4 per cent), Sri Lanka (4.2 per cent) and Indonesia (3.5 per cent). India ranked 2nd among the 20 APO member countries for which the study has been made. The comparison of labour productivity measures in terms of GDP (Purchasing Power Parity) per person employed per hour and Overall Productivity–Real Growth, that is, percentage change of Real GDP per person employed in Asian Countries and four benchmark countries during 2013 reveals that productivity level per person employed per hour in India during 2013 in comparison with other selected nine Asian countries is the lowest at 4.78 US$. The labour productivity in selected nine Asian Countries has been reported to be the highest for Singapore (47.25 US$) followed by Hong Kong (43.77 US$) and Japan (36.33 US$).[19] While growth

in labour productivity has been impressive, in terms of absolute level of productivity India lags behind and has to meet this challenge to remain competitive.

Thus, Government faces several challenges in skilling—improving quality of basic education and stemming dropout rate from schools, improving skills of casual labour, majority of whom are illiterate and can benefit little from classroom based trainings, increasing labour productivity, designing proactive strategies to ensure that women are not left behind in work participation and last, designing skilling programmes to meet the aspiration of the youth but not the least ensuring career progression of already employed with appropriate skilling so that overall productivity increases and Indian industries can compete globally.

Initiatives for skill building[20]

The Government has recognised the need for Skill Development with the 11th Five Year Plan providing a framework to address the challenge. The first National Skill Development Policy was framed in 2009 and subsequently a National Skill Development Mission was launched in 2010. Over the last seven years, from Eleventh Plan period, India has made some progress towards developing the institutional efforts to drive skills training at scale. The establishment of the NSDC in 2009 to promote private sector participation via short duration courses was a significant initiative. The NSDC has tied up with more than 207 training providers, of which many have started scaling up their operations. NSDC also supported and incubated 33 Sector Skills Councils (SSCs) that are intended to facilitate the much needed participation and ownership of the industry to deliver needs-based training courses.

The National Skills Development Agency (NSDA) is working with the State governments to rejuvenate and synergise skilling efforts in the State. The National

---

[18] GoI, Annual Report of Ministry of Labour and Employment, 2014–15.
[19] GoI, Annual Report, 2014–15.

[20] The state of the sector reports on livelihoods for the years 2011 and 2013 had in-depth coverage of skill development. This chapter builds on them.

Skills Qualification Framework (NSQF) has been anchored at NSDA and efforts have been initiated to align all skilling and education outcomes with the competency based NSQF levels. These efforts builds on the 60 year old legacy of vocational training infrastructure which now number about 11,964 Industrial Training Institutes and 3,200 polytechnics.

Targets set for skilling by government

The Government of India (GoI) has set a target to impart the necessary skills to 500 million people by 2022, in line with its forecast of a significant requirement of skilled manpower over the next decade. However, some experts have raised concerns over the magnitude of the target. The Institute of Applied Manpower Research (IAMR) (a government think-tank) has computed

new skill gap figures to arrive at a 'realistic' overall target. According to IAMR's analysis, the total number of people who need to be trained by 2022 ranges between 249 and 290 million across differing skill requirement scenarios. The Twelfth Plan has embarked on a relatively modest target of skilling 80 million people until 2017. It aims to increase the percentage of workforce with formal skills to 25 per cent at the end of the plan.[21]

The major ministries and departments that impart skill development, their key schemes and their target for skilling till 2022 are given in Table 6.3.

Apart from the seven ministries/ institution mentioned in Table 6.3, there are 13 other ministries/departments that impart skill training.

Central Government Programmes: At central government level, presently 73 different skill development schemes are

Table 6.3: National vocational and skill development schemes planned by the major departments

Ministry/ Department/ Organisation	Key schemes/Programmes/Institutions with a provision for vocational education and training programme	Projections of trained individuals in 2022 (in million)
National Skill Development Corporation (NSDC)	By the end of March 2015, the NSDC Board has approved 203 skilling proposals and 37 Sector Skill Councils with total financial commitment of over ₹2500 crore. There are 207 NSDC approved training partners, 2,904 operational NSDC partner centres, including 676 mobile centres with coverage across 28 States and 5 UTs in 471 districts across India.[22]	150
Labour and Employment	**Craftsmen training scheme:** Aims to provide a supply of semi-skilled labour and reduce unemployment among the educated youth. (through 11,964 Industrial Training Institutes ITIs (2284 in Government and 9680 in Private Sector) having a seating capacity of 16.92 lakh.[23]	100
	Apprenticeship scheme: It aims to provide in-house training to employees working in the company.	
	Center of excellence scheme: The scheme discusses the facilitation of multiskilling courses in 21 industry sectors.	
	Modular employable skills scheme: Focuses on the delivery of short-term courses of the National Council for Vocational training. Most of the trainings are provided through 11,964 Industrial Training Institutes.	

(Continued)

---

[21] GoI, 2013, Twelfth Five Year Plan (2012–17), 'Faster, More Inclusive and Sustainable Growth', Volume I. Available at http://planningcommission.gov.in/plans/planrel/12thplan/pdf/12fyp_vol1.pdf

[22] GoTN, 2015, Skill India. Available at http://www.pibchennai.gov.in/one%20year%20achievement/03062015e14.html

[23] GoI, 2015, Annual Report, 2014–15.

(Continued)

Ministry/ Department/ Organisation	Key schemes/Programmes/Institutions with a provision for vocational education and training programme	Projections of trained individuals in 2022 (in million)
HRD Higher Education	**Vocationalisation of secondary education**: It has created infrastructure of 21,000 sections in 9,619 schools and a capacity of about 1 million students at the 12th level.	50
	Community polytechnic scheme: Acts a focal point to promote the transfer of science and technology to the rural sector.	
	Jan Shikshan Sansthan: It has 157 vocational training centres that are run by NGOs offering more than 250 courses.	
Agriculture	Providing training in agriculture extension, training in the use of agricultural implements and machinery, soil conservation. A number of ongoing schemes and programmes of the Ministry of Agriculture have an inbuilt component of capacity building and skill development training of farmers. At least 16 different missions/programmes have such components.[24] Most are aimed at self-employment and per person budget is also very low at ₹540 in 2012–13 but was only ₹97 in 2013–14.[25]	20
Textiles	Decentralised training programme with 24 weavers' service centres, 13 power loom centers and many other boards and councils. Apparel Export Promotion Council.	10
Department of Heavy Industry	Counselling, retraining and redeployment of rationalised workers of CPSEs.	10
Department of Information Technology	Conducts courses in the field of electronics, telecommunications, IT, process control and instrumentation.	10
Food Processing Industries	Training courses run by various research institutes such as: Central Food Technology Research Institute, Paddy Processing Research Centre, Council of Entrepreneurial Development Programme, Establishment of food processing and training centers.	5

Source: Presentation by Government of Tamil Nadu on National level policy on skill development, Global Investors meet, September 2015 http://tamilnadugim.com/wp-content/uploads/2015/04/Skill-Development.pdf

implemented by 20 different ministries/departments of Government of India as indicated in Table 6.4. These include wage employment as well as self-employment. A ministry-wise list of targets and achievement in skill development is provided in Annex 6.1.

The major ministries/agencies for skill development for 2014–15 as per targets set are: NSDC (3.3 million), Ministry of Agriculture (2.2 millions), Ministry of Labour and Employment (1.62 million),

Ministry of MSME and Ministry of Housing and Urban poverty alleviation, (0.65 million each), Ministry of Electronic and Info Technology (0.61 million) and Ministry of Rural Development (0.56 million). Overall, as of February 2015, approximately 5,872,800

Table 6.4: Persons trained by different ministries for last four years

Year	Number of persons (millions)		
	Target	Achievement	% of annual target
2011–12 (13 ministries)	4.65	4.57	98%
2012–13 (19 ministries)	7.25	5.19	72%
2013–14 (21 ministries)	7.34	7.64	104%
2014–15 (21 ministries)	10.51	7.61	72%*

Source: Answer to the Parliament Question on 25th November, 2014. Available at http://pib.nic.in/archieve/others/2014/dec/d2014122401.pdf
Answer to Parliamentary question No. 858 on 30 April 2015 in Rajya Sabha.

[24] Answer to starred question no. 72 in Lok Sabha. Available at http://164.100.47.132/Annexture_New/lsq15/15/as72.htm
[25] Rajya Sabha, Unstarred Question No. 1772 on skill development and training programme for farmers answered on 13 March 2015.

people were trained by Central Ministries/ Departments in the financial year 2014–15 which was 51 per cent of the target set.

The five major programmes in terms of outreach (apart from vocational training through ITIs) are: (a) Deen Dayal Upadhyaya Grameen Kaushalya Yojana (earlier Aajeevika Skills Development Programme), Ministry of Rural Development, (b) NSDC, (c) Skill Training for Employment Protection amongst Urban Poor (STEP-UP) under Swarna Jayanti Shahari Rozgar Yojana (SJSRY) which has been restructured into National Urban Livelihoods Mission (NULM) since September 2013, Ministry of Housing and Urban Poverty Alleviation, (d) Rural Self-Employment Training Statute (RSETI), Ministry of Rural Development, (e) Skills Development Initiative Scheme (SDIS) of Ministry of Labour. NSDC programme is fee-based while others are subsidy-based. Apart from Central Ministries, states allocate budgets for skilling. RSETIs (sponsored by banks) provide short and focused skill training for self-employment. Some of the industries take their own initiatives in skilling their employees. Despite this massive effort by different agencies in public and private sectors, it appears that the Twelfth Plan targets of skilling 80 million are unlikely to be achieved.

State Government initiatives: Most of the states have set up skill missions under suitable legal forms. Apart from implementing the central government schemes, state governments have taken measures to improve skills by setting up separate institutions, allocating budgets for specific schemes etc., for example, Government of Tamil Nadu has set up a Tamil Nadu Skill Development Corporation, a section 25 company and allocated ₹100 crores for last two years (2013–14 and 2014–15) for undertaking skill development training of 2 lakh candidates every year (TNSDC 2015).[26]

The corporation implements only state schemes and also acts as nodal agency guiding 21 major departments in skill training. Similarly Government of Gujarat has funded skill development out of state budget which has been equivalent or more than central government budgets for the state. While some of the budget allocation has been for gap filling measures, some budgets are earmarked for skill training. However, there is little segregated data on outreach under state programmes and budgets.

State governments have come up with innovative models that are being upscaled in the country. One such initiative is by Government of Gujarat to provide need-based skill training in rural areas. According to the summary report on skill development prepared by the Federation of Indian Chambers of Commerce and Industry (FICCI) and presented at the global skill summit in 2013: 'People in urban areas have a 93 per cent higher chance at vocational training than those in rural areas. Furthermore, a person with a high school degree has a 300 per cent higher chance at getting trained than an illiterate person.'[27] Recognising the low enrolment of women and rural youth in ITIs, Government of Gujarat decided to adopt a flexible approach to strengthen the skill development sector, making it more accessible for women and rural youth, keeping in mind their aspirations, needs and problems and thus established Kaushalya Vardhan kendras (Box 6.1).

Brief analysis of the major programmes and results

Vocational training

1. Ministry of Labour and Employment implements skill development to school leavers/school dropouts through a number of schemes and also institutes such as

---

[26] TNSDC, 2015, Presentation on TNSDC, made to National Skill Development Agency, New Delhi on

8th January 2015. Available at https://c27web2.saas. talismaonline.com/NSDA/Tamil%20Nadu.pdf
[27] FICCI, Reaping India's Promised Demographic Dividend—Industry in Driving Seat, 2013.

Box 6.1: *Kaushalya Vardhan Kendras of Gujarat*

The concept of Kaushalya Vardhan Kendras (KVK) in Gujarat was launched in 2010. The idea behind KVKs was to promote entrepreneurship and strengthen skill development especially among the youngsters in rural areas. The programme has reached 1.37 million people since inception through a network of 500 KVKs established in four phases.[28] About 63 per cent of the trainees were women and 63 per cent are from SC/ST/OBC backgrounds. KVKs are functional in villages having population of 5000 and more (2500 in case of tribal villages) and provide skill training for a cluster of villages within a radius of 15 km.

KVKs adopt a decentralised, cluster based approach for skill development that is responsive to local cultures, traditional skills and industry needs. Kaushalya Sabhas organised in all villages within the catchment area. In the Kaushalya Sabhas, KVK coordinators interacted with potential training seekers and interested groups to decide type of courses, time schedules and infrastructure requirements for the KVK. Once the courses were identified, outsourced manpower including faculties from registered manpower agency were deputed at the KVKs.

Courses were selected on the basis of employment and self-employment opportunities available in the locality and cluster of villages. Courses are designed on the basis of the participatory approach of Kaushalya Sabhas based on the WISH concept: W—Women Oriented Courses, I—Industry Oriented Courses, S—Soft Skill and Service Sector Related Courses, H—Hard Core Traditional Courses.[29]

The courses also promote home-based employment and entrepreneurship. 512 short term courses were designed, considering local need (40 to 576 hours of instruction each). The courses that were most popular and hence were introduced in most of the KVKs, included computer fundamentals, tally software, basic welding, electric wiring, beauty and make up, hair dressing, tailoring and garment stitching, domestic appliance repairing, mobile repairing, plumbing and motor driving. Apart from these, life skills in 1980 aspects are also imparted.

Some of the successful elements of KVK included:

- Utilization of existing institutions and infrastructure—available government buildings were identified and infrastructure upgraded. Doorstep delivery of training.
- Awareness campaigns were launched to advertise the programme through a host of meetings held at local schools and panchayats. Street plays and folk theater were staged along with staging signage and information boards.
- The KVK staff also establishes key linkages with industries, companies and job providers in the proximity of KVK and helps the trainees acquire jobs.
- Apart from funding from the state government, a nominal fee of ₹50 is charged from the candidates (no fees taken for SC/ST/Women/Specially abled and BPL candidates).
- There is no upper age limit for candidates.
- The hiring of faculty and trainers has been formalised and outsourced.
- The trainees receive a formal certificate from Gujarat Council of Vocational Training on course completion.

An annual budget of ₹20–25 lakhs for non recurring expenses and ₹16 lakhs for recurring expenses is allocated per KVK.[30] For purposes of centralised monitoring by Commissionerate of Employment and Training (CET), the National Information Centre (NIC) has developed an online portal. The coordinator at each KVK updates information regarding enrolments.

The scheme was conferred the Prime Minister's Award for Excellence in Public Administration for the year 2013.

Source: http://darpg.gov.in/darpgwebsite_cms/document/file/KVK_case.pdf

---

[28] Discussions with Dr Sandhya Bhullar, IAS, Director, Employment and Training and MD, Gujarat Skill Development Mission, Government of Gujarat.
[29] Skill Development in India–present status and recent developments, Swantini. Available at www.swantini.in.
[30] Kaushalya Vardhan Kendra, Pioneering a flexible approach of skill development in rural Gujarat, a case study, 2014. Available at http://darpg.gov.in/darpgwebsite_cms/document/file/KVK_case.pdf

Craftsmen Training Scheme (ITI/ITCs), Apprenticeship Training Scheme (23,800 establishments), Modular Employable Skills, Crafts Instructor Training Scheme (6 institutes), Advanced Vocational Training Scheme and Hi-tech Training Scheme (65 centres), Supervisory Training (2 institutes), Women Training Institutes (11 institutes), Central Staff Training and Research Institute Model Training Institutes and Model Industrial Training Institutes. For more than six decades the Ministry of Labour and Employment has been implementing some of the long term courses of two years available in the country. Training is imparted in 126 trades[31] of duration 1–2 years. National Trade Certificate—nationally and internationally recognized under the aegis of National Council for Vocational Training (NCVT)—is awarded to successful trainees.[32]

ITIs are the key institutions through which vocational training is imparted. Since Vocational Training is a concurrent subject, central government is entrusted with the responsibility of framing overall policies, norms and standards and examination for vocational training while day-to-day administration of Industrial Training Institutes rests with the State Governments/Union Territories Administrations. Upgradation of ITIs especially the tools and facilities, and skills of trainers and teachers is essential. Some of the ITIs are being upgraded to centers of excellence through central assistance. Central government provides interest free loan to for upgradation of ITIs through civil works, purchase of tools and equipments and recruitment of instructors. There is a provision of multi entry and multi exit facility with the course curriculum designed in consultation with the Industry. This is done under public–private–partnership in the form of Institute Management Committees with

---

Box 6.2: *Prime minister at the launch of Skill India Mission*

'If the 20th century saw India's foremost technical institutes—the IITs—make a name for themselves globally, the 21st century require that India's ITIs (Industrial Training Institutes) acquire global recognition for producing quality, skilled manpower.'

Source: PM's speech on 15 July 2015.

---

representatives from industries, government and academic organisations who play a major role in terms of providing practical training and the identification of emerging skill demands in the local industry.

While the intake capacity of ITIs in some states including Himachal Pradesh, Punjab, Haryana, and Uttarakhand is very large compared to the eligible population, it is very low in some states like Uttar Pradesh, West Bengal and Bihar.[33] The capacity in ITIs needs to be judiciously expanded, after conducting a study of the demand and supply in the catchment area. Some stakeholders also mention that courses taught in ITIs mainly impart basic skills in specific trades and most of their teaching staff is not well trained. They mainly run courses and training programmes for mechanics, electricians and plumbers. If India is serious about educating and providing skills to the country's youth—65 per cent of the country's population is under the age of 35—to compete in the global economy, a new paradigm in vocational education is needed.[34] Some of the state governments like Gujarat and Tamil Nadu have invested significantly in the improvement of ITIs.

---

[31] 73 Engineering, 48 Non-engineering, 05 exclusively for visually impaired.

[32] Available at http://www.dget.nic.in/content/institute/key-statistics.php

[33] Technopak, 2014, Skilling Indian Workforce, A Blueprint for Setting up National Institutes of Skill Development, a white paper. Available at http://phdcci.in/image/data/Upcoming%20Event%20 2014/Dec-2014/PHD-Chamber-Technopak-Skiling-Whitepaper2014.pdf

[34] Syed Iqbal Hasnain, 2015, Modi's National Skill Development Mission doomed to fail, *American Bazaar*, July 22 2015. Available at http://www.americanbazaaronline.com/2015/07/22/modis-national-skill-development-mission-doomed-to-fail/

Box 6.3: *Strengthening ITIs and educational qualification framework*[35]

The Government of Gujarat established the CET to facilitate vocational training and other skill development programmes, which are responsive to the industry needs. To strengthen the vocational training sector, the Government of Gujarat has embarked upon several initiatives including revamping existing ITIs, establishing new ITIs, setting up of Superior Technology Centers (STC), and introducing special training programmes in emerging sectors like IT.

There are 779 ITIs (282 Government, 113 grant-in-aid and 384 self-financed) in the state covering all 26 districts and 225 talukas. To make the ITIs more effective, the Government of Gujarat has embarked upon a major initiative to upgrade them with modern technology, high tech classrooms and state of art labs and workshops. The course structure and curriculum at the institutes has been modified to make it more relevant to industry needs.[36] The Government has also recognized a two year ITI course after 8th standard equivalent to a 10th standard certification. Similarly, a two year ITI course after 10th standard is recognised as equivalent to 12th standard certification. These systemic changes allow ITI graduates to enter the formal education stream, and will also significantly enhance the acceptability of vocational training programmes.

Source: Dr Sandhya Bhullar, IAS.

Comprehensive and reliable data on employment of ITI passed students and their monthly earnings is not readily available. Data collected under the World Bank funded project throws some light on the ground level situation. Government is implementing World Bank funded project for upgradation of 400 ITIs into Centers of Excellence and 33 state governments/UTs are participating under the project. The scheme is funded in the ratio of 75:25, that is, 75 per cent is the central share and 25 per cent is the state share. The project commenced in 2007 and came to a close by September 2015. The salient features of the project include providing infrastructural facilities, introduction of multi-skill courses catering to the need of a particular cluster of industry around an ITI to produce multi-skilled workforce of world standard.

The key results achieved are presented in Table 6.5.

The increase in wages after training at about 50 per cent is impressive. But even at the increased level, the real monthly earnings of skilled workers are very low as

Table 6.5: Results of the upgradation project of ITIs[37]

	Base line—Jan 2007	As of April 2015
% of passouts with a NVCT certificate	All—61% Male—61.5% Female—74.2%	All—78% Male—78% Female—71%
% of passouts finding employment within a year of passing out	All—32% Male—33.4% Female—18.7%	All—60% Male—64% Female—38%
% real monthly earnings measured one year after completing training (in INR)	All—2,421 Male—2,474 Female—1,961	All—3,553 Male—3,800 Female—3,200

compared to even minimum wages fixed by the government for unskilled labour.[38] Under such circumstances, the relevance and utility of vocational skills training has to be examined.

Skill training

2. Ministry of Housing & Urban Poverty Alleviation implements urban livelihood mission under which skill training is

---

[35] Discussions with Dr. Sandhya Bhullar, IAS, Director, Employment and Training and MD, Gujarat Skill Development Mission, Government of Gujarat,

[36] Kaushalya Vardhan Kendra (KVK), Pioneering a flexible approach of skill development in rural Gujarat, a case study, 2014. Available at http://darpg.gov.in/darpgwebsite_cms/document/file/KVK_case.pdf

[37] World Bank, 2015, Implementation Status Results, Vocational Training Improvement Project: P099047—Sequence 15. Available at http://documents.worldbank.org/curated/en/2015/05/24435905/india-india-vocational-training-improvement-project-p099047-implementation-status-results-report-sequence-15

[38] On the basis of increase in the Consumer Price Index, the central government has fixed the National Floor Level Minimum Wages from ₹115 to ₹137 per day w.e.f. 01 July 2013.

provided. During 2014–15, 49,809 candidates were trained, out of which 10,958 had been placed and 5,166 were aided to set up individual and group enterprises which translates to about 34 per cent placement ratio. In order to give boost to the skill training, a Memorandum of Understanding (MoU) has been signed by the Ministry with NSDC in September 2014, for facilitating training of approximately one lakh urban poor by engaging with training partners of NSDC and leveraging the existing training infrastructure created by them across the country.

3. Ministry of Rural Development implements two major programmes, Deen Dayal Upadhyaya Grameen Kaushalya Yojana (erstwhile SGSY and Aajeevika skills) and trainings through RSETIs.

i. Deen Dayal Upadhyaya Grameen Kaushalya Yojana

During the year 2014–15, Deen Dayal Upadhyaya Grameen Kaushalya Yojana—DDU-GKY was launched. The programme has its roots in SGSY which was restructured to NRLM. In July 2014 standard operating procedures were issued for Aajeevika skills. In September 2014, Aajeevika skills was renamed as DDU-GKY with some new features and operational improvement. The targets and achievements discussed are regarding these three programmes.

The placement linked training target for the ministry for the Twelfth Plan period is 10.5 lakh jobs (reduced from the earlier target of 33 lakhs). Achievement from 2012 till March 2015 has been just above 5 lakhs; Andhra Pradesh (20 per cent), Odisha (10 per cent), Madhya Pradesh (9 per cent), Tamil Nadu and Jammu Kashmir (8 per cent each) have the major shares. Candidates placed are reported to be 362,631[39] (72 per cent). During 2014–15,

against the annual target of training 2.10 lakh candidates, a total of 46,998 candidates were trained till December 2014 and a total of 23,001 (49 per cent) have been placed.[40]

The key changes under DDU-GKY[41] as compared to Aajeevika skills programme are as follows:

- Prioritisation of sectors/projects and project implementing agencies has been sharply focused by laying down criteria or prioritisation. Eligibility criteria for PIAs has been streamlined and definition of PIA categories has been expanded to include partners with experience in priority areas. A special feature is where an enterprise/company acting as Project Implementing Agency (PIA) can enroll with DDU-GKY as 'champion employer'—one that has the capacity to place 10,000 candidates in the first two years. Three PIAs have signed MOU with the Ministry.

- Foreign placement is being given a push under the programme. Since by 2020, developed countries are predicted to face a shortfall of over 57 million semi-skilled manpower while India is expected to have a surplus of 47 million, the emphasis is on training which meets global standards. Training partners who can train and support overseas placement and captive placements are given primacy. It is mandatory for every PIA to provide placement to at least 75 per cent of trained candidates.[42]

- The programme has specific targets to be achieved by SC, ST, women, and minorities thus ensuring sharp targeting. While these were continued from the earlier

---

[39] GoI, 2015, Presentation to Performance Review Committee, 9th July 2015, DDU-GKY, MoRD. Available at http://ddugky.gov.in/ddugky/DocumentsForDownload/PRC_9_July_2015.pdf

[40] GoI, 2015, Annual Report of Ministry of Rural Department, 2014–15. Available at http://rural.nic.in/netrural/rural/sites/downloads/annual-report/Annual_Report_2014_15_English.pdf

[41] GoI, 2015, Programme Guidelines DDU-GKY, Ministry of Rural Development, Government of India.

[42] Placement is defined as employment for a minimum of three months.

programme the expansion of target group has been made more inclusive (youth from MGNREGA household, household under auto inclusion parameters as per SECC, 2011, family member of SHG member under NRLM etc.).

- The programme is designed to be a major contributor to the Prime minister's 'Make in India' campaign with industry internships, where funding support is provided for 12 months with 75 per cent placement guarantee.

- The programme emphasizes monitoring through online MIS and also concurrent monitoring through reputed institutions such as NIRD, NABCONS etc. Post programme placement tracking and counselling for one year has been introduced.

The programme has a three tier implementation model with (a) DDU-GKY unit at MORD providing policy support, funding, facilitation and technical support; (b) state skill mission embedded in state rural livelihood mission is expected to provide co-funding and also ensure proper implementation; (c) PIAs implement the programme by providing skill training and placements. The strategy of the ministry has been to move from direct implementation by the central government to further build capacities of state governments for implementation of DDU-GKY and to help build coordination mechanisms at central level to improve the skilling delivery process. Nine states are categorised as Action Plan states where their plans are approved by the Ministry and the states implement the programme. The other states are Year Plan (YP) states where MORD supports implementation. The state governments are expected to undertake skill gap assessment, hold job melas, migrant support centres, develop and disseminate communication materials and also provide alumni support.

The action plans of the different states show that most of the trainings proposed are of three months duration.[43] For example, Maharashtra State Rural Livelihood Mission will conduct skill training for 58,335 youth during the next two years out of which 56,335 are to be trained for three months. Similarly Karnataka has proposed training 118,173 youth out of which 113,238 will undergo three month course. However, 1095 candidates are expected to be trained for 12 months. How far such short term courses improve the skill sets and enhance productivity of the trainees is a question that will be raised by the prospective employers.

Cost norms and wages expected: This has been worked out on the basis of a course of 576 hours duration in case of a three month training only. The cost norms have been worked on the basis of a six day week with a minimum duration of eight hours per day. Therefore the duration of the three month, six month, nine month and 12 month courses will be 576 hours, 1152 hours, 1728 hours and 2304 hours respectively. Minimum wages expected are also related to the duration training—₹6000, ₹8000, ₹12,000 and ₹15,000 for the different courses. Minimum wages for foreign placements is ₹25,000. While it is commendable that the minimum wages have been prescribed, there is little detail as to how this will be ensured. There are no disclosures in the annual report and other materials on the past track record of wages achieved during the Twelfth Plan.

Incentivising retention and career progression: Additional resources are being made available to the PIA for retention of employment of trained candidate at the rate of ₹3000 per person retained in employment for 365 days. A major challenge is to assist those already placed to progress in their careers. This has been addressed in the form of an additional payment to PIAs at the rate of ₹5,000 for every person trained by the PIA

---

[43] GoI, 2015, Minutes of the Empowered Committee held on 22nd June 2015, Ministry of Rural Development. http://ddugky.gov.in/ddugky/DocumentsForDownload/Minutes_EC_meeting_22nd_June.pdf

who crosses a salary of ₹15,000 per month and holds it for a minimum of 90 calendar days within one year of completion of training. It is envisaged that this will be possible only if the PIA invests in handholding and skill upgrading activities after placement.

Regional focus: Roshni is a special initiative under DDU-GKY for skill development of 50,000 youth in 27 most critical left wing extremism districts, in Jharkhand, Odisha, Chhattisgarh and Bihar. The programme launched in June 2013 is facing implementation difficulties as seen from minutes of the recent performance review by the MORD.[44] The progress appears to be tardy with alerts being issued to PIA to improve performance. Out of the 10 project implementing agencies, nine agencies have a shortfall of more than 70 per cent in the targets in trainings as agreed in the project work schedule. There is little information provided by these agencies on placements and also salaries.

Himayat, launched in 2012, is aimed to train 100,000 youth of Jammu and Kashmir. As of March 2015, 40,253 youth have been trained and 32,331 (80 per cent) are reported to be placed.

ii. Rural Self Employment Training Institutes

The GoI has facilitated setting up Rural Self Employment Training Institutes, one in each district of the country for basic and skill development training of the rural BPL youth to enable them to undertake micro enterprises and wage employment. These are bank led institutions, that is, managed and run by the public sector/private sector banks with active cooperation from the state governments.[45] There were 587 RSETIs by end March 2015, offering intensive short-term residential self-employment training programmes with free food and accommodation, designed specifically for rural youth. Most of the training courses are aimed at self-employment. RSETIs are graded at least every two years and the performance monitoring of RSETIs is also ensured by the monitoring cell of RSETIs under the Ministry of Rural Development. National Institute of Rural Development and Panchayati Raj Hyderabad is the nodal agency to implement the RSETI project.

As seen from Table 6.6, the number of RSETIs and number of trained persons has been increasing year after year. Settlement of candidates into enterprises has been satisfactory. However, less than half the settled candidates have been able to access bank finance (only 27 per cent of the trained persons had been able to get bank loan to start their enterprise). Why the bank loan access is low when the RSETIs are sponsored by leading banks is a question that banks have to ask themselves and find effective solutions. While the reported settlement

Table 6.6: Performance of RSETIs

	2011–12	2012–13	2013–14	Cumulative at end of 2014–15
No. of RSETI				587
Number trained	126,432	284,912	340,148	1,319,285
Number settled	28,801	194,181	229,314	807,019
% of settled candidates	23%	68%	67%	61%

Source: RSETI Quarterly Newsletter Jan–March 2015 quarter, National Institute of Rural Development and Panchayati Raj, Hyderabad.

---

[44] GoI, 2015, Minutes of the Meeting to Review Implementation of Projects under Roshni Project under DDU-GKY, held on 21 July, 2015. Available at http://ddugky.gov.in/ddugky/DocumentsForDownload/Minutes_of_Roshani_Meeting.pdf

[45] Ministry of Rural Development bears the one time expenditure, up to a maximum of ₹1 crore per institution, on infrastructure development and DRDAs provide support towards cost of training for rural BPL candidates to the sponsored banks. State governments provide land, free of cost, to these institutions on priority basis. Banks are responsible to manage day to day functioning of the institute.

and placement rate is reasonably high at 61 per cent, the impact study carried out by World Bank (discussed further in the section 'Impact evaluations of skill training') mentions several weaknesses of the RSETI programme, such as the absence of clear-cut guidelines for the selection of trainers leading to different methods and qualification criteria across states, a curriculum that has not been updated since 2010, and the limited acceptability of RSETI certificates for loan provision (despite the programme focusing on self-employment and implementation through the banking network). Those weaknesses, jointly with the lack of positive impact on employment found by the quantitative analysis, suggest the need for a thorough review and detailed evaluation of this particular programme.

iii. Rural development and self employment training institute (RUDSETIs)

There are 27 RUDSETIs in the country of which seven are in Karnataka. The RUDSETIs follow the pioneering model based in Ujire, Karnataka, set up jointly by SDME Trust (Shri Dharmasthala Manjunatheswara Educational Trust), Syndicate Bank and Canara Bank. RUDSETIs have traditionally reported a higher placement of trainees through self-employment and wage employment. In 2014–15 candidates placed formed 67 per cent of those trained (Table 6.7). About one-third of the settled candidates have been able to take a bank loan to set up their business.

4. National Skill Development Corporation

NSDC, is mandated to skill 150 million persons by 2022 and is an important institution in the skilling landscape. Formed under the Ministry of Finance, in 2010,

Table 6.7: RUDSETIs' performance in 2014–15

No of Institutes	27
Number trained	23,692
Number settled	16,534
Number with bank finance	5,510
Settlement %	67

Source: Yashogatha, A Newsletter of RUDSET Institute, Volume 13 Issue 1, April–June 2015.

presently NSDC works under the newly formed Ministry of Skill Development and Entrepreneurship. NSDC is a public–private partnership with 51 per cent equity held by private sector and the balance 49 per cent by the Union Government. NSDC works with a wide variety of partners ranging from private sector for profit training providers, universities,[46] state governments, and public sector companies.

NSDC is funded for its programmes through National Skill Development Fund (NSDF).[47] Till 31st March 2015, NSDF has released ₹23,330 million to NSDC towards skill development programmes including National Skill Certification and Monetary Reward Scheme—Standards Training Assessment and Reward (STAR) and UDAAN Scheme (J&K oriented).[48]

NSDC has three core activities—implementing skill training programmes through partner institutions, funding SSCs especially for skill certification and implementing specific government schemes such as STAR, now renamed and revamped as Pradhan Mantri Kaushal Vikas Yojana (PMKVY).

Funding for skill training

NSDC calls for proposals from training providers and adopts a multi-stage selection process with the help of professional organisations to identify proposals for funding. The two most important criteria for selection are sustainability of the business model and linkages with employers. The NSDC provides skill development funding

---

[46] NSDC has entered into collaboration with 27 universities in the country for cooperation in skill development. Unstarred question 424 of Rajya Sabha, answered on 23 July 2015.

[47] The National Skill Development Fund was set up in 2009 by the GoI for raising funds both from government and non-government sectors for skill development in the country. The Fund is contributed by various government sources, and other donors/contributors to enhance, stimulate and develop the skills of Indian youth by various sector specific programmes. A public trust set up by the government of India is the custodian of the Fund.

[48] Available at http://www.skilldevelopment.gov.in/nationalskilldevelopmentfund.html

either as soft loans or equity, and supports financial incentives to select private sector initiatives to improve financial viability through tax breaks etc.

NSDC has 232 training partners with 3127 training centers which have cumulatively trained 5.51 million people and placed 2.35 million.[49] Data on active partners and progress over different periods is difficult to come by in NSDC's website. However, not all partners are active as can be seen from the impact assessment report of Deloittee[50] which mentions that as on 31 December 2014 NSDC has approved more than 159 training partners, of which 90 are active.

Similarly, placement is also not very robust in some states. For example, till 31st March, 2015, NSDC trained 187,220 persons in Rajasthan out of which 9,273 persons got placement.[51] The Minister, Shri Rudy, has also mentioned that the monitoring and accountability aspects are being improved in NSDC.[52]

NSDC, has disbursed ₹7440 million over the five year period Q4 FY10–Q3 FY15 for skill development.[53] Of the total fund disbursed, about 86 per cent was disbursed to various training partners, 11 per cent to SSCs and the balance 3 per cent towards Innovation and special projects. The mode of fund disbursement by NSDC is primarily through soft loans (78 per cent), followed by Grant/Marketing Development Assistance (19 per cent) and equity (3 per cent).

Sector Skill Councils (SSCs) complement the existing vocational education system for the Industry Sector in meeting the requirements of appropriately trained manpower in quantity and quality. SSCs are funded from the NSDF through the NSDC.

The SSCs have the following functions:

(i) Conducting research: Building up skill inventory database for the industry sector, skill-wise, region-wise, reviewing international trends in skill development and identifying skill gaps and technology to be taken up for teaching.

(ii) Improving the delivery mechanism: Partnering with educational institutions to train trainers and upgrade skill sets of existing industry employees, and those in the industry value chain, e.g., dealer and service networks.

(iii) Building quality assurance: Setting up a robust and stringent certification and accreditation process for industry sector facing skill development institutes to ensure consistency and acceptability of standards.

SSCs operate as autonomous bodies with their own governance and eventually the SSCs will be self-funded, for-profit organisations. One of the important function of the SSCs is developing the national occupational standards and qualification packs (NOS/QPs).

National Skill Certification and Quality Assurance (NSQF): NSDC has approved 33 Sector Skill Councils as of 31 March 2015 which play a vital role in bridging the gap between what the industry wants and what the skilling curriculum ought to be. The NSQF initiative seeks to transform the way skills training are done. If implemented well it will transform the way skills qualifications are received by the employers both in recruitment and pricing of skilled persons. It will also make the training institutes responsible and accountable for the quality and detail in skills training (Box 6.4).

---

[49] This data was displayed on the home page of NSDC web site on 29 August 2015 and the information period is not displayed.

[50] NSDC, 2015, Executive Summary of Impact Assessment Study, 2014–15. Available at http://www.nsdcindia.org/sites/default/files/files/pdf/Executive-Summary-Impact-Assessment-Study2014-15.pdf

[51] Unstarred Question No 2017 in Rajya Sabha Answered on 06 August 2015.

[52] *Outlook*, 2015, The NSDC had no Accountability, 10 August 2015. Available at http://www.outlookindia.com/article/the-nsdc-had-no-accountability/294976

[53] NSDC, 2015, Executive Summary. Available at http://www.nsdcindia.org/sites/default/files/files/pdf/Executive-Summary-Impact-Assessment-Study2014-15.pdf

Box 6.4: *Skill standards and certification*

The NSQF is a competency-based framework that organises all qualifications according to a series of levels of knowledge, skills and aptitude. The NSQF is anchored in the NSDA and is being implemented through the National Skills Qualification Committee (NSQC). These levels, graded from one to ten, are defined in terms of learning outcomes which the learner must possess regardless of whether they are obtained through formal, non-formal or informal learning. NSQF in India was notified on 27th December 2013. All other frameworks, including the National Vocational Educational Qualification Framework (NVEQF) released by the Ministry of HRD, stand superceded by the NSQF.

The NOS specify the standard of performance an individual must achieve when carrying out a function in the workplace, together with the knowledge and understanding they need to meet a standard consistently. Each NOS defines one key function in a job role. Each NOS must be a concise and readable document, usually consisting of no more than five or six pages (some are only one or two). In their essential form, NOS describe functions, standards of performance and knowledge.

The NOS are laid down by employers (through their SSCs). A set of NOS, aligned to a job role, called Qualification Pack (QP), is to be available for every job role in each industry sector. These drive both the creation of curriculum, and assessments. Thus NSQF will theoretically make it possible to drive competency based training for every job role in industry. It would be possible for all current vocational courses, like MES, ITI Courses, or similar vocational courses in schools, colleges and polytechnics to be aligned to job roles at specific NSQF Levels. An ITI course in plumbing will need to declare they are training for plumbers at NSQF Level 3. Similarly a polytechnic, training in fashion design, may say it is training for NSQF Level 5 for Garment Cutters.

Key benefits expected out of such initiative are:

a. Mobility between vocational and general education by alignment of degrees with NSQF,
b. Recognition of Prior Learning, allowing transition from non-formal to organised job,
c. Standardised, consistent, nationally acceptable outcomes of training across the country,
d. Global mobility of skilled workforce from India, through international equivalence of NSQF,
e. Mapping of progression pathways within sectors and cross-sectorally,
f. Approval of NOS/QPs as national standards for skill training.

By December 2016, adoption of these norms will be mandatory for accessing government funding for skill training. The recruitment rules of the GoI and PSUs of the central government shall be amended to define eligibility criteria for all positions in terms of NSQF levels. By December 2018, it will be mandatory for all training courses to be NSQF compliant.

Source: NSDC.

As of 31 March 2015, across 28 Sectors, standards for 1319 job roles pegged at NSQF levels 1 to 8 have been defined by the Sector Skill Councils. Fourteen SSCs have covered development of 80 per cent of entry level workforce QPs. These and NOSs have been developed in association with industry (Figure 6.6). The adoption of these norms is slowly being incorporated into training eligibility criteria by the training establishments. The challenge is in disseminating the standards to the training institutions and making them understand the differentiated levels in each skill set. Trainer training and competence building is a necessary corollary to the implementation of the NSQF standards. More than trainees, the teachers will require considerable competence building to make the NSQF work.

Standards Training Assessment and Reward (STAR): The government started a scheme titled STAR during 2013–14 to motivate a large number of youth to voluntarily join skill development programmes. The NSDC implemented the scheme wherein on successful completion of training and obtaining a certificate, every candidate was provided with a monetary reward of an average of ₹10,000/-.

Figure 6.6:   Integration of NSQF with academics and industry[54]

Creating Career Pathways
Academia/Industry integration through NSQF

Education	Academic Level	Skill	NSQF Level Interpretation
Class 9	1	No Skill – Educated/Uneducated	1
Class 10	2	Skill with some experience	2
Class 11	3	Semi Skilled	3
Class 12	4	Skilled	4
1st Year of Graduation	5	Supervisor of Skilled Worker	5
2nd Year of Graduation	6	Supervisor's Supervisor	6
3rd Year of Graduation	7	Manager of Supervisor	7
1st Year of PG	8	Junior Management	8
2nd Year of PG	9	Middle Level Management	9
PhD	10	Senior Level Management	10

QP/NOS created by SSCs are NSQF compliant and ready for adoption by Central Ministries, State Governments, Regulatory Institutions, Training Providers organisations etc.

Source: NSDC. 2015.

Small sample independent evaluation of STAR: An independent evaluation of STAR was conducted in 2014[55] and the key findings of the study are:

a. Retail SSC alone accounted for 36.9 per cent of total candidates enrolled under STAR. Retail and IT-ITES sectors in aggregate accounted for 60.2 per cent of total candidates. Remaining 39.6 per cent of candidates are distributed unevenly across 14 other SSCs.

b. The highly populous and economically lagging states are not able to benefit as much as the more prosperous ones. AP, Haryana, HP, MP, NCT, Rajasthan, Punjab & TN having higher coverage; Assam, Bihar, Chhattisgarh, J&K, Jharkhand, NE States, Odisha, Maharashtra, UP, Uttarakhand & West Bengal are not availing due share of benefits.

c. While the Scheme was designed to provide training for L1 to L4 level job roles, 51.6 per cent of candidate respondents were studying for a graduate degree, or were graduates or post graduates. If the intent of the Scheme was to benefit school-leavers and school dropouts, that does not seem to be happening. Also noteworthy is that in 43 per cent of the cases, actual educational qualification reported by candidates during evaluation is higher than recorded in the skill development management system (SDMS).

d. Calls were made to 546 candidates, out of which only 219 were responded to.

   • According to responses received, 20 per cent of candidates got training for less than 30 days. Minimum duration of a course should be 30 days. SDMS does not show any course having a duration less than 30 days, but respondents reported otherwise.

   • The Scheme requires that at the time of the enrolment for the course, the trainee needs to pay

---

[54] NSDC, 2015, National Workshop with States, Vigyan Bhawan, New Delhi, 9 May 2015, Skilling with Scale at Speed, a presentation.

[55] NSDA, 2014, an independent evaluation done in April and May 2014 of the Performance of STAR, by Saurabh Kumar Singh and Kumar Devashish Chandragupta Institute of Management, Patna. Available at https://c27web2.saas.talismaonline.com/NSDA/Independent%20Evaluation%20of%20STAR%20-%20Report%20by%20NSDA%2013th%20June%202014.pdf

some part of the course fee, presumably to ensure her/his sustained interest in the completion of the course. 54 per cent of the students have not paid any amount for their course. Even among those who paid some money, none was aware of what they were paying for.

- Of the 72 per cent respondent candidates who have appeared for assessment, only 24 per cent candidates received their result. Against the Scheme requirement of results being uploaded within two working days of completion of the assessment, 67 per cent of candidates were waiting for 20 days or more to receive their results.
- A very large number of candidates do not even know what the STAR scheme is. NSDC mentions that they did not receive the funds for promotion of the scheme to create awareness.
- The SDMS records the name of the Training Partner which is the entity approved by the concerned Sector Skill Council and is supposed to have trained the given individuals. The response received from candidates showed that 66 per cent of them were being trained by an entity that was not the training partner recorded in the SDMS.
- 84.6 per cent candidates who report having bank accounts are not recorded on SDMS.

e. NSDC provided a list of 18,537 candidates who are supposed to have received the reward money. Sample from this list showed that:

- 16 per cent of the candidates have not even received their results.
- Of those who had got their results, only 54 per cent have received certificate and 59.5 per cent have received reward money. But of the actual sample only half of the candidates received reward money.

- Of those who received reward money, 59.1 per cent of the candidates reported receiving amount less than ₹5,000/- whereas minimum reward is ₹7,500 as per the Scheme.

f. Some of the responses received from candidates point to anomalies in the Scheme:

- There are persons who are either working or are already undergoing some training of their own accord. Their names are being added as STAR beneficiaries and a small amount paid to them if they pass the tests.
- Candidates are being asked to sign debit notes as part of the account opening formalities—and the reward money coming to their accounts is being taken away by the training providers.

g. Large-scale franchising is in evidence. All training providers denied any sub-franchising is taking place, though complaints received suggest otherwise. Training providers are supposed to be accredited with the SSCs and NSDC after a due process. However, permitting accredited training partners (TPs) to appoint franchisees raises issues about the validity of accreditation as also the skill level of those trained.

Pradhan Mantri Kaushal Vikas Yojana (PMKVY): Government has streamlined, revamped the STAR scheme and launched it as the Pradhan Mantri Kaushal Vikas Yojana (PMKVY). The programme will reimburse anybody who develops a certain skill certified by a relevant 'assessment agency' (one of three key pillars of the programme). If an individual already has a skill and only gets assessed and certified, they are reimbursed less—around ₹2,000. If an individual undergoes training, too, they are reimbursed more, an average of ₹8,000 (actual payments are on a graded scale depending on the sector and type of the specific skill). The training needs to be done at an approved training partner (the second key pillar), and the pedagogy along with skills trained are decided by the Sector Skill Councils (the third key pillar), thus ensuring that because of industry–government coordination, training for only in-demand skills get subsidised. Private sector companies offering skill development courses will be offered a level playing ground with government bodies, and the same standards will be applied to those wanting to partner with the state to deliver training (hence, there will be no crowding out of the private sector from this public–private partnership social scheme).[56]

However, NSDC will have to come to speed in implementing PMKVY by improving the partner selection and monitoring systems to ensure that the difficulties faced in implementation of STAR and lessons learnt are effectively used to implement PMKVY.

Industry engagement and perspective

While placement of candidates after training has been an issue, the industries have also been reporting shortage of man power. The Quarterly Report on Changes in Employment in Selected Sectors (October 2014 to December 2014) by Ministry of Labour and Employment notes that, 'during discussions with the managements, of sample units, it is revealed that most of them are facing shortage of labour in their respective units. A mismatch between requirement and availability of skills is also felt by employers. According to them multi-skilled workers are needed to compete in the globalised economic environment'.[57] Since India has more number of MSME units and they tend

to have a small number of employees, they need persons with multiple skills. Steps need to be taken to identify the group of skills that each group of MSME unit needs and design programmes to meet these multi-skilling requirements rather than single skill training being imparted now.

During the round table across sectors conducted by PHD Chamber in December 2014, the key competencies that industries require in their employees were identified as:

- Ability to collaborate with others
- Good knowledge and understanding of an area
- Ability to work as a team member
- Good communication skills
- Ability to solve problems
- Practical exposure to the industry and develop understanding of work life
- Positive attitude and willingness to learn
- Ability to deploy technology meaningfully
- Language competencies
- Good organisation skills
- Adaptability
- Attention to detail
- Ethical orientation and respect for standards

Thus, the requirements of soft skills are highlighted by the industrial employers. Many skill development courses have started including soft skills development.

Government and NSDC recognise that industries need to be essential partners in skill development. Industry and corporate sector linkage is being established through Sector Skill Councils which needs to be strengthened further. The SSCs are to act as the effective bridge between industries on the one hand and the government/academia on the other so that the needs of industries are accurately reflected in the skill development programmes of the government, and the curriculum of academic institutions.

Industries need to take a more proactive role so that more apprenticeship opportunities are created and the industries starts funding part of the training cost

---

[56] Rajiv Mantri and Harsh Gupta, 2015, IITs to ITIs—Modi's Voucher Revolution in Skill Development? *Live Mint*, 13 August 2015. Available at http://www.livemint.com/Opinion/9n9WeI5C5ISJI4FJ6CNBHN/IITs-to-ITIsModis-voucher-revolution-in-skill-development.html

[57] GoI, 2015, Quarterly Report on Changes in Employment in Selected Sectors (Oct 2014 to Dec 2014), Ministry of Labour and Employment, Government of India. Available at http://labour.gov.in/content/reports/QES_24th_final.pdf

as an investment for its own developed manpower, adopting skill development as a significant component of their CSR efforts and providing differential wages to skilled workers and also incentivizing unskilled persons to acquire skills.

Perspectives of training providers

Six training providers were interviewed as part of the discussions for this chapter. While three are Pan-India skill providers and the other three are confined to individual states. All of them have been providing skill training for more than five years. They largely provide grant based training courses to students, mobilising funding from various skilling programmes of the government. About 10 per cent of the programmes are paid programmes. While 50 per cent to 70 per cent of the programmes are placement linked, the others are for upskilling. The large training providers offer training in as many as 16 sectors and 40 trades whereas the small ones offer in three trades in one sector. They are short term courses of two to three months. They endeavour to provide at least half the class hours as industrial on-the-job-training. In the last two years, the training providers are adhering to NSQF and training content are approved by SSCs. The councils insist on quality and standardisation for which industry acceptance is high. Placement rates have been increasing in the last two years.

The student age ranges between 18 to 35; though students dropout from school 8th standard onwards, parents don't allow students to go out for jobs till they are 18–20. Industry also does not want to employ very young labour and employ labour after the age of 18 to be clearly outside the ambit of law relating to child labour. Student selection is the biggest challenge being faced by the training institutions. In some states the acceptance of skill training among students and industries is high; Andhra Pradesh is an excellent state for skill training. In some

states students do not have employment opportunities and the candidates need to migrate. North-east students when they work in plains find climate and food habits difficult to adjust. In Assam there are lot of migrants from neighbouring countries and according to the training providers, they want free support from the government and do not want to work.

On account of the need to go to a distant place for training and the need to migrate after training for a job, enrolment of women candidates in well paying high-skills training courses has been low. Government is spending a lot of money for skilling but students do not want jobs where they need to do hard physical work. In some southern states casteism is high and so students from five to six districts are taken in one batch to manage the social dynamics.

Awareness building on what to expect from skill training, and also in jobs is key part of initial counseling. Training institutions also bring in employers to talk to prospective students. Managing with a salary of ₹6000 to ₹7000 in metros is difficult. They also identify industries where boarding, lodging and subsidised food are provided and cost deducted from salary. Salary is a key issue, not many industries follow minimum wages and insufficient salary is one of the key reasons for student dissatisfaction.

Training providers find that on an average within the first three months, 10 per cent leave the job. Within six months about 25 per cent of the students move to other companies. Lot of job hopping happens in the first year. Students expect higher salary of ₹15,000 where as they are offered ₹8,000. This is one of the major reasons for turnover. When one person decides to leave, the others from the batch/village also leave together. Though work place adjustments, people management and anger management are taught in the skilling course, industry feedback shows that students often lack these skills.

The training providers have invested in necessary infrastructure but also use infrastructure and machinery of ITI/Polytechnic.

Training providers find the funding from NSDC soft loan with usually two to three years moratorium at 6 per cent and equity a scalable and sustainable funding mechanism. With sponsored programmes, the institutes can turn around in four to five years. NSDC's role is appreciated by all the training providers. A key recommendation they have is that skill training should be imparted from schools with a bouquet of courses of interest to the students. Once a foundation is laid, acceptance and idea of having a skill can be built upon.

Impact evaluations of skill training

Two impact assessments of skill training have been carried out during 2014–15 by World Bank at the behest of NSDA and another by Deloitte and Tata institute of Social Sciences commissioned by NSDC. An analysis of findings is presented further.

World bank impact evaluation[58, 59]

World Bank carried out evaluation of five largest skill development programmes—Aajeevika Skills Development Programme (ASDP), Ministry of Rural Development, NSDC, STEP-UP, Ministry of Housing and Urban Poverty Alleviation, RSETI, Ministry of Rural Development, SDIS of Ministry of Labour during 2014.

The study was carried out in five states of Assam, AP, MP, Odisha and Rajasthan. The study analysed the outcomes, justification of public investment costs, administrative aspects that affect delivery and earnings premium of short duration courses. The five programmes target different population groups: two of them focus on rural youth, one on urban youth, and the remaining ones cover both. They all prepare the trainees for

wage or self-employment but emphasize one or the other.

The sample for the study included 2,620 present trainees, 1,979 past trainees, control group of 2,017 persons, 669 employers and 400 training providers. The key findings of the study are:

- Education level of trainees is fairly high except in RSETI; Less than 15 per cent have up to nine years of schooling and others are with secondary education and above. Disadvantaged and low income groups are well represented in all programmes.

- Eighty-nine per cent of employers in the sample (n = 669) recruit trainees from one scheme; remaining recruit from more than one scheme. Around 35–42 per cent of employers in the sample hire SDIS or NSDC trainees; Enterprises are private (> 90 per cent). Employers are mostly in the service sectors for most RSETI and ASDP trainees. For other schemes, 66–77 per cent are in the service sector and 22–31 per cent in manufacturing. Majority of employers have less than 10 employees.

- The placement rate of trainees (shortly after the end of the training period) is modest: 27 per cent overall, ranging from 23 per cent to 36 per cent across programmes, but with substantial state-wide variations. One or two years after training, the employment rate of trainees is not much different: 28 per cent. However, significant labour market churning has occurred over the period of one or two years after training: trainees initially placed have left their jobs, looking for other opportunities (or simply quit); others have entered the labour market later. This strongly suggests that, although initial placement facilitates insertion in the labour market, it does not ensure a good job match and sustainability of employment.

- Andhra Pradesh stands out, with at least 50 per cent placement rate across programmes (except in SDIS where no trainees have reported as received placement support); MP is second-best performer

[58] World Bank, 2015, Skills Development Programmes in India, Labor Market Impacts and Effectiveness Findings of an Evaluation Study, March 2015. Key findings.

[59] Meky, Muna Salih, 2015, Labor Market Impacts and Effectiveness of Skills Development Programmes in India. Washington, D.C.: World Bank Group. Available at http://documents.worldbank.org/curated/en/2015/04/24616611/labor-market-impacts-effectiveness-skills-development-programs-india

with 32 per cent. The placement rate is lowest in Odisha at 12 per cent.

- Sustainability of employment is a critical issue; a large proportion of those placed after the training with TP support do not work several months later. Evidence of short job tenure is also provided by employers who report that many newly hired leave their jobs after two to three months of employment. Around one-third does so because of other job opportunities but others, according to employers, leave because of low pay, distance from home or for family reasons.
- Although all programmes aim at providing gainful employment, a large proportion of trainees (28 per cent) indicate that they do not intend to work after training, but rather to pursue further studies. This lack of motivation raises questions about the adequacy of the selection process of participants and also the value attached to the jobs available at the end of training.
- Skill development programmes give a positive earnings premium: trainees who have got a job earn on average about 21 per cent more than non-trainees (with same age, education, marital status, state of residence). There is a stronger effect on women. They give access to better quality jobs (as measured by proxies, such as a job contract, shorter work hours, and access to pension plan).
- Skill development programmes have made a difference and contributed to increase in the employability and earnings of participants, and to give them access to better quality jobs (even if most jobs are still in the informal sector).
- When programmes are considered separately, positive employment and earning's effects are only observed for NSDC, SDIS, STEP-UP. No impact could be detected for RSETI and ASDP trainees.
- Selection of training providers: Selection is based on competition, mostly cost with insufficient attention to quality of offerings, and labour market demand. Franchising is widely used and not subject to competition and quality control.

There is insufficient use of labour market analysis to select courses and training providers. There is concentration of offerings over a limited number of trades with high variance in quality. At least two-thirds of providers are located in urban areas and the remaining in rural areas.

- Assessment and certification: Large differences across programmes are found, not all mandate third-party assessments and certification. Insufficient availability of qualified assessors is an issue. Lower cost and more rapid process with training providers carrying out assessments resulting in higher risk of quality compromise and lack of standardisation of certificates.
- Monitoring: Monitoring reports are mainly used to claim reimbursements. Verification of data is uncertain. Cases of duplication in accounting of beneficiaries are reported.

The study concludes that even if most skill development programmes are found to have positive labour market effects, expectations of their overall impact on the Indian economy need to remain modest. Courses are of short duration and cost is low. The amount of human capital that can be provided through those programmes is likely to remain modest. While these courses can be a useful instrument to facilitate insertion in the labour market, these cannot be expected to yield huge productivity increases and need to be complemented by other types of human capital investments. Their targets should be adjusted accordingly.

NSDC's impact assessment

NSDC commissioned during 2014–15 an impact assessment of its activities. The specific objectives of the assignment were: (a) study the impact of training on the livelihood of the skilled candidates under NSDC, (b) assess the effect of its training partners on the skilling ecosystem.

NSDC mandated Deloitte to conduct impact assessment of the skilling initiatives in three regions, that is, North, South and East. Tata Institute of Social Sciences (TISS) carried out the study in west and north east regions. While the observations and key findings are presented in detail by Deloitte team, the TISS report carries limited analysis at this stage and the full report is expected to contain all the key findings. Deloitte's report is summarized below:

- A total of 4,800 persons were met and interviewed during the study covering 111 training centres of 75 training partners.
- The business model of operation of the NSDC training partners is pre-dominantly through the network of franchised centres (76 per cent) with a core of own centres (24 per cent).
- The total number of skill training courses offered across the country by the sample training partners is 4,502 across 28 priority sectors as identified by NSDC. Highest number of courses is being offered in southern region (39 per cent), followed by eastern (23 per cent) and northern (20 per cent) regions. Sectorally, 74 per cent of the courses are in the Services sector, followed by Industry/manufacturing (23 per cent) and Agriculture (3 per cent). Sixty-one per cent of the courses being offered are of short duration (<200 hours).
- Fifty-five per cent of the TPs reported customising skill training courses according to the company/industry demands. Majority of the training partners (around 70 per cent amongst the ones who responded) have collaborated with industry for organising demonstration classes and expert sessions and inviting guest lecturers etc. for training delivery. According to 62 per cent of students/alumni surveyed, the training centres have an on-the-job training component.
- Ninety per cent of the students/alumni across the three regions responded that their centre has provided soft skills training; 99 per cent of the TPs stated to have a pre \-joining counselling process at their training centres, which was corroborated by 95 per cent of the students/alumni who attributed a high quality rating to the same.
- Fifty-seven per cent of the TP management reported that they are conducting entry level assessment when students join the courses. Regarding end term assessment, it was reported that it is outsourced by the TPs in 65 per cent of the cases. In case of outsourced assessments, 74 per cent TPs said that it is conducted by an SSC approved agency. Assessment practices needed improvement.
- Total number of trained students by NSDC training partners in the period Q1 FY 14–Q3 FY 15 including all regions was about 27.5 lakhs. This includes 13.5 lakh students who have been trained under non-STAR and 14 lakh students who have been trained under the STAR scheme. The drop-out rate (difference between enrolment and training) is 10 per cent. Further, the failure rate of those who complete the training and attempt certification is also 10 per cent. In the north, south & east, 60 per cent, 71 per cent and 74 per cent of the alumni respectively are employed after the skill training programmes.
- On an average, 81 per cent, 81 per cent and 77 per cent of the employers in the northern, southern and eastern region respectively either 'agreed' or 'strongly agreed' that the alumni of NSDC's training programmes display better performance as compared to other employees/workers.
- Majority of the beneficiaries surveyed find the skill training course to be easily affordable to affordable (ranging between 64 per cent and 71 per cent) across all the regions surveyed. The average fees is (as reported by TPs)—₹4,900.
- As per data reported by 53 TPs to NSDC, the operating expenses as percentage of revenue is 129 per cent for all partners combined together since they have received NSDC funds. It is heartening that 20 per cent of TPs exhibit overall turnaround and earned more revenues than expenditure on cumulative basis.

Key Initiatives taken in the years 2014 and 2015

All these policy and operational measures (Box 6.5) are expected to yield better outcomes in the coming years.

Box 6.5: *Key initiatives taken in the years 2014 and 2015*

Institutional alignments: Skill development and entrepreneurship efforts across the country have been highly fragmented so far. Recognising the need and urgency of quickly coordinating the efforts of all concerned stakeholders the Department of Skill Development and Entrepreneurship was created which was later made into a full-fledged Ministry of Skill Development and Entrepreneurship on 9th November 2014. The National Skill Development Agency (NSDA), an autonomous body that was created with the mandate to co-ordinate and harmonise the skill development activities in the country, has been made a part of the Department of Skill Development and Entrepreneurship, along with the NSDC, 33 SSCs, NSDF and the National Skill Development Trust (NSDT).

To create further convergence between the Vocational Training system through ITIs and the new Skill Initiatives of the government, two verticals from Directorate General of Employment and Training (DGET)—DDG (Training) and DDG (Apprenticeship Training) have been transferred to the Ministry of Skill Development and Entrepreneurship on 16th April 2015. Thus, the major institutions/departments involved in skill development now are under one ministry.

Revision of the National Policy on Skill Development: The National Policy on Skill Development (NPSD) was first formulated in 2009. It has been reviewed and the draft new policy has been formulated in July 2015. The policy addresses the key obstacles in the skilling and entrepreneurship landscape, including low aspirational value, non-integration with formal education, lack of focus on outcomes, quality of training infrastructure and trainers, etc. Further, the policy aims to align supply with demand, bridge existing skill gaps, promote industry engagement, operationalise a quality assurance framework, leverage technology and promote apprenticeship to tackle the issues in the skill space.

Improving standards of skilling at state level: NSDC during the year has signed MoUs with several states for collaboration in skill development. A sub-group of Chief Ministers on Skill Development have been constituted by National Institute for Transforming India (NITI) Aayog to suggest measures for strengthening State Skill Development Missions to enhance capacity and improve standards of skilling at the state level.

New schemes launched: PMKVY is a Flagship outcome-based skill training scheme of the newly created Ministry of Skill Development and Entrepreneurship launched in 2015. The scheme has an outlay of ₹1,500 crore, with a target to cover 24 lakh persons in its first year of implementation, (including 10 lakh under Recognition of Prior Learning). The training under PMKVY is based on the NOSs/QPs developed by the Sector Skill Councils to improve employability of the skilled manpower. To promote placements, the scheme also has a component of incentives linked to placement of people skilled under the scheme. The scheme will be implemented through NSDC.

The Ministry of Rural Development has started a new version of the existing Aajeevika Skills Scheme as the Deen Dayal Upadhyaya Grameen Kaushalya Yojana (DDU–GKY). The programme aims to provide placement linked training to one million youth by the year 2017.

The Ministry of Labour & Employment has launched a new scheme 'Establishment of National Career Service'. The national web portal that is being established as part of the scheme will facilitate users to register and seek/access counselling and employment related services while industries will be encouraged to register and post vacancies on the NCS portal and access the database of registered users.

Rationalisation of the Skill Development Schemes of the Government of India: The wide variations in the norms for costs, duration of training, outcomes, monitoring requirements etc., across about 70 skill development schemes being run by the 20 Ministries/Departments of the GoI is causing problems at the implementation stage. Based on the Committee set up to make recommendations on rationalisation of these schemes, the government has approved Common Norms in July 2015 to rationalise more than 70 skill development programmes being implemented by different Central Ministries/Departments. The Common Norm addresses the whole spectrum of skill development processes and systems including inputs, outputs, funding/cost norms, third party certification and assessment, monitoring/

tracking mechanisms and empanelment of training providers.

The outcomes of these skill training programmes have been defined in terms of placement achieved in wage and self–employment.[60] Every training programme and training provider will be judged on the results—in terms of the employment being procured by the persons trained and the salaries being paid for these jobs.

Making Skill Development an Integral Part of all Government of India Schemes: The government is keen to ensure that skill development become an integral part of all GoI schemes.[61] For instance, a scheme to build roads and highway should earmark a certain minimum percentage of the funds to skill persons to use the road (as drivers), maintain the road (as maintenance workers) etc. Ten per cent of Special Central Assistance to Scheduled Caste Sub Plan, 10 per cent Special Central Assistance to Scheduled Tribes Sub Plan, 5 per cent of Border Area Development Programme, 20 per cent of funds under Building and Other Construction Workers Welfare Cess, 10 per cent of allocation under Integrated Action Plan for LWE districts have been earmarked for skill development.

Creation of Additional Training Capacity: To ensure that there is sufficient skill development capacity in the country, a number of steps are being taken such as: (a) Determination of the Capacity Gap, so that the shortfall in capacity can be gauged and a plan for meeting this shortfall can be formulated and implemented, (b) Targeted approach to creation of Capacity, for ensuring greater accessibility and equity, for certain specific sectors and geographies where training capacity is clearly inadequate, such skill development needs of infrastructure sector, skill development for LWE areas, north-eastern and hilly states, skill development for women, persons with disabilities, etc. (c) Opening the doors for new training providers, by developing appropriate accreditation norms for training providers.

International expertise: The NSDA has signed a Technical Assistance Agreement (TA) with the Asian Development Bank, with the objective to enhance the capacity of NSDA to effectively implement its mandate of guiding quality skills development initiatives across Central Ministries, States, and the private sector. Similarly, an India–European Union Skill Development Project has been signed. The project is designed to impact on the capacity development of the key government and the private sector institutions and individuals as well as strengthening the implementation of the National Policy on Skill Development.

Source: GoI, 2015, Programme Guidelines DDU-GKY.

Conclusion

The current year is a watershed in skill development and entrepreneurship. With a slew of government strategies and policy initiatives, the focus is on creating skill building institutions that work to a set of standards resulting in certification of trainees, the landscape of skill based employment is set for a significant change. The perception is that NSDC, while launching new schemes and enrolling new partners has not been able to fulfil its mandate through effective coordination and monitoring of results. With the government launching a number of new schemes in the recent past, the challenges of effective, coordinated implementation magnify. The concentration of skill development in urban areas, lower enrolment of women, low wage levels even after skill acquisition, lack of focus on quality in training, rent seeking behaviour on the part of skill providers, continuing skill gaps despite training, lack of quality trainers, lack of adequate arrangements for trainer training and upgradation are some of the difficulties that bedevil this important national movement (Annexure 6.1).

---

[60] Unstarred question no 2012 in Rajya Sabha answered on 6 August 2015.

[61] GoI, 2014, Initiatives, Achievements, Policies and Roadmap for the Future, Ministry of Skill Development, Entrepreneurship, Youth Affairs and Sports, Government of India.

The ambitious but necessary targets entail training of 250 million people in next five years. At an estimated cost of ₹20,000 per individual, this requires ₹5 trillion funding. With industry not keen to reskill their own employees, the likelihood that they will contribute significant sums is remote. While trainees can be asked to contribute, there are limits to their financial capacity as these are either unemployed or lowly paid before training. Very clearly financial resources have to be found for meeting the targets of skilling 250 million youth. The possibility of attracting CSR funding to the skilling initiative should be fully explored. Employers that gain from skilled manpower can also be approached to pay a placement fee, offsetting the costs of training to some extent.

Apart from financial resources, technical and knowledge resources are likely to prove more elusive. Finding adequate number of trainers with relevant skills, training them to be competent faculty and ensuring adherence to quality standards are the prime challenges that need to be faced. A massive coordination effort is seen as critical to bring the variety of stakeholders together in order to unify the efforts on a uniform quality platform for skill development.

The hope of youth rests on skill building. Their dreams ride on skill acquisition leading to viable livelihoods opportunities. To provide sustainable skill building to the millions, the policy and strategy elements should be long-term. The investments in institutions should also prioritise sustainability and accountability for results.

ANNEXURE 6.1
Ministry-wise performance in skill training 2014–15

S. No.	Ministry/Organisation	Target for 2014–15	Cumulative achievement for 2014–15	
			Number	% of annual target
1.	Ministry of Labour & Employment	16,25,000	16,85,000**	103.70%
2.	Ministry of Agriculture*	22,00,000	11,43,671	51.98%
3.	National Skill Development Corporation*	33,00,000	34,42,422**	104.31%
4.	Ministry of Rural Development	5,62,950	3,95,201	70.20%
5.	Ministry of Micro, Small & Medium Enterprises	6,50,000	5,52,386	84.98%
6.	Department of Higher Education	1,21,800	30,055	24.67%
7.	Department of Electronics & Info Technology	6,10,000	–	–
8.	Ministry of Housing & Urban Poverty Alleviation	6,50,000	47,922	7.37
9.	Ministry of Women & Child Development	96,000	–	–
10.	Ministry of Textiles	1,20,000	–	–
11.	Ministry of Social Justice & Empowerment	96,050	23,752	24.72%
12.	Ministry of Tourism*	80,800	97,986**	121.27%
13.	Ministry of Minority Affairs	95,000	40,924	43.08%
14.	Ministry of Tribal Affairs	50,000	–	–
15.	Ministry of Home Affairs	8,000	626	7.83%
16.	Ministry of Road Transport and Highways	17,500	–	–
17.	Ministry of Chemicals & Fertilisers	42,900	24,864	57.96%
18.	Ministry of Commerce and Industry	1,38,000	93,105	67.46%
19.	Department of Heavy Industry	31,000	24,339	78.51%

(Continued)

(Continued)

S. No.	Ministry/Organisation	Target for 2014–15	Cumulative achievement for 2014–15	
			Number	% of annual target
20.	Ministry of Development of North Eastern Region	4,000	–	–
21.	Ministry of Food Processing Industries*	9,000	9,506**	105.62%
	Total	1,05,08,000	76,11,759	72.43%

Sources: National Skill Development Agency, Government of India, 2015.
Notes: * *As per data received from the Ministry bill March, 2015.*
        ** *Achievement exceeds against the target.*

Non-farm Sector Enterprises and Employment

For distinguishing livelihoods that are in artisanal crafts, manufacturing and services, the term non-farm sector is traditionally used. There are also occupations that are based on farming but carried out off-farm such as in agro and food processing. To capture non-farm livelihoods comprehensively is a major challenge. Non-farm livelihoods are a significant means of sustenance, both in rural and urban areas. These livelihoods are also in the nature of wage employment or self-employment including running of enterprises. The livelihoods are based on large organised sector entities, unorganised sector entities as well as own- account enterprises. Khadi and village industries, individual craftsmen, weavers and workers of different kinds make up the spectrum of off-farm livelihoods. Medium, small and micro enterprises, Khadi and village enterprises, household businesses, own-account unorganised units, self-employed entrepreneurial units and non-agricultural labour of all kinds form the core of off-farm livelihoods. This chapter focuses on handicrafts, handlooms and wage employment in the non-agricultural sectors in general.

There has been an ongoing structural shift in the economy–away from agriculture and towards services. Manufacturing sector share of GDP has been growing marginally, whereas services sector has shown vigorous growth (Table 7.1). Agricultural sector that used to contribute to national income significantly in the past has been having lower shares in GDP year after year. It is not on account of lack of growth in agriculture but due to aggressive growth in services sector. Nearly two-thirds of the GDP is contributed by services sector.

Table 7.1: Trends in share of services sector in GDP

	2000–01	2011–12@	2012–13*	2013–14**
Trade, hotels, and restaurants	14.5 (5.2)	17.4 (1.2)	17.2 (4.5)	24.0 (3.0)#
Trade	13.2 (5.0)	15.9 (1.0)	15.8 (4.8)	–
Hotels and restaurants	1.3 (7.0)	1.5 (3.8)	1.4 (0.5)	–
Transport, storage, and communication	7.6 (9.2)	7.3 (9.4)	7.5 (6.0)	–
Railways	1.1 (4.1)	0.7 (7.5)	0.8 (0.3)	–
Transport by other means	5.0 (7.7)	5.4 (8.6)	5.6 (6.6)	–
Storage	0.1 (6.1)	0.1 (2.9)	0.1 (8.6)	–
Communication	1.5 (25.0)	1.1 (11.2)	1.1 (6.5)	–
Financing, insurance, real estate, and business services	14.1 (3.5)	16.5 (11.3)	17.2 (10.9)	18.5 (12.9)
Banking and insurance	5.4 (–2.4)	5.7 (12.9)	5.9 (11.8)	–
Real estate, ownership of dwellings, and business services	8.7 (7.5)	10.7 (9.9)	11.4 (10.0)	–
Community, social, and personal services	14.7 (4.6)	13.8 (4.9)	14.3 (5.3)	14.5 (5.6)
Public administration and defence	6.5 (1.9)	5.9 (4.2)	6.0 (3.4)	–
Other services	8.2 (7.0)	7.8 (5.4)	8.2 (6.8)	–
Construction	6.0 (6.1)	8.2 (10.8)	8.1 (1.1)	7.8 (1.6)
Total services	51.0 (5.1)	54.9 (6.6)	56.3 (7.0)	57.0 (6.8)
Total services (including construction)	57.0 (52)	63.1 (7.1)	64.4 (6.2)	64.8 (6.2)
Total GDP	100.0 (4.1)	100.0 (6.7)	100.0 (4.5)	100.0 (4.7)

Source: Central Statistics Office (CSO).
Notes: Shares are in current prices and growth in constant prices; Figures in parentheses indicate growth rate; * first revised estimates, @ second revised estimates, ** provisional estimate; # includes the combined share and growth of trade, hotels, and restaurants and transport, storage, and communication for 2013–14.

The structural changes are reflected in the employment-based livelihoods too. The 2011–12 survey on informal employment brought out that 242 million people were engaged in employment in non-agriculture related activities which was more than those employed in the agriculture sector. The major industries in which people were employed or engaged were trade hotel and restaurant services, manufacturing, construction and transportation, storage and communications (Figure 7.1). The remaining sub-sectors such as mining, education, insurance and health had a much smaller share of people engaged in livelihoods. In terms of percentage, 49 per cent of employment was in agricultural sector, 13 per cent in manufacturing, 12 per cent in non-manufacturing and 27 per cent in services.

There had been a significant shift of livelihoods from agricultural sector to other-than-agriculture sector (Table 7.2). Agriculture-based livelihoods accounted for 58.5 per cent of people employed in 2004–05. By 2011–12, this declined to 48.9 per cent. The non-manufacturing and the services sectors had a share of around 30 per cent of all livelihoods in 2004–05. In 2011–12, this increased to 38.5 per cent. Manufacturing sector increased the proportion of livelihoods from 11.7 per cent to 12.6 per cent which is a negligible increase. The growth rate in jobs was the highest in non-manufacturing sub-sectors, driven mostly by a booming construction sector. Among services, trade, transport, storage and communication sectors registered a strong employment growth. The change in nature of livelihoods is discernible and there is a distinct shift away from agriculture to non-farm sector with agricultural employment declining by 13.8 per cent in the seven year period from 2005 to 2012. While agriculture shed about 37 million workers, non-farm sector created more than 51 million jobs during the seven-year period. But for growth of the non-farm sector, the employment situation could have rendered livelihoods unsustainable.

The 68th round of NSSO survey (Table 7.3) brought out that more workers are

Figure 7.1: Change in employment trends across sectors

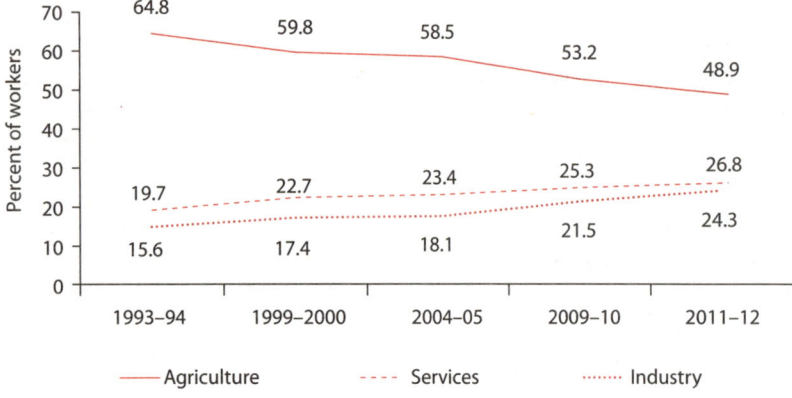

Source: Excerpted from Chapter 10, *The Economic Survey 2013–14*, Ministry of Finance, GoI, 2014.

Table 7.2: Employment trends in farm and non-farm sectors

Sector	Number employed (millions)		Share to total (%)		Growth rate in jobs (%)
	2004–05	2011–12	2004–05	2011–12	
Agriculture	268.93	231.90	58.50	48.90	(−13.8)
Manufacturing	53.91	59.75	11.73	12.60	10.8
Non-manufacturing	29.41	55.25	6.41	11.65	87.9
Services	107.36	127.33	23.36	26.85	18.6
Total	459.61	474.23	100	100	3.2

Source: NSSO surveys, various periods; Ministry of Statistics and Programme Implementation, GoI.

Table 7.3: Informal workers employed by various sector (%)

Sector	Rural workers	Urban workers
Agriculture	11.4	1.6
Mining and quarrying	1.2	
Manufacturing	21.3	24.9
Construction	27.3	9.8
Wholesale and retail trade, auto repairs	13.9	20.7
Transport, storage	7.1	7.8
Hotel and food service	2.2	4.0
Information, communication		2.7
Public admin, defence	1.9	4.3
Financial services	0.8	2.6
Education	5.1	5.8
Scientific, technical, professional activities	0.4	1.7

Source: Informal Sector and Conditions of Employment in India 2011–12, NSSO 68th round, July 2014.
Note: The data relates to wage labour and hence the agriculture sector numbers are lower than others.

Figure 7.2: Rural households by main source of income

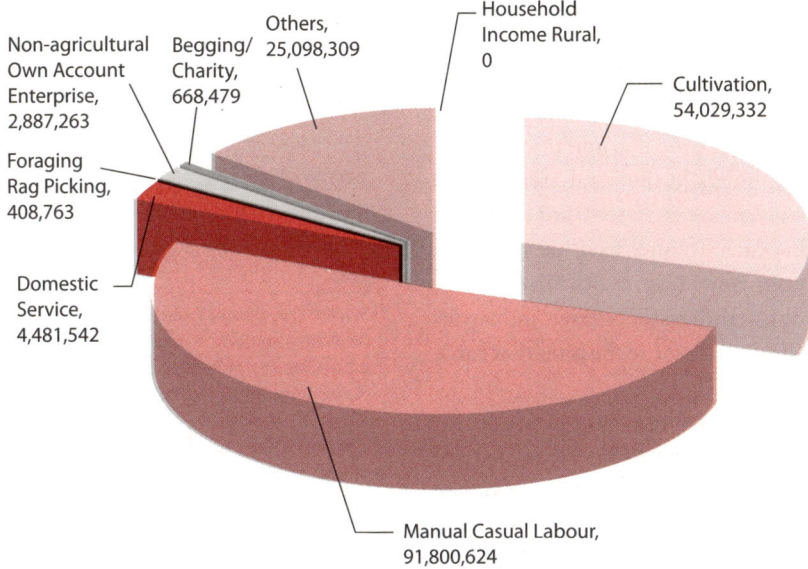

Source: Socio Economic Caste Census, 2011, Ministry of Rural Development, GoI.

employed in construction in rural areas than in urban areas. Manufacturing, construction and trade sectors constituted the bulk of employment-based livelihoods according to the survey.

In the Economic Census, the main source of income reported by the respondents is a useful proxy for livelihoods that the people can pursue. 30.1 per cent of those surveyed, reported cultivation as the source of income and 51.2 per cent were engaged in manual wage labour (Figure 7.2). Part or full time domestic services were rendered by 2.5 per cent of people for earning their livelihoods. The shift in nature of livelihoods even in rural areas is amply demonstrated by the majority of households that depend on non-agricultural activities for their main source of income. For about 70 per cent of the households, non-farm sector economy is more critical than the farm sector. This shift has occurred for a number of reasons. Firstly, the increasing labour force and the pressure on agricultural land has rendered many livelihoods unviable. Secondly, economic growth since the 1990s fuelled construction, transport, microenterprises and several new economic sectors in finance, information, communication and technology. The

growing aspirations of rural people created an urge to migrate rather than to work in the fields, as was revealed in the Situation Assessment Survey of farmers in 2005.[1] However, the growth in new livelihoods came not so much from manufacturing but from non-manufacturing and the services sectors. Shift from agriculture requires new skills and competencies. Unskilled jobs can be found in construction-related works but not much in other sectors. Non-farm sector has become the major sector that sustains livelihoods, whether in rural or in urban areas. This is in keeping with the pattern of economic growth and aspirations of the people. A critical point to note is that the livelihoods provided by the services sector is not proportional to its share of national income. Despite 63 per cent share in GDP (in 2011–12), services sector offered only 38 per cent jobs. Agriculture provided 48 per cent jobs but had a much smaller share in GDP. This is indicative of the fact that those in agriculture are likely to be poorer whereas those in the non-farm sector livelihoods are likely to be comparatively better off.

---

[1] More than 40% of the farmers surveyed expressed a desire to quit farming.

The issues of manufacturing sector employment in the organised sector are no doubt important but not within the scope of the kind of livelihoods that are a part of this Report. The kind of livelihoods that we seek to cover relate to informal and unorganised sector livelihoods in the rural areas as well as in the urban areas. In terms of identified sectors in which attempts have been made by the government to improve the livelihoods, handloom, handicrafts, village industries and small enterprises are the ones that catch attention.

The handloom and handicraft sector is looked after by the Ministry of Textiles. The khadi and village industries are looked after by the Ministry of Micro, Small & Medium Enterprises (MSME). There are some overlaps between handloom and handicrafts, especially in case of carpets and *zari* work. Similarly, there are also overlaps between khadi and village industries (KVIs) and handloom and handicrafts in several artisanal products. KVI is the description of an enterprise form whereas handloom and handicrafts could be in enterprise form or just wage labour. The number of people employed in these three sectors is estimated at 35 million.

While the Development Commissioner of Handicrafts and Handlooms looks at sustaining the artisans' and craftsmen's livelihoods through improving their skills and providing linkages, KVIC—with the support of KVIB—is helping rural enterprises develop in those sub-sectors where there is potential. The nature and contents of support programmes thus differ. However, in capacity building of the persons involved and marketing their products, different agencies have similar interventions.

Handicrafts

"Handicraft can be defined, which is made by hand; should have some artistic value; they may or may not have functional utility."

The handicrafts sector is reportedly the second highest non-agricultural livelihood

Table 7.4: People employed in handloom, handicrafts and KVIs

Sectors	No. of people employed (millions)
Handloom (2009–10)	4.3
Handicrafts	9.8
Khadi and Village Industries (2013–14)	21.2
Total	35.3

Source: Handlooms from Census Data of 2009–10.
Notes: No updates to this are available. Handicrafts employment is estimated by the Taskforce on Handlooms set up by the Planning Commission. The KVIs data is as per the KVIC Annual Report 2013–14. The data is likely to err on the side of excess on account of overlap between the three categories.

sustaining sector in terms of self-employment. The estimated employment as per the 12th Five-Year Plan Task Force in handicrafts was 9.8 million in 2014–15, rising to 12.3 million in the year 2016–17 (Table 7.4). In case of handicrafts mostly, people have been pursuing their traditional skills passed on from generation to generation. The major activities in handicrafts are under different materials such as wood, metal, leather, natural fibre, coir, stone, terracotta, horn- and-bone-utilising artisanal skills such as carving, casting, painting, stitching, embroidery, zari work, spinning, weaving, twisting, pottery and carpentry. The Development Commissioner of Handicrafts identified a list of 32 handicraft categories (Table 7.5).

Current data on the number of people employed in each category of handicraft is not available. No recent surveys/census of handicraft households and workers has been made in the recent past. The last survey was carried out in 1995–96 by National Council of Applied Economic Research (NCAER). Some estimates of artisans working under some categories was made in a monograph released by the Madras School of Economics. These estimates are in Table 7.6.

Men dominate the handicrafts' sector. In some categories such as stone and leather, no women craftsmen are seen (Table 7.6).

Table 7.5: Major categories under handicrafts (Development Commissioner of handicrafts, GoI)

S. No.	Name of the craft	S. No.	Name of the craft
1.	Bidri	17.	Musical instrument
2.	Cane & Bamboo	18.	Pottery and clay objects
3.	Carpet	19.	Rugs & durries
4.	Conch-Shell	20.	Stone (carving)
5.	Doll & Toys	21.	Stone (inlay)
6.	Filigree & Silverware	22.	Terracotta
7.	Folk Painting	23.	Theatre, Costumes & Puppet
8.	Furniture	24.	Textile (handloom)
9.	Grass, leaf, read & fiber	25.	Textile (Hand embroidery)
10.	Horn & Bone	26.	Textile (Hand printed)
11.	Jewellery	27.	Wood (carving)
12.	Leather (footwear)	28.	Wood (inlay)
13.	Leather (other articles)	29.	Wood (turning and lacquer ware)
14.	Metal ware	30.	Zari
15.	Metal images (classical)	31.	Coir twisting
16.	Metal images (folk)	32.	Miscellaneous crafts and Paintings

Source: Website of the Development Commissioner Handicrafts: www.Handicrafts.in

Table 7.6: People engaged in different categories of handicrafts (2004–05, in lakhs)

Medium used	RURAL			URBAN			Grand total
	Men	Women	Total	Men	Women	Total	
Earth	5.06	2.85	7.91	1.24	0.60	1.84	9.75
Fiber	17.63	14.84	32.47	18.10	7.41	25.51	57.98
Metal	4.55	0.43	4.98	4.43	0.41	4.84	9.82
Wood	5.65	5.47	11.12	0.50	0.52	1.02	12.14
Stone	0.40	0.01	0.40	0.66	0.00	0.66	1.07
Leather	0.24	0.00	0.24	0.75	0.00	0.76	0.99
Others	0.07	0.00	0.07	0.05	0.00	0.05	0.12
Total craft	33.61	23.59	57.19	25.72	8.95	34.67	91.86
Share of craft (%)	**1.6**	**2.0**	**1.8**	**3.5**	**4.2**	**3.7**	**2.2**
Non Craft Sector	2010	1160	3170	708	202	910	4080
Total Working Population	2044	1184	3227	734	211	945	4172

Source: Based on National Sample Survey 2004–05. Excerpted from Enumeration of Crafts Persons in India by Brinda Viswanathan in *Monograph 25/2013.* Madras School of Economics, 2013.

In rural areas, more people are dependent on handicrafts than urban areas. Overall, 2.2 per cent of workers in the country gain their livelihoods from handicrafts sector.

The Development Commissioner (DC) of Handicrafts has the responsibility of planning and implementing measures for development and growth of the handicrafts sector. A design and technical upgradation scheme will cater to enhancement of artisans' skills through development of new design and supply of prototypes of improved/modern equipments to the craft persons and revival of rare crafts. Apart from skills training, tool kits are provided and market information on colours and designs is gathered and disseminated to weavers.

The Development Commissioner (handicrafts) runs a number of schemes for supporting handicrafts. These cover training, design, marketing, market support, exhibition, publicity, export, planning and research and artisan welfare. Five different training schemes address the needs of entry-level skills as also master craftsmen. There are two design support schemes and eleven schemes on marketing and support for marketing. The market-related schemes range from construction of physical markets to meeting the cost of travel of craftsmen to participate in trade fairs and exhibitions. There are also 10 schemes for supporting the export of handicrafts. Six different welfare schemes recommend building work sheds and houses, providing support for indigent artisans, providing group insurance schemes relating to life and health as well as awards for master craftsmen and community organisations of craftsmen.

The Babasaheb Ambedkar Hastshilp Vikas Yojna has the objective of developing artisans' clusters into professionally managed and self-reliant community enterprises on the principles of effective member participation. One hundred and fifty weaver clusters with 50,000 weavers are covered under this scheme. In the Outcome Budget 2014–15, the Ministry of Textiles noted:

> During the year 2013–14, ₹4.00 crores have been allocated under the Baba Saheb Ambedkar Hastshilp Vikas Yojana Scheme (Including NER). Out of ₹4.00. Crores, an amount of ₹3.98 Crore has been sanctioned during Financial Year 2013–14 for 116 new projects and reimbursement cases. No fresh cluster projects have been sanctioned because of non-finalization of location of clusters.

Under marketing and support services component, the DC (handicrafts) undertakes marketing events in India and abroad. He also organises the Gandhi Shilp Bazaar and Crafts Bazaar. The craftsmen's groups are also facilitated to participate

in exhibitions in India and abroad. Life insurance cover is made available to all artisans between 18 and 60 years under the Handicraft Artisans Comprehensive Welfare Scheme. There are also special schemes to develop crafts in Jammu and Kashmir and setting up a Hast Kala Academy in Delhi. The Outcome Budget 2014–15 of the department notes "₹21.94 crores have been incurred in respect of committed liabilities during Financial Year 2013–14 and 2,18,106 artisans have been covered under Rajiv Gandhi Shilpi Swasthya Bima Yojana. No coverage of Handicrafts Artisans could be undertaken under the Bima Yojana due to non-approval of EFC". It is strange that despite allocations, specifically to mitigate risks in vulnerable livelihoods, insurance cover could not be provided.

The allocations for handicrafts declined in 2013–14 (Table 7.7). While in 2014–15 there was an increased allocation, in the current year the allocation has drastically declined. There is a need to look into the requirements of the sector and provide adequate funding for critical aspects such as raw material linkages, marketing support and introducing design and technology changes. The Skill India programme might be able to take up the tasks of training and capacity-building professionally but other aspects of artisans' livelihoods should also be taken care of.

A major challenge for craftsmen is the limited availability of remunerative markets, both in India and abroad. While niche markets that are remunerative are available to a select few artisans and craftsmen, the general majority has to move through either a public sector entity that organises marketing or through voluntary sector organisations that link the artisans with the market. Technology, availability of raw materials, advise on design and customer preferences as well as skills training are all in short supply. Availability of finances and also hassle-free marketing channels are the continuing issues. There have been a number of schemes of the government implemented through

Table 7.7: Budget allocations for schemes of handicrafts

Scheme	2012–13 achievement	2013–14 budget	2013–14 achievement	2014–15 budget allocation	2015–16 budget allocation
National Handicrafts Development Programme	95.79	110	103.27	101	27
Babasaheb Ambedkar Hastshilp Yojana	44.98	3	3.98	6	3
Marketing Support and Services	46.27	37	42.87	34	56
Handicrafts Artisans Comprehensive Welfare Schemes	26.67	24	21.94	32	8
Research and Development	4.75	8	7.66	6	7
Mega clusters	23.38		0	249	123
Total	241.84	182.00	179.72	428	224

Source: Outcome Budget 2014–15 of Ministry of Textiles, GoI, 2015.

multiple channels but access to scheme benefits has always been limited. A number of programmes by the states and central government have been initiated for skills training and for establishing raw materials supply, either through state organisations or through collectives of handicrafts men. Credit through banking system at subsidised rates is facilitated and market linkages through Khadi and Village Industries Boards (KVIBs), Handicrafts Development Corporations, Export Promotion Council for Handicrafts (EPCH) and periodic sales campaigns in different cities. But the reach of all these development programmes has been limited. Except in niche markets, remunerative prices for handicrafts are normally not available and artisans are unable to recover the total cost of production and materials along with the labour component. Very often, the livelihoods of craftsmen are at a subsistence level despite the support available from different agencies.

There are a few well organised value chains within the handicrafts sector that have been able to provide a steady and reasonably remunerative market. Institutions like FabIndia, Tribes India, Cottage Industries Exposition Limited (CIE), Ode to Earth, ANTS Foundation, Urmul and Bandhan Creations etc., have managed to secure fair prices for artisans' products through their marketing initiatives. The number of such market-oriented institutions which can link with craftsmen at the backend should

increase. Without substantial investments in marketing, it would be difficult to achieve the projected growth in gainful employment of people in the handicrafts sector.

KPMG, in a paper prepared for NSDC, pointed out that lack of adequate data on the number of craftsmen, their socio-economic status, livelihood conditions and details of families, is a major bottleneck that affects planning and policy making. It also listed lack of access to credit at reasonable rates, problems with raw material supply, infrastructure and technology gaps, technical resource gaps and inefficient programme implementation by administrators as impediments to the growth of the sector. Further, other issues related to the handicrafts sector are economies of scale not being achieved on account of geographic dispersion and lack of uniform-quality protocols that prevent aggregation. The dubious role played by some entities in the private sector which also handle marketing has come for criticism. Unfair trade practices, delayed payments, using initial advances to craftsmen to keep the final payments low, use of craftsmen as bonded-piece-rate workers by master craftsmen and traders, are some market related-problems that still persist. Cheap imports of substitutes for artisanal products also eats into the market as well as their margins. The current focus on training and building physical infrastructure can help only to a limited extent. Dignity of work of the craftsmen should be recognised by the public at large. We need awareness campaigns that make people think of the nature of work that these craftsmen do and also develop willingness to pay an appropriate price for artisanal products.

Handlooms

India has been a traditional power house in hand weaving. Cotton, silk, wool, jute and other fibres have been traditionally used in handlooms. India is the only country to use all varieties of silk—Mulberry, Tassar, Eri and Muga varieties. In different parts of the country there are different weaving cultures that have given rise to geographically identified material. More than 4.3 million weavers were engaged in the sector as per the Handloom Census 2009–10.[2] The Census brought to light the fact that North-eastern states have more than 60 per cent of the weaver population. Assam has more than 40 per cent of the all India population of weavers. West Bengal and Andhra Pradesh are the two other states having a significant weaver population. Of the 4.33 million weavers, 78 per cent are women and 87 per cent rural (Table 7.8). Most weavers attain weaving skills by working in the family occupation and hence a significant proportion of them are not literate. Even those that are literate are not well educated. 57 per cent of the households were classified as Below Poverty Line. The census

reveals the erosion in traditional livelihoods as the number of weavers and looms had declined by about 34 per cent over a period of 15 years. The reduced numbers seem to have strengthened the livelihoods of those who remain in the sector as seen from the increased proportion of full time weavers and reduction in idle looms.

The Annual Report of Ministry of Textiles 2014–15 observes that adoption of modern techniques and economic liberalisation, however, has had a serious impact on the handloom sector. Competition from power looms and mill sector, availability of cheaper imported fabrics, changing consumer preferences and alternative employment opportunities have threatened the vibrancy of the handloom sector.

In the recent past there had been significant improvements to raw material used as also the designs to cater to niche markets where good quality handloom products fetch a premium price. Apart from quality and design issues the competition from power looms which were able to produce a much better quality material at a lower price and at the same time compete not just with handlooms but also with mill-made fabrics had come in the way of handloom development. However, the burgeoning power loom industry also led to significant increase in employment opportunities and that too at higher wage levels on account of its requirement of semi-skilled labour. But

Table 7.8: Highlights of handloom census 2009–10

Description	2009–10 Census	1995–96 Census
No. of weavers and allied workers (million)	4.33	6.55
No. of weavers households in NER (million)	1.51	1.45
No. of looms (million)	2.37	3.48
Women weavers (%)	77.9	60.6
Share of full-time weavers to total %	64	44
Proportion of households reporting more than 60% income from weaving (%)	35	31
Idle looms	4%	10%
Production of fabrics (million metres)	6930	3120

Source: Handloom Census of India 2009–10.

---

[2] Handloom Census of India 2009–10, National Council of Applied Economic Research, New Delhi.

in the rural areas and in weaving clusters a number of livelihoods depend on the market for handloom fabrics being improved.

The handloom weavers face rising input costs, low credit availability and high cost of credit, marketing hurdles, infrastructure gaps and low education and skill levels. Yarn supply is a perennial problem. Availability of good quality yarn at reasonable prices is hard to come by. Mostly yarn has to be transported from southern India (where it is produced) to North-east (where most looms and weavers are located) at high freight costs. The National Handloom Development Corporation (NHDC) set up 788 yarn depots in different parts of the country to provide reasonably priced yarn to weavers. But the supply from yarn depots of NHDC caters to only 15 per cent of the demand. There is also a geographical skew in presence of depots. Assam for example has 44 per cent of weavers but has only 5.6 per cent of yarn depots! Availability of azo-free quality dyes is also an aspect deserving attention. Yarn depots can also attend to supply of dyes with NHDC's support. Upgradation of dye infrastructure is enabled through GoI scheme for handloom cluster development. The dye houses are exclusively used by master weavers and the other weavers are unable to access dye houses for their requirements. This needs to remedied by investing in more dye houses in the clusters.

Lack of financial literacy and lack of collateral drives weavers to access credit from informal sources. They depend on the trader or the master weaver for their credit needs. The raw material is taken on credit and even advance wages are availed from the master weaver or trader. This creates problems in pricing and marketing. The weavers have to remain content with the wage employment. The government schemes under which weavers either individually or in cooperative society groups can avail loans are useful for a small number of weavers. The large majority of weavers are starved of funds from formal sources which can improve their ability to market products at a better price.

The Handloom Mark has been launched to serve as a guarantee to the buyers that the handloom products being purchased by them are genuine hand-woven products and not power loom or mill-made products. A number of design interventions have been introduced in key handloom clusters with the support of leading institutes such as National Institute of Design, National Institute of Fashion Technology, etc. Skill building of the weavers is also necessary to try out new and contemporary designs. Research and development work on loom design for improving productivity and reducing weaver fatigue are aspects that need more focus. Private sector partnerships can bring in the technical and marketing resources to the advantage of all. In developing Khadi Denim (Box 7.1), private sector initiative yielded good results.

While the value of domestic sales of handloom products is not reported, exports amounted to ₹22.46 billion in 2014–15, declining from the peak of ₹28.12 billion achieved in 2012–13.[3] The industry has to reorient itself to meet the marketing challenges that are being faced on account of economic, social and technological changes. Improving the production process to ensure defect free fabrics that cater to the modern consumer preferences is a good starting point. Branding and geographical identification of speciality handloom products will go a long way in establishing a remunerative and sustainable market which avoids competition from power loom goods (Box 7.2). Given that India has a rich variety of handloom catering to different tastes and requirements, a concerted attempt at brand based marketing is essential.

Currently, the major programme supporting this sector is Comprehensive Handloom Cluster Development Scheme (CHCDS) which has the objective of assisting the entrepreneurs/weavers to set up facilities with modern infrastructure. This intervention seeks to enhance the competitiveness

---

[3] Source: Handloom Export Promotion Council. 2015. Available at: www.hepcindia.com

Box 7.1: *Handloom denim story*

Arvind Mills, India's largest denim manufacturer, is a key player in bringing khadi-denim to market, having spent the last four years in R&D understanding the commercial, social and marketing angle that fits in with an of-the-moment East-meets-West narrative. Sharp branding of the three could propel the birth of a new textile, with a long life ahead of it.

The company's internal product development lab has since researched and brought in consultants for extensive studies. Arvind's Executive Director, Kulin Lalbhai, believes that he is seeing the birth of the product in its truest form only now, years into R&D. He explains, 'Denim is quite a technical product, it requires specific treatments for indigo to react to the fibre. And then it needs to be woven in a certain way with a certain weight. It's an incredibly difficult thing to marry khadi with denim technology.' Speaking about the prospects and challenges associated with its developments, Lalbhai says,

> Khadi and denim have very different supply chains. Spinning the yarn used for khadi is a completely manual process, done on the charkha, and so the major challenge with this product begins with how to source it. Arvind has been working with various

intermediaries in Gujarat as well as direct sources to set up an entire supply chain to procure khadi yarn. Production is complicated as well because the yarn is inherently imperfect, and quite delicate. Retro-fitting the weaving and processing of this yarn with what's required for denim manufacturing has been our second big contribution.

Arvind has also been working with designer Rajesh Pratap Singh for whom weaving and R&D is core to his business. Rajesh has worked extensively with khadi throughout his career and began experimenting with natural indigo-dyed plain weaves five years ago. Over the past two years, he has been purchasing Arvind's khadi-denim twill fabric. The alliance has grown into setting up a joint R&D unit to explore aesthetical and technical improvements that would make it easier to construct garments with. What excites him about the product? 'It is hand-spun, hand-woven—completely hand made. It has a softness and beauty that comes from the natural indigo dyeing process, that involves no chemicals. And finally, it is intrinsically Indian.'

Source: Based on an article by Nikita Doval in *Livemint* 17 June 2015. Available at www.livemint.com

Box 7.2: *Handloom branding initiative*

India Handloom Brand, recently launched in Chennai (under Development Commissioner of Handlooms, GoI) seeks to ensure production of high quality, defect free, hand-woven, authentic 'niche product'; zero defect; authentic traditional design; zero impact on environment; and social compliance. The weaver will be able to get bulk orders and higher wages by interacting directly with the market. It will also help weaver entrepreneurs (from younger generation) to take up the traditional profession of production of quality handloom fabrics in bulk and marketing within and outside the country.

Products identified for branding:

Cotton Sari: Jamdani, Tangail, Shantipiri, Dhaniakhali, Bichitrapuri, Bomkai, Kotpad, Pochampalli, Venkatgiri, Uppada, Siddipet, Narayanpet, Mangalagiri, Chetinad, Balaramapuram, Kasergod, Kuthampally, Chendmangalam Dhoti.

Silk Sari: Baluchari, Mugasilk, Sulkuch silk, Khandua, Berhampuri, Bomkai Silk, Benares Brocade, Tanchoi, Benarasi, Butidar, Jangla, Benarasi Cutwork, Pochampally, Dharmavaram, Kanchipuram, Arni Silk, Molkalmuru, Paithani, Patola, Champasilk, Ashawali Silk, Salem Silk (Dhoti), Uppada, Jamdani.

Cotton Silk Sari: Chanderi, Maheswari, Kota Doria, Ilkal, Gadwal, Covai Kora Cotton.

Dress material: Cotton—Odisha Ikat, Pochampalli Ikat; Silk—Tanchoi, Benarasi, Cutwork, Odisha Ikat, Pochampally Ikat, Tassar Fabric, Muga Fabric, Mekhala/Chadar

Bed sheet: Odisha Ikat, Pochampally Ikat.

Scarf/shawl/chadar: Kani Shawl, Kinnori Shawl, Kulu Shawl, Tangaliya Shawl, Kutch Shawl, Wangkhei Phee.

Branding process: The following entities will be eligible to apply for 'India Handloom' brand registration:

Genuine firms/institutions dealing with production of handloom fabrics including: Primary Handloom Cooperative Societies; SHGs, consortia, producer companies, Joint Liability Groups (JLGs); and weaver entrepreneurs.

Producers of garments and made-ups with the condition that they will use 'India Handloom' branded fabric and also comply with additional quality parameters regarding stitching, standard sizes etc., as may be laid down by the Development Commissioner for Handlooms.

Source: Website of Development Commissioner Handlooms, Ministry of Textiles, GoI.

of the clusters in terms of increased market share and ensuring increased productivity by higher unit value realisation of the products. The Scheme seeks to meet the discerning and changing market demands both at the domestic and at the international level and raise living standards of the weavers. The facilities are to be set up in six mega handloom clusters. To provide skills, upgradation, design and technological support to handloom weavers and to liaise with the state governments, a scheme to support the operations of weavers' service centers is also in pipeline.

The GoI has schemes for consolidation of existing clusters, setting up of new clusters and support to smaller groups of weavers. Two new mega[4] handloom clusters (with 15,000 looms each) are to be started during the current year in Bihar and Tamil Nadu. In marketing apart from participation in international fairs and buyer–seller meets abroad, several domestic marketing campaigns are carried out. A marketing complex in Delhi has been completed which will provide outlet for handloom fabrics from different parts of the country. A health insurance for weavers which covered 17.5 lakh weavers till September 2014 has been discontinued

from 1 October 2014 and the insurance scheme is expected to be now carried out by Ministry of Health. A life and accident insurance scheme covers 1.90 lakh weavers. Apart from the Development Commissioner (Handlooms), other agencies such as Silk Board also provide support to weavers.

The budget allocations show a declining tendency (Table 7.9). Some of the older schemes do not find any funding support. The weavers' debt waiver scheme does not find any allocation in this year's budget. Even allocation to the welfare scheme which is basically for insurance of the weavers has been drastically cut. The budget allocations indicate

---

[4] Under the scheme, components like conducting Diagnostic Study, formulation of Detailed Project Report (DPR), engaging Designer, Product Development, Corpus for raw material, Worksheds (for BPL weavers), Skill upgradation etc. are fully funded by GoI, while the components like Technology upgradation, Design Studio, including the Computer Aided Design System, Marketing Complex, Value Addition (setting up of garment unit), Dye House, Common Infrastructure, Publicity etc., are part-funded by the GoI.

Table 7.9: Budget allocations for handlooms sector

				(in ₹ millions)
Scheme	2012–13	2013–14	2014–15	2015–16
National Handloom Development Programme			2,880.0	1,250.0
Comprehensive Handloom Development Scheme		1,070.0	–	
Integrated Handloom Development Scheme (CSS)	1,700.0			
Revival reforms and restructuring package for handlooms (CSS)	2,2050.0	1,570.0		
Market and Export Promotion Scheme (CSS)	480.0			
Diversified Handloom Development Scheme	200.0			
Weaver Service Centre	325.0	350.0	330.0	380.0
Handloom Weavers Comprehensive Welfare Scheme	1,050.0	650.0	550.0	150.0
Mill Gate Price Scheme	3,500.0	965.0	1,250.0	1,400.0
Scheme for grant of special rebate		0.10	0.10	
Trade Facilitation Centre and Crafts Museum				800.0
Others	300.0	329.9	375.0	420.0
CHCDS – Handloom Mega Cluster		260.0	260.0	66.0
Lump sum provision for Northeast and Sikkim			570.0	400.0
Grand Total	**29,605.0**	**5,195.0**	**6,215.1**	**4,866.0**

Source: Web pages of Development Commissioner, Handlooms, Ministry of Textiles, GoI.

a direction contrary to what has been said earlier[5] about the kind of support required by the handloom sector. Dr Narasimha Reddy in his critical article[6] comments,

> Per capita spending of the government on handloom sector, a labour intensive textile manufacturing section, spread all over India, does not exceed ₹500. But, it is ready to spend ₹1,000 crores on Self-Employment and Talent Utilization (SETU). Government's target of encouraging self-employment would have been reached with smaller investments in handloom sector. Thousands of handloom weavers are becoming poorer by the day, as their wages are not increasing…

Despite the efforts taken by the weavers and the supporting organisations, the sector could face threats to its existence in a rapidly changing market. Unless customer, market and weaver interface is continuous, the products may not command a good price. Skilled weavers are in short supply. More than 25 per cent of existing weaver households did not want their children to continue in the profession. Unless the weaver secures a place of dignity and views the vocation with pride, the number engaged in the sector is bound to dwindle. The incomes from weaving should be at par with or better than the alternative employment opportunities. This would be possible only when credit and

marketing bottlenecks are sorted out. The increasing exports offer a positive signal. How to improve domestic marketing and increase visibility and desirability of handloom fabrics in the eyes of community at large is the question that requires answers. As Dr Narasimha Reddy says, 'We need to actively invest in the sector's strengths, not subsidise its weaknesses. Give it access to the same R&D, credit, raw materials, technology, education, social security and infrastructure that other growth sectors of the economy automatically get.'

Khadi and village industries

The Khadi and Village Industries is an important segment of the rural economy. The Khadi and Village Industries Commission (KVIC) at the central level (under the ministry of MSME) and the Khadi and Village Industries Boards (KVIB) in the states provide support of different kinds for the enterprises in this space to be set up, nurtured and sustained. KVIC has classified the village industries into seven classes (Table 7.10).

KVIC has been implementing schemes for creating self-employment and wage employment through the Khadi and Village Industry enterprises. The economic objective of KVIC programmes is that the supported units should produce marketable goods and

Table 7.10: Classification of village industries

Agriculture based	Pulses & Cereals Processing Industry, Gur & Khandsari Industry, Palmgur Industry, Fruit & Vegetable Processing Industry, Village Oil Industry
Forestry based	Medicinal Plants Industry, Bee Keeping Industry, Minor Forest Based Industries
Handmade paper and Fibre	Handmade Paper Industry, Fibre Industry
Mineral Based	Pottery, Lime
Polymer and Chemical based	Leather Industry, Non Edible Oils & Soap Industry, Cottage Match Industry, Plastic Industry
Rural engineering and bio-technology	Non Conventional Energy, Carpentry & Blacksmithy, Electronics
Service and textile	

Source: Website of KVIC. Available at www.kvic.org.in

---

[5] The Prime Minister spoke of 'global branding and data mapping', of 'improving quality, technology and materials', and 'working capital and finance', rather than the usual sad subsidies and sops. None of these found space in the recent budget.

[6] Dr Narasimha Reddy, Talk and Walk: Not Together—Handloom Sector in Union Budget 2015–16. Available at https://factly.in/handloom-sector-budget-2015-16-talk-and-walk-not-together

socially the entrepreneurs should become self-reliant over time (Box 7.3). The schemes of KVIC are aimed at development of Khadi, welfare of artisans and village entrepreneurs, market development and strengthening infrastructure of existing weak Khadi institutions. The following table contains the achievements of KVIC and KVIBs (Table 7.11).

The production and sales performance show a reasonable growth rate, especially in case of village industries. The sector employs more than 21 million people, which indicates the significance of the sector. As stated earlier in the chapter some overlap of these operations with that reported from handicrafts and handlooms sector is inevitable.

Box 7.3: *Khadi going places[7]*

'Khadi has come to represent a handmade-in-India product of value and pride. And while it continues to be a symbol of freedom, it also represents an evolving India—the best of India's past endures in this ancient weave, yet it embraces elements of contemporary India to find a new synthesis and relevance', said designer Deepika Gehani. These days khadi silk and khadi cotton are finding prominence and khadi-viscose blends are also used extensively by stylists. Rahul Mishra, fashion designer says he has showcased a 'khadi collection in various forms like jumpsuits, skirts, tunics and trousers; so the designs are many'.

He adds that fabrics look elegant when kept simple. 'There is no need to glamorise khadi. Those who want a minimal look with a deep sense of Gandhian aesthetics will enjoy khadi in its natural form. If you really want to go for bling and shimmer, then go for satins, linens and chiffons,' he added.

'Silk khadi, which is available in a variety of hues and shades, adds elegance and a touch of royalty to any space. The dye gives the cloth a whole new dimension and looks great on cushions, tablecloths, runners, curtains, or sofa covers. Beautifully textured, sensuous and skin friendly, it also makes for great sofa covers,' said Parul Jain. With increased demand for khadi fabrics and with designers like Ritu Kumar, Sabyasachi Mukherjee, Rahul Mishra and Anand Kabra using khadi extensively, it's is obvious that prices will shoot up.

The price of cotton khadi in local market is somewhere between ₹34 and ₹82 per metre, while if you want to buy a designer scarf, you may have to shell out ₹4,000. Rodricks feels with increased demand, prices have increased, but what worries him is the condition of weavers as they are not getting their due.

Table 7.11: Khadi and village industries operations

	2012–13		2013–14		Total		
	KVIC	KVIBs	KVIC	KVIBs	2012–13	2013–14	Growth rate
Production (in Rupees billion)							
Khadi	7.62	2.63	8.11	2.85	10.25	10.96	6.9%
Village Industries	232.62	149.46	252.98	164.94	382.08	417.92	9.4%
Sales (in Rupees billion)							
Khadi	10.22	3.09	10.81	3.5	13.31	14.31	7.5%
Village Industries	268.18	164.28	300.73	187.51	432.46	488.24	12.9%
Employment (in million)							
Khadi	1.07	0.27	1.1	0.32	1.34	1.42	6.0%
Village Industries	11.41	7.32	11.94	7.83	18.73	19.77	5.6%

Source: Annual Reports 2012–13 and 2013–14 of KVIC. Available at www.kvic.org.in

---

[7] This has been excerpted from an article, 'Thanks to Modern Designers, Khadi is Going Places and Earning its Pride of Place', by Nivedita Sharma. Available at http://www.theweekendleader.com/page.php?id=746&title=Haute%20 Khadi&h=54#sthash.KnXcIwzl.dpuf

KVIC implements two important schemes for the sector. The Khadi Reform and Development Programme has funding support from the ADB and aims at positioning Khadi in consonance with the emerging market needs, expanding employment for Khadi craftsmen and enhancing their income levels. The PMEGP was initiated in 2008–09 by merging Prime Ministers Rozgar Yojana and Rural Employment Generation Progamme. The objective of the PMEGP is to provide sustainable employment to youth through self-employment and enterprise creation through rural industrialisation (Box 7.4). PMEGP provides margin money assistance, facilitates banks loans, provides entrepreneurship training and other support relating to technology and marketing. More than 450 model projects have been prepared and made available to prospective applicants. EDP training had also been arranged for 38,000 people during the last year. Under PMEGP so far 290,000 enterprises have been set up providing cumulative employment to 2.55 million persons. The provision of margin money and the eligibility for interest subsidy on bank loan have been the major instruments used by KVIC, KVIB and the District Industries Centres in PMEGP.

Table 7.12: PMEGP performance

Aspect	2013–14	2014–15
Number of projects (no)	50,493	18,141
Margin money provided (Rupees billion)	10.76	4.28
Production (Rupees billion)	64.59	NA
Sales	80.73	NA
Employment (millions)	0.38	0.14

Source: website of KVIC - www.kvic.org.in

The PMEGP appears to be doing well in terms of enterprise creation and employment (Table 7.12). The reasons for the reduced number of enterprises created in 2014–15 is not clear. KVIC had also arranged for Janashree Bima Yojana, a life insurance cover for 0.28 million people from among its units. During the year 2013–14 KVIC received an allocation of ₹16.14 billion of which it had utilised ₹14.31 billion. The employment and enterprise creation performance in terms of numbers is noteworthy.

Other non-farm sector activities

The government's efforts towards improving and strengthening livelihoods outside the farm sector have been to ensure flow

---

Box 7.4: *PMEGP: An outline*

Objective

- To generate continuous and sustainable employment opportunities in rural and urban areas of the country.
- To provide continuous and sustainable employment to a large segment of traditional and prospective artisans, rural and urban unemployed youth in the country through setting up of micro enterprises.
- To facilitate participation of financial institutions for higher credit flow to micro sector.

Features

- The Scheme is implemented through KVIC and State/UT KVIBs in rural areas and through District Industries Centres in urban

and rural areas in ratio of 30:30:40 between KVIC/KVIB/DIC respectively.
- No income ceiling for setting up of projects.
- Assistance under the Scheme is available only to new units to be established.
- Existing units or units who have already availed any govt subsidy either under state/central govt schemes are not eligible.
- Any industry including Coir based projects excluding those mentioned in the negative list.
- Per capita investment should not exceed ₹1 lakh in plain areas and ₹1.5 lakhs in hilly areas.
- Maximum project cost of ₹25 lakhs in manufacturing sector and ₹10 lakhs in service sector.

Source: www.kvic.org.in

of credit from formal financial institutions, support for technology upgradation and modernisation, provision of infrastructural facilities, testing facilities and quality certification. Developing entrepreneurship and the technical skills through training, support for product development, design interventions and packaging, risk mitigation of artisans and works through different social sector interventions and safety nets, support for accessing domestic and global markets, organisation of people and their collectives in order to facilitate easy delivery of all kinds of services. The ministry of MSME works through the Khadi and Village Industries Commission, the Coir Board and other such institutions to deliver its services. For the coir sector through Coir Board an export market promotion scheme has been implemented. This popularises coir and coir products in markets abroad and supports the industry to modernise itself in order to orient its products for exports. The ministry has also initiated a scheme for promoting innovation and rural entrepreneurship.

The non-agricultural livelihoods at the lower end of the spectrum have significant challenges. Each sub-sector of activity needs to be studied in detail and the value chains fully mapped. Those which have a viable market should be taken up for improvement. The improvements should seek to provide technology, ideas, raw material and marketing support if over the medium term. The enterprises and the craftsman are able to pay for the services and cover their costs in full so that the livelihoods become more certain and sustainable. Revival plans that merely aim at sustaining employment but without a viable market may not be the most appropriate way of protecting livelihoods. It would be a far superior option to shift people engaged in such marginal livelihoods dependent on charitable support from others to more viable new economy livelihoods. Administratively the bulk of non-farm livelihoods are divided between two ministries, Textiles and MSME. MSME supported efforts seem to be doing well compared to the other efforts. Since most of the base level work is in creating enterprises and provide opportunities to other artisans and craftsmen employment opportunities, harmonisation of the schemes is a clear need. The National Policy on Skill and Enterprise Development should ensure that harmonisation across schemes and ministries takes place and the potential entrepreneurs do not need to arbitrage between schemes and ministries.

Private Sector Engagement in Livelihoods and Corporate Social Responsibility

Corporate Social Responsibility (CSR) became a statutory responsibility for the Indian companies with the passing of the Companies Act, 2013. In the last year's report the theme of CSR has been dealt with in the great detail in a separate Chapter.[1] by Manas Ratha. Companies are required under the Act to spend a part of their profits on specific themes that have a social welfare objective. The companies are required to frame policies, commit funding, ensure oversight and report results in order to ensure that the money spent is well spent.

The private sector and corporates' involvement in promoting welfare of community and achieving economic and social empowerment of vulnerable people is much older than the recent government initiative. A survey of top 300 companies in India carried out showed that 142 of these companies had set up a separate foundation. These foundations had mostly been set up before the year 2010 and some of the foundations more than 50 years old. These foundations had taken up a wide variety of activities in education, health, livelihoods, community empowerment and other related areas. While quite a significant part of the welfare activities had been in areas where the manufacturing units were situated or targeted at potential customers of these companies, a large part of the welfare measures went much beyond their areas of operations or their customers. In effect a number of initiatives carried out by these foundations addressed general issues of people with whom the company did not have any commercial or business dealings. In these cases the companies went far beyond being a mere donor to the foundation's activities. The companies allowed the use of their name to lend credibility to the foundation, took care of administrative, infrastructural and structural needs and bore the expenses on employees. The companies also provided senior management expertise from the companies' rolls for the foundation in order to manage the operations of the foundation well. The study carried out by Prakruthi[2] found that a large part of the work done by the foundations was in partnership with NGOs. This enabled the foundations to leave the detailed field related implementation aspects to institutions that are competent and retain the planning and strategic aspects of development interventions with themselves. This appears to have been a win-win situation that had developed over a period of time.

After the Companies Act, 2013 came into effect there have been several doubts raised on the nature of interventions, eligibility of certain types of existing development works

---

[1] Chapter 4: Corporate Social Responsibility and Livelihoods, Manas Ratha, SOIL, 2014.

[2] Archana Shukla Mukherjee, Sunanda Poduwal, Viraf M. Mehta, 2015, Study on Corporate Foundations: An Emerging Development Paradigm? India: Prakruthi.

being carried out by companies and the kind of supervision arrangements required for the purpose of the Act. The Ministry of Corporate Affairs has provided detailed clarifications.[3] Now most of the companies have framed their own CSR policies established by CSR committees of the board and also invested in monitoring systems that would measure and report results. In a number of cases, the CSR policy mimics the guidelines given by the Ministry of Corporate Affairs with no additions. But there are also companies that have framed very focussed and at the same time elaborate CSR policy. Some of the policy documents reviewed contained detailed measures on governance of the policy, procedures for preparation of projects and sanctioning and implementation, monitoring and reporting. The companies with detailed CSR policies were engaged in doing CSR for a long time much before introduction of the Companies Act, 2013.

The CSR policies of a few companies were taken up randomly to examine their outlook on supporting livelihoods. Bayer Crop Sciences for example has proposed to design a well-planned initiative to provide vocational and skill development training, support identification and adoption of new income generation livelihood opportunities with new technologies and improved agricultural and non-agricultural incomes. The company also proposes to work towards creating markets for local commodities, products and skills. Rural Electrification Corporation Ltd. proposes to promote rural enterprise and livelihoods including skill development and training, providing development support to common facility centres and production centres in rural areas, promoting and developing rural technologies for micro enterprise promotion, undertaking relevant community development programmes. It also proposes to support vocational, technical

and higher education to disadvantaged and marginalised sections.

Dr Reddy's Laboratories has set up a foundation named the Dr Reddy Foundation which among other things focuses on rural livelihoods. It aims at ensuring regular income to farmers by introducing technology interventions in their doorsteps. It had the objective of reaching 22,000 farmers by March 2015 in nine states and 29 locations across the country. Its primary and peripheral interventions are in major crops such as paddy, maize, cotton, sugarcane, vegetables and pulses. The foundation also is engaged in skilling rural youth. Presently there are five projects in skilling rural youth being run. A livestock improvement programme focussing on animal healthcare for prevention of major disease such as foot and mouth disease has also been initiated.

In case of livelihoods the CSR interventions are both in the farm sector and nonfarm sector area. In the farm sector the interventions relate to soil and water conservation, optimising use of water, improved crop practices, attention to crop and animal health care and introducing package of practices and production advisories that will improve productivity. There are very few interventions that focussed on linking farmers with markets. However some corporates have taken up linkage with markets as part of their overall livelihood development strategy. On the non-farm sector the focus of CSR has been on supporting creation of micro enterprises as also building up skills among youth for improving employability. In fact investments in skill building have been a strong area that attracts corporates because it directly benefits the corporates with improved quality of labour force on a variety of sectors. The industry collaborations with skill training institutes seem to be strengthening. Under the government programme 1,227 ITIs across the country have industry partnerships where the corporate sector provides faculty training, lab upgradation and placement support. Apart

[3] General Circular No. 21/2014 dated 18 June 2014 by Ministry of Corporate Affairs, GoI.

from this, some of the corporates collaborate directly with government programmes aimed at improving and stabilising livelihoods.

Further, we have described the interventions carried out by a few large corporates in the sphere of livelihoods to get a flavour of what corporates can do. The Adani group invests in promotion and nurturance of SHGs and also the village development committees which plan, implement and monitor the activities. The Adani Foundation also works on programmes for enhancing employability of youth. Basically the type of courses that are offered in skill development relate to the manpower requirements at the Mundra Port (where Adani is operating the port), motor vehicle repairing and training in English speaking skills. The Adani Foundation (AF) has set up an Adani Skills Development Centre and it supports the ITIs in Gujarat and Maharashtra. Further skill development training for traditional occupations is carried out in technologies relating to micro irrigation and drip irrigation systems, innovative farming with efficient use of water, land and energy, training in garment making, beautician courses, bag making for women especially and training in masonry and mobile repairing. The foundation also provides a one-time economic support for marginalised groups such as persons with disabilities and widows in the form of seed money so that they can initiate income generated activity. The support ranges up to ₹10,000 per person and it can be given either to an individual or in groups in case there are viable group income activities. The AF also reports that it supports traditional artisans in Kuchh in weaving, dyeing, printing, bandhani, embroidery, leather work, pottery, metal work and wood work. This support is mainly to ensure that their traditional crafts which are on the decline are sustained and improved upon. There are a number of other activities in the real sector relating to organic agriculture, social forestry, pulping of mangoes and improved animal husbandry which are being supported by the foundation.

The Aditya Birla Foundation covers about 5,000 villages with a population of 7.5 million people. The annual expenditure of the group is about ₹2.5 billion. In sustainable livelihoods the Aditya Birla Group carries out its projects under Aditya Birla Centre for Community Initiatives and Rural Development. It focuses on SHGs to facilitate micro finance for farmers and women, integrated agricultural development, integrated livestock development, watershed management, micro enterprise development and skill development through vocational training. It has a number of partners from among the NGO sector for implementing its various livelihood related programmes.

Box 8.1: *Comprehensive and end-to-end solutions in poorly endowed areas: Lupin group story*

The Lupin Foundation has been a significant CSR focussed institution set up by Lupin Laboratories. Apart from Lupin Foundation, the group also has set up a Desh Bandhu and Manju Gupta Foundation (DBMGF) which operates in Dhule district of Maharashtra. Their field operations were visited as part of the ground work for preparation of this report. The foundation has the target of reaching 130,000 families in the district. The focus of their intervention in the field is on women and youth farmers especially the poor. The objective of the project is to lift these poor families above the poverty line. Starting in 2010–11, so far the project has covered 95,000 households. The project intervention covers economic development activities under agriculture, animal husbandry and non-farm sectors, natural resource management in both land and water and social development aspects in health, education and women empowerment. Some of the innovations introduced have been in health where mobile medical diagnostic unit visits the villages and carries out pathological testing as well as providing ECG and X-ray testing facilities. In education, the tribal ashram schools have been taken up for intensive support and e-learning programmes have been introduced. Fifteen villages in a contiguous area are put into a cluster and the staffs of the foundation attend to the requirements of farmers in those areas from the cluster office. The people have been organised into family development groups and each family is required to prepare a plan and get it approved by the groups in which they are members. Service delivery is through the family development group to individual families based on their plan. An elaborate database at the district level has been set up so that family level monitoring of progress become possible. The experience of the foundation has been positive in the real sector and natural resource management aspects. Microfinance activities which were set up as part of the foundation's work to ensure that people will get access to loan have not done well. Since staff involved in development were also involved in providing loans, the recovery rates have been poor and the project has found it difficult to instil the required credit discipline. The foundation is considering exiting from the microfinance activities so that the other activities are intensified. As a strategy to provide formal options both for accessing inputs and selling outputs in the market, a producer company has been formed with 1,000 shareholders in one of the project blocks. The company has already commenced supplying inputs to its members. It is hoping to start aggregating outputs for selling at remunerative prices in the larger markets.

The foundation listed the following as the challenges. The monitoring mechanism despite being elaborate is unable to produce real time data of the kind required for effective monitoring. The targets set seem to be ambitious for the very short time frame in which it has to be achieved. The tribals in the area with whom the project is working show a low response especially on the micro finance part of the programme. Family based plans produce demands for a wide variety of activities which are difficult to coordinate because some of the activities do not have the kind of numbers for the project to provide close attention. A number of people that are landless remain in the households for whom finding viable local livelihoods options is difficult. Marketing of produce that is arising from improved productivity has become one of the most important issues to be addressed in the near future.

Despite the challenges, the DBMGF is bringing hope to the people in a dry district in Marathwada region of Maharashtra. It provides technical services, new ideas on how better and more viable livelihoods can be undertaken in the local area, aggregating and organising people into community entities that can work together in common interest, providing solutions for water and soil through appropriate interventions and also providing knowledge skills through the entire gamut of activities. When corporate organisations invest on end-to-end solutions in a given geographical area where skills, ideas, actual livelihood activities, investments required for the same and education and health are woven together in a complete fabric then they really make a huge difference.

Source: By the author based on field visit to their project location and discussions with the staff.

Funding under CSR

Last year, back-of-the-envelope calculations had been made that the corporate sector may spend about ₹200 billion on CSR activities based on numbers of their past profits. A report during the current year shows that the CSR spending for the year 2014–15 is likely to be around ₹50 billion. The Indian Institute of Corporate Affairs (IICA) had estimated that 16,300 companies that attract the CSR provisions of Companies Act would spend about ₹200 billion each year. A recent paper[4] states that the actual CSR spend might be higher than ₹250 billion. Satish Deodhar says,

As per the union budget of 2015–16, the corporate tax will amount to a whopping ₹470,628 crore for the financial year 2015–16 (MF, 2015). Second, their estimates are based on the Prowess data provided for the

[4] Satish Y. Deodhar, 2015, India's Mandatory CSR: Process of Compliance and Channels of Spending. Ahmedabad: IIM.

financial year 2012–13. Net profit, net worth, and turnover for the current and future financial years will be much higher than the financial year 2012–13. Therefore, both on account of 2 per cent calculations on corporate tax and many more companies exceeding the net profit, net worth, and turnover criteria, the CSR spending for the current and future years will be much larger than ₹25,000 crore.

According to IICA, More than 30,000 directors on the boards of these companies will be involved in implementing the CSR policy of these institutions. The Companies Act and the CSR guidelines very clearly place the responsibility for CSR activities on the board and make CSR an integral part of the corporate governance of the institutions. The requirement to set up a CSR committee and also preparation of a CSR policy that is approved by the board ensure that this gets the best of attention and that companies actually focus on the people who may or may not be the stakeholders of the company itself. In this manner the CSR is integrated into the overall governance practices of companies. Increasingly companies find that their ability to run businesses sustainably is possible only when they have the support of not only their customers but also the community at large. The guidelines on CSR and sustainability for Central Public Sector enterprises states, 'Since Corporate Social Responsibility and sustainability are so closely entwined it can be said that CSR and sustainability is a company's commitment to its stakeholder to conduct business in economically, socially and environmentally sustainably manner that is transparent and ethical.'

There are also challenges in the manner of companies' engaging themselves in CSR. In several places the companies have to look for implementation partners on the ground to run some of their CSR projects. The projects are focussed on education, health, basic amenities for livelihoods. In each case it becomes necessary to deal with individuals and families and almost at their doorsteps. The kind of delivery capability required both in terms of manpower and technical resources is scarcely available with either the companies or even their dedicated foundations. But one of the insights of companies is also that there are not enough well-managed voluntary sector entities available to implement these projects for best results. This requires the companies to invest HR capacities for strategising, planning and monitoring implementation. The last mile delivery aspects alone are outsourced in favour of agencies that have the ability to put staff in but their performance needs to be closely monitored and guided by more professional staffing by the company itself. If the partnership with voluntary sector agency is for the long term then the corporate starts investing in the capacity building of the partner first. This pushes up the cost and also reduces the ability of the companies to execute very large projects or cover large geographies. The second area of discomfort is when working side by side with government projects. In almost all the areas where the CSR activities can be focussed there is a government programme being run (with varying degrees of efficiency). While in some cases because of the government's own commitment or because of the local government officials' positive outlook, it has been possible for the corporate to work in close co-ordination and avoid duplication and overlap of efforts. But there are other locations where it's difficult to work alongside or in partnership with the government department or agencies. There have been complaints of difficulties in holding health camps, in entering villages for training of rural youth or undertaking watershed projects or afforestation programmes for which clearances from Department of Agriculture or forests are required. In many cases the corporates find that as per records the work that they want to do has already been done and because of this reason the permissions from the concerned government department do not come through. Such areas of difficulties need to be smoothened so that corporate sector can collaborate with government departments in a seamless manner.

The third issue is that of human resources. CSR for many of the companies which for the first time have to plan, implement and monitor these kind of projects is a very new discipline. Their current competence in running their business could range from manufacturing, IT services, transportation or finance with very little domain knowledge or understanding of livelihood projects. The kind of competence required to design and a run livelihood project is not common place and a dedicated cadre of CSR professionals needs to be developed. The estimates[5] are that 30,000 professionals in the CSR space are required and there are no short term solutions to produce CSR professionals. Already a number of organisations have taken up designing and conducting training courses for honing the skills of professionals and also training new university passouts into becoming CSR pointspersons in the corporate sector. And this is not likely to happen soon because of low capacities in the education and training system to produce such professionals overnight.

The companies therefore might take the easy route such as contributing to Prime Minister's Relief Fund or missions of national importance such as Swachch Bharat Abhiyan. But contributions to funds are not a good substitute for actually engaging with people and trying to solve their problems. The option available for companies for contributing to funds rather than designing and running projects should be discouraged. A further issue has been that local administration in the CSR project areas finds it challenging to utilise state and central funds. The companies provide gap funding even in such places where the public funds have not been actually put to use. There are other instances where the companies are expected to hand over the funds earmarked for CSR and not actually participate in the initiatives. The companies apprehend that this fund can be misused or misappropriated. It would

be useful to evolve a protocol of how and where funds can be utilised and where they would have the maximum impact as also an accounting for the moneys that are received and used especially where the work is done in collaboration with local administration.

The top ranked companies in CSR

The top ten companies in the CSR space (2014) were identified through a jury based process by the IIM Udaipur and Economic Times.[6] The top companies were (a) Tata Steel, (b) Tata Chemicals, (c) Mahindra Group, (d) Maruti Suzuki, (e) Tata Motors, (f) Siemens, (g) Larsen & Toubro, (h) Coca-Cola India, (i) Steel Authority of India and (j) Infosys.

An analysis of the Sustainability Reports of some of these top companies shows that many of them invest in skills and vocational training; not all of them work in real sector livelihoods. Investments in rural livelihoods projects are not common. *Tata Steel* has a comprehensive range of interventions in rural livelihoods. It works on real sector livelihoods in the rural and semi-urban areas to harness the available skills and resources and improve agricultural productivity of their lands. The interventions aim at improvement of productivity and crop yield, dry land farming, wasteland development and horticulture, enhancing irrigation facilities, and enhancing capacities of rural communities through skill-based trainings in farming techniques. The report by the company states that System of Rice Intensification (SRI) method of paddy cultivation was rolled out in more than 1,100 acres of land, benefitting over 2,000 farmers across locations in 2013–14. The paddy productivity increased by four times from 0.5 tons to 2.5 tons per acre. Further 1,000 acres of wasteland was developed benefiting

[5] Source: Indian Institute of Corporate Affairs, New Delhi.

[6] *Economic Times*, - http://economictimes.india-times.com/magazines/corporate-dossier/indias-best-companies-for-csr-2014

more than 200 farmers. Cumulatively more than 16,000 acres of wasteland have been brought under cashew, mango and lemon plantations in partnership with National Horticulture Mission. Tata Steel also created 152 irrigation structures including lift irrigation facilities, creation/renovation of ponds etc. in Jharkhand and Odisha. Over the years several water harvesting structures have been created irrigating more than 5,000 acres of land, benefiting 6,000 farmers. Further, more than 700 SHGs have been promoted covering for 9,000 plus women facilitating small business units operated by them. The women are supported in poultry farming, pig and goat rearing, soap making, phenyl making, mushroom cultivation, nurseries to raise sapling, seedless tamarind making, tailoring, paper bag making etc. The company also invests in skill development for employability. The skill programmes are designed to train youth for entry-level positions in the organised sector. In 2013–14, nearly 2,000 youth were trained in various vocational trades across locations with 30 per cent of them being gainfully employed.

The *Mahindra Group* in a unique intervention partnered with Naandi Foundation to work with the Adivasi community in Araku Valley. The centuries-old cropping pattern of Adivasi community in Araku was not adequate to feed an increasing population. Naandi Foundation evolved a horticultural development project on marginal, degraded community lands to enrich their local nutrition, their ecosystem and augment the community's income. The participating Adivasi farmers grew Arabica coffee through organic agriculture and have started earning an annual income of more than ₹100,000.

Maruti Suzuki apart from other CSR activities, supports skill development for employability of youth. The Company is currently working with 85 ITIs spread across 21 states to upgrade automobile related trades. This initiative covered over 5,500 students in 2013–14. The Company undertakes faculty training, students' training and organises job placement fairs at the institutes. A large number of students passing out of these ITIs secure employment at the Maruti Suzuki dealer workshops. In the last three years, over 2,800 students from these ITIs were employed in service workshops of the Company's dealers.

L&T also is focused on skill development in the livelihood spectrum of activities. It has set up eight Construction Training Skills Institutes to train youth in trade skills relating to construction industry. Carpentry, bar bending, masonry, electrician, welding and scaffolding are the usual trades in which courses are conducted, lasting three months to six months. In 2013–14 the institutes trained 45,000 candidates. The trained students are provided certificates of proficiency in the trade. They are free to work anywhere or start own enterprise too. Many trainees are placed on suitable jobs with L&T's subcontractors in the different projects across the country. L&T also runs a Project Neev for differently abled people. These candidates are trained in making handicrafts and other products. L&T arranges for marketing of the products made by these persons through different channels.

NGO Box and Renalysis Consultants carried out a study of selected 100 BSE-listed companies on their CSR spending in 2014–15. These 100 companies are a good representation of large and medium companies listed in the BSE. Nearly one-fourth (27 per cent) of the companies spent more than the prescribed CSR spend and about two-third (64 per cent) of the companies spent less than the prescribed CSR spend. Two per cent of the companies spent zero amount from their prescribed CSR spend and 9 per cent of the companies spent exactly same as the prescribed CSR amount. Thirty-nine per cent of the companies spent more than 50 per cent of the prescribed CSR spent but missed the target of the prescribed CSR spend. Reliance Industries emerged as the largest spender with CSR spend of ₹7.6 billion. It is clear that the companies struggle to spend the CSR outlays in the initial years.

Key factors for a successful CSR strategy

Frederick Allen identified five key factors for a successful CSR strategy.

1. **Business-based social purpose:**[7] There have been too many examples of CSR programmes that ignore business fundamentals. Leadership-level CSR programmes always directly reflect what the business is and what it does.

2. **Clear theory of change:** CSR is becoming mandatory in all Indian companies. It will get harder to distinguish one company's efforts from another's. Well strategised CSR programmes will drive measurable social change. The good examples are of Tata Steel and Lupins DBMGF described earlier.

3. **Quality and depth of information:** Merely identifying social priorities for community investment isn't enough. Leadership comes from providing all stakeholders with a significant depth of information about the social issue through credible research, white papers and so on.

4. **Concentrated effort:** It won't do to go through the motions and show that money is spent. Leadership is shown by corporations that focus their efforts on one social issue and align all their internal and external resources with this issue.

5. **Partnering with experts:** Leadership requires establishing a high degree of credibility. This is best done through relationships with social issue experts and not-for-profit organisations which many of Indian companies do.

All the five key factors apply in case of livelihood projects. The results from livelihood projects would be measurable and hence can demonstrate leadership of the corporate to others in a telling manner.

CSR activities are a new area of practice for many Indian companies. Despite the fact that many Indian companies have done social work in the past, part of what was done will not qualify as CSR in the sense defined in the Companies Act. The study of 100 companies referred earlier shows that companies are struggling with the idea of CSR and how to spend their money for good effect. Companies require not only good ideas, but also well designed projects and delivery capabilities. The personnel to do the CSR planning, projectisation and implementation is not likely to be available in-house for many companies in the near future. The voluntary sector with its richer experiences, should put in place a shelf of project ideas backed by implementation strategies. A national or regional platform of project ideas for CSR and a database of possible implementing organisations will be a boon to the corporate sector. This would help the companies take decisions and start using their CSR budgets effectively.

---

[7] Frederick E. Allen, The Five Elements of the Best CSR Programmes, Forbes, April 2011.

Conclusion: How will livelihoods be meaningful and inclusive?

Chapter 9

While not being an exhaustive stock taking, a number of livelihood related themes, policies and programmes have been covered in the earlier chapters. Livelihood as a body of knowledge and a field of practice is complex and diverse. The diversity in natural resource endowments and local cultures make it difficult to have a common approach across the country. If there is one key element that we wish for in the conceptualisation of livelihood development, what would it be? According to us, it should be the autonomy of action in the choice of livelihood and the practice of it in the hands of household. Policies and programmes on livelihoods are usually meant for vulnerable people who lack own resources to pursue gainful employment or vocations. Since the policies are framed for the have-nots, considerable supply side thinking enters the design and implementation. The assumptions in the supply stage indicate that the intended target of the programmes cannot be trusted to do a good job of his/her livelihood. Hence, we see a number entry barriers, operational conditions, requirements of proving one is on the right path at regular intervals and prove that the programme design was right. Never for a moment the supply side thinkers pause to reflect whether they can do the same things expected of the programme target population.

If autonomy of action has to prevail, then planners should learn to whittle down their conditions to the barest minimum. Livelihood project designs can do with a healthy dose of realism. People participation has been a buzzword for a long time. In all the projects a participation of people is ensured and there is adequate documentation to prove people participated. But the question is how their participation was made use of to improve the programme design and delivery? When was the last time a significant change resulted from consulting people who are supposed to benefit from the programme? Why people still do not own programmes where people's institutions have been built up painstakingly? Trust is an important factor in the government and people interface. When trust goes missing, ownership even in a participatory programme shifts to the government functionaries. The NRLM is a case in point. The design prioritised channeling money into groups through grants, infrastructure and bank loans. Had the individuals and groups been asked to come up with a clear plan of how they will use the money (if it is a grant) and how they will use and repay (if it is a loan), the outcomes could have been different. We may not see a number of groups leaving corpus funds idle in bank accounts or one in three groups defaulting on bank loan repayment. The assumption from the supply side was that lack of funds was the reason for people not having sustainable livelihoods. The reality is that there were not enough good ideas on what sustainable income generating activities can be pursued. If ideas were in short supply, sequencing of interventions should have been very different. NREGS and NRLM can gain from conscious attempts at building ownership among the benefiting people. Building ownership in people is not a job that the government departments do well. They need to look for support outside the government sector.

The statutory obligations cast on the government to provide 100 days of employment at the minimum wage for each household that demands work, are difficult to fulfil. First is the question of resources to fulfil the mandate. A three-fold increase over the current budget was required to provide 100 days of work to families that demanded work last year. Assuming that funds are available, how to create meaningful work in the rural areas where people can be employed is the next challenge. Some participatory planning carried out last year has brought a change to the nature of works to be carried out. There are far less roads, and far more irrigation and water related works planned in 2015–16. NREGS has to find ways of making village communities plan their requirements and implement the same over a long period if the works cannot be completed in a year. This is an area where demand side contributions will bring much better results—as the participatory watershed projects have demonstrated.

Building ownership into livelihood support programmes is a critical requirement. This is cognitively understood as seen in the documents that are put out by different schemes and programmes. How to build ownership among the target people is a skill issue in the implementing agency. When large programmes are implemented, the frontline staff normally deals with 'knowledge dissemination' with the benefiting people. The frontline staff have for the most part never carried out livelihoods similar to what is advocated by them. The resultant

lack of clarity and lack of conviction alienates the beneficiaries psychologically. In the public sector, training of such people is not given adequate importance. The difference between some of the well-run programmes and the poor ones is the staff capacities and their understanding of the local context. Typically voluntary sector organisations train their staff and bring in necessary technical expertise. The reason for some NGO run projects doing well is their understanding of the local needs and staff training. The public sector projects, in contrast, believe in achieving targets. While spending targets and physical number can be achieved, what about results and impact? The lack of attention on impact and quality of results has to be remedied in project design and implementation.

This report recognises the radical shifts taking place in the livelihoods of the poor. The typical land and agriculture dependant poor households are moving away for other jobs and vocations. The services—led by construction sector—have been able to wean away unskilled labour into their fold. These jobs are low end, but not dependent on the monsoon or crop prospects for wages. Further with some development of skills and experience there is a possibility of earning a higher wage, whereas in agricultural labour the opportunities to earn more with higher skills are very limited. Another influencing factor is the possibility of migrating to towns and cities with all their attractions. The inability of land to support a large part of population is well understood and internalised by the people which is clear from the shifting employment patterns. Instead of trying to arrest such shifts and the accompanying migration, the people should be provided skills and competence to handle new jobs better and improve their quality of life. The Skill India framework has rightly addressed the issues involved in shifting labour from agriculture to non-farm sector and from rural areas to other areas. However the large target of training

500 million people in the next seven years is not only overly ambitious,[1] but also likely to result in low quality courses that might not produce competent, skilled manpower for the employer. The need in skilling is to moderate the ambition, invest in quality and make the trainees employment-ready. Another aspect of skill initiative is the shift in the mindset to be achieved among youth on educational choices they make after leaving school. Guidance to students on career choices should be available from their secondary school onwards. The functionality of artisan, craftsmen, tradesmen skills and how these can lead to better livelihoods should be fully explained so that students can make the right choices. Aspirational education in universities leads to disappointments and a large well educated but unemployed labour force. Scarce resources utilised for a university education without clear career options can be applied for technical/vocational skill development with all options of wage and self-employment.

Agriculture based livelihoods suffer from a crisis of confidence. The suicides as an extreme decision are a powerful reminder of the fragility of the livelihoods based on farming. Except in niche crops and well-endowed states with all linkages, farming is not a profitable vocation. Those who practise farming in vulnerable conditions, do so for want of a better choice. They farm more for the cash flow rather than for profits; with passage of time these farmers are becoming bankrupt. The debt build-up in farming in some states is far in excess of their yearly income. Situation Assessment Survey (SAS) of farmers reports that in AP the annual income of an average farmer is about ₹72,000; the debt level is about ₹123,400. If the surplus of income over expenditure is taken as the benchmark,

barring states such as Haryana, Punjab and Karnataka, farmers elsewhere will find it difficult to repay the loans. At all India level SAS reports the average loan outstanding per farm household is about ₹47,000 and the net surplus of income above expenditure[2] is about ₹2,400 per annum. The risks in farming are far too varied and idiosyncratic that even the best risk managers will find difficult to contain. In farm livelihoods, the focus of government should be to develop efficient and transparent markets with a sound price discovery mechanism, invest in farmers' collectives and overhaul the crop insurance arrangements. The crop insurance should be converted in to a safety net instead of pretending that crop insurance can be a commercial proposition. The restructuring of crop insurance will be a better alternative to providing interest subsidies which reach only 50 per cent better-off farm households that are lucky enough to get a bank loan.

The dairy sector is a mixed bag. The resounding success of cooperative milk societies and their higher level organisations has not provided enough learning for replication of the AMUL and GCMMF model successfully in other states. Success in organising livelihoods is not just about having sound ideas, but also the passion and commitment. For a sector that provides sustenance to a majority of vulnerable people, dairying does not attract adequate attention. Since small dairy holders are numerous, their capacity to negotiate with the market for inputs, technical services and marketing outputs should be improved. The milk procurement arrangements in many states do not seem to prioritise farmer interests. The extension services run by governments are unable to provide satisfactory quality services in a timely manner. A number of good organisations that provide dedicated service such as BAIF and JK trust could

---

[1] In 2014–15 all ministries and NSDC together trained less than eight million people. In seven years, at the current rate of workflow, about 10 per cent of the target, that is, 50 million can be trained.

[2] The expenditure interest on loans but not the principal repayment.

be valuable resources to learn from. As an experiment, the extension services in some small states can be totally handed over to such committed agencies in the interest of the farmers.

In the handloom and handicrafts sectors the feeling is that those in charge are going through the motions. Neither funding, nor the expenditure has a reasonable relationship with the number of people dependent on these sectors. The attempted interventions do not seem sustainable in the long run. Providing health insurance cover for artisans and craftsmen is a laudable act, but not something a technical department should prioritise as an objective. Skills, technology, infrastructure and markets are areas where the Development Commissioners' interventions are needed. The Khadi and Village industries sector seems to focus well on creation of enterprise and employment. The numbers reported under PMEGP show that with some margin money support and project ideas entrepreneurs are willing to take risks of setting up their own production units. The need is to expand the outreach of such programmes that provide autonomy to the entrepreneur on what to do and provide support appropriate for that choice.

While compulsory CSR by legislative fiat has come into force, the socially relevant interventions by corporate sector have been in place for a long time. But the new entrants to CSR have faced difficulties in the first year of implementation in finding their feet in an unfamiliar terrain. The CSR space urgently needs professionals to man positions in the companies and give direction to CSR activities. Livelihoods do not seem the first choice for many corporates. Many are comfortable with vocational skills training, but not livelihoods in the real sector. Voluntary agencies working in the field should come up with good designs in real sector livelihoods that the companies can take up.

The past year has witnessed the launch of a number of programmes and campaigns by the government. These are well meaning and aim at making a difference to common man in terms of not just livelihood opportunities but also an improved quality of life. The focus on natural resources, climate change issues, improving the quality of labour force and their working conditions, improving the ease of doing business, institutional and product interventions not just in high finance and large projects but also in microenterprises and microfinance offers a welcome change agenda for the government and the public alike. In the midst of the urgency to change what does not work, there should be no haste to dismantle what works or what can be made to work. Some of the plans seem an ambitious overreach in terms of the numbers targeted (skilling). Some might not find the financial resources required (NREGS, NFSA). In some, the operational modalities will require extensive work in the last mile (JAM). But on the whole the urgency and commitment shown reflect a willingness to tackle the problems and find solutions. The global situation of low oil and commodity prices is a key support that can hold inflation under check and facilitate a low interest rate regime. It is up to the private sector—not just the mega enterprise, but microenterprises too—to step up and do their best.

The questions for the future lie in the present. What if with increased devolutions, the states neglect the livelihoods and social sector programmes? Where do we find funds for the NFSA and NREGS to fulfil the legislative mandate? If it is far too large a burden, should we not get the legislations amended to bring in a dose of realism? What is the state of readiness of private sector to employ the skill trained people, especially in the context of jobless growth experienced in the current millennium? How to bring in voluntary and private sector into livelihood programmes of the government to promote people participation and improve delivery efficiency? When do we plan to have a ministry or a department to look at livelihoods issues in an integrated manner instead of in different silos? The hard questions do not have easy answers. We need to work at them.

References

Achievements of Ministry of Rural Development, Ministry of Rural Development, GoI 2015.

Agarwal, Ranjana, Manish Pruthi, Pallavi Kumar and Pawan Lodhi A Case Study of Training in Handicrafts for Primitive Tribal Groups in Jharkhand, - www.indiacsr.in/en/?p=10843

Agricultural Statistics at a Glance 2014, Ministry of Agriculture, Oxford University Press.

Aharam Traditional Crop Producers Company India, Equator Initiative Case Study Series. New York, NY. United Nations Development Programme, 2012.

Aharam Traditional Crop Producers Company India, Equator Initiative Case Study Series. New York, NY. United Nations Development Programme. 2012.

All India Baseline Study on Producer Companies & Contract Farming Practices, Dr Amar KJR Nayak, XIMB, 2014.

Annual Policy Review April 2014–March 2015, PRS Legislative Research, Institute for Policy Research Studies, August 2015.

Annual report 2013–14, BAIF, Pune 2014.

Annual Report 2013–14, KVIC.

Annual Report 2014–15, Ministry of Agriculture.

Annual Report 2014–15, Ministry of Finance.

Annual Report 2014–15, Ministry of Housing & Urban Poverty Alleviation.

Annual Report 2014–15, Ministry of Labour and Employment.

Annual Report 2014–15, Ministry of Medium Small and Micro Enterprises.

Annual Report 2014–15, Ministry of Rural Development.

Annual Report 2014–15, Ministry of Textiles.

Annual Report 2014–15, National Bank for Agriculture and Rural Development.

Annual Report 2014–15, Reserve Bank of India.

Annual Report, 2013–14, NDDB, Anand, Gujarat.

Annual Report, 2014–15, Department of Animal Husbandry, Dairying & Fisheries, Ministry of Agriculture, Government of India.

Ansari, Shah Nawaz, Socio-economic Aspect of Artisans in India in 20th Century, *International Journal of Humanities and Religion* (IJHR), February 2014.

Babu, Ram, A. N. Panda, Performance Assessment Study of Mahatma Gandhi National Rural Employment Guarantee Scheme: An Overview, Vol. 4, Issue 2, January 2015, *Global Journal of Multidisciplinary Studies.*

Biswas, Indranil, Vocational training in India, India, Science and Technology, 2008, Available at: http://www.nistads.res.in/indiasnt2008/t1humanresources/t1hr2.htm

Budget Briefs Volume 7/6 MGNREGS, GoI 2015–16, Accountability Initiative, Research and Innovation for Governance Accountability 2015.

Case study of India, in Smallholder Dairy Development: Lessons learned in Asia, January 2009, FAO, Rome.

Case Study on Livestock Service Center (LSC) in Kachchh, Access Livelihood consulting, Hyderabad, 2012.

Dairy Industry Vision 2030, Suruchi Consultants, 2014. Available at: www.suruchiconsultants.com/pageDownloads/report/63_Surchi_DIV_2030.pdf

Dholakia, Ravindra H., Manish B. Pandya, Payal M. Pateriya, Urban–Rural Income Differential in Major States: Contribution of Structural Factors, W.P. No. 2014-02-07 Indian Institute of Management, Ahmedabad, February 2014.

Economic Survey 2013–14, Ministry of Finance, Government of India, July 2014.

Economic Survey 2013–14, Ministry of Finance, Government of India, February 2015.

Education, Skill Development and Labour Force, Vol. 3, 2013–14, Government of India, Ministry of Labour & Employment Labour Bureau Chandigarh, GoI, 2014.

Employment and Unemployment Situation among Social Groups in India, NSS 68th Round (July 2011–June 2012).

Enterprise, NIRDPR Quarterly Newsletter, March 2015.

Evaluation of Placement Linked Skill Development Special Projects under SGSY.

Executive Summary of Impact Assessment Study, 2014–15, NSDC, 2015, Available at: http://www.nsdcindia.org/sites/default/files/files/pdf/Executive-Summary-Impact-Assessment-Study2014-15.pdf

Final Report on National Level Consultation on Skill Development, Employment and Mobility in India National Institute of Advanced Studies, Bangalore, 22 December 2014.

Final Report: Vol. II, Ministry of Rural Development, March 2013.

Gupta, Sanjay, Will producer Companies Act Change farmers' fortune? Rural Marketing, June 2015, Available at: www.ruralmarketing.in

Hasnain, Syed Iqbal, Modi's National Skill Development Mission Doomed to Fail, 2015, American Bazaar, 22 July 2015, Available at: www.americanbazaaronline.com/2015/

Impact Assessment of Marketing Assistance Schemes of MSMEs: With Special Reference to Vaishali, Bihar K Aashish Entrepreneurship Development Institute of India, Gandhinagar.

Implementation Status Results, Vocational Training Improvement Project: P099047, Sequence 15, World Bank, 2015, Available at: http://documents. worldbank.org/curated/en/2015/05/24435905/ india-india-vocational-training-improvement-project-p099047-

Informal Sector and Conditions of Employment in India, NSS 68th Round, NSSO, Ministry of Statistics and Programme Implementation, GoI, July 2014.

Initiatives, Achievements, Policies and Roadmap for the Future, Ministry of Skill Development, Entreprenuership, Youth Affairs and Sports, GoI 2014.

Jatav, Manoj, Sucharita Sen, Drivers of Non-Farm Employment in Rural India Evidence from the 2009–10 NSSO Round, Economic and Political Weekly, June 2013.

Jha, Praveen and Nilachala Acharya, December 2015, Expenditure on the Rural Economy in India's Budgets since the 1950s: An Assessment, *Review of Agrarian Studies.*

Joining Both Ends of the Supply Chain, Rabo Bank Industry Note#500, Rabo Bank, July 2015.

Joining Both Ends of the Supply Chain, Rabo Bank Industry note#500, Rabo Bank, July 2015.

Kaushalya Vardhan Kendra (KVK), Pioneering a flexible approach of skill development in rural Gujarat: A Case Study, 2014, Available at: http:// darpg.gov.in/darpgwebsite_cms/

Key Indicators of Debt and Investment in India, NSS 70th Round, NSSO, Ministry of Statistics and Programme Implementation, GoI, December 2014.

Key Indicators of Land and Livestock Holdings in India, NSS 70th Round, NSSO, Ministry of Statistics and Programme Implementation, GoI, December 2014.

Key Indicators of Situation of Agricultural Households in India, NSS 70th Round, NSSO, Ministry of Statistics and Programme Implementation, GoI, December 2014.

Key Indicators of Urban Slums in India, NSS 69th Round, NSSO, Ministry of Statistics and Programme Implementation, GoI, December 2013.

Kumar. Nanda T, 2015, CII: Dairy Vision 2025 Delhi: Keynote Address speech at CII, Available at: http:// www.nddb.org/about/speech/dairyvision

Leitch, Helen, Producer Companies in India: Potential to support Productivity Profitability of Poor Smallholder Farmers, World Bank, 2014.

Making Indian Dairy Farming Competitive, The Small Farmer Perspective, A White Paper, Yes Bank, 2015.

Mantri, Rajiv and Harsh Gupta IITs to ITIs—Modi's Voucher Revolution in Skill Development, 13 August 2015, 2015.

MDG India Country Report 2015, Social Statistics Division Ministry of Statistics and Programme Implementation, GOI 2015.

Meena, D. L., D. K. Jain Economics of Milk Production in Alwar District (Rajasthan): A Comparative Analysis, *International Journal of Scientific and Research Publications*, Vol. 2, Issue 8, August 2012.

Mehrotra, Santosh, Ankita Gandhi, Bimal Sahoo, Estimating the Skill Gap on a Realistic Basis for 2022, IAMR Occasional Paper No. 1/2013, Institute of Applied Manpower Research, Planning Commission, GoI, February, 2013.

Meky, Muna Salih, Skills Development Programs in India, Labor Market Impacts and Effectiveness Findings of an Evaluation Study. World Bank, 2015, Available at: http://documents.worldbank. org/curated/en/2015/04/24616611/labor-mar-ket-impacts-effectiveness-skills-development-programs-india

MGNREGA – Roundup of 2014–15 and Way Ahead for 2015–16 – An End Year Assessment Report – Ministry of Rural Development, GoI 2015.

Mid-Term Assessment Report, NRLM—National Mission Management Unit, National Rural Livelihoods Mission, MoRD 2015.

Minutes of the Empowered Committee held on 22nd June, 2015, Ministry of Rural Development, GoI, 2015, Available at: http://ddugky.gov.in/ddugky/ DocumentsForDownload/Minutes_EC_meeting_

Minutes of the Meeting to Review Implementation of Projects Under Roshini Project Under DDU-GKY, held on 21 July, 2015. GoI, 2015, Available at: http://ddugky.gov.in/ddugky/ DocumentsForDownload/Minutes_of_Roshani_ Meeting.pdf

Misra, Sangita, and Anoop K. Suresh, Estimating Employment Elasticity of Growth for the Indian Economy; RBI working paper 06/2014.

Moinak, Maiti, Understanding the Employment Challenges in India, *International Research Journal of Social Sciences*, January 2015.

MSME at a Glance, Ministry of MSME, GoI 2015.

Mukherjee, Sacchidananda, Debashis Chakraborty, Satadru Sikdar, Three Decades of Human Development across Indian States: Inclusive Growth or Perpetual Disparity, Working Paper 2014/139, National Institute of Public Finance and Policy, New Delhi, June 2014.

National Policy for Skill Development and Entrepreneurship, Ministry of Skill Development and Entrepreneurship, GoI, 2015.

National Workshop with States, Vigyan Bhawan, New Delhi 9 May 2015 Skilling with Scale at Speed: A Presentation. NSDC, 2015.

Nayak, Amar K. J. R., All India Baseline Study on Producer Companies & Natural Farming

Practices: Part 1 Producer Companies in India, XIMB, 2014.

NDSP, Project appraisal document, World Bank, Available at: documents.worldbank.org/curated/en/2010/04/12157650/india-national-dairy-support-project 2010

Of Bold Strokes and Fine Prints, An Analysis of the Union Budget 2015–16, Centre for Budget and Governance Accountability (CBGA), March 2015.

Outcome Budget 2014–15, Ministry of Agriculture, 2015.

Outcome Budget 2014–15, Ministry of Finance, 2015.

Outcome Budget 2014–15, Ministry of Housing & Urban Poverty Alleviation, 2015.

Outcome Budget 2014–15, Ministry of Labour and Employment, 2015.

Outcome Budget 2014–15, Ministry of Medium Small and Micro enterprises, 2015.

Outcome Budget 2014–15, Minstry of Textiles, 2015.

Prabhu, Nagesh, Milch Cattle, Buffaloes to Be Covered Under Livestock Insurance, *The Hindu*, 2 August 2015. Available at: http://www.thehindu.com/news/national/karnataka/milch-cattle-buffaloes-to-be-covered-under-livestock-insurance/article7492039.ece

Praneet Mutha, Director, Vippy Industries Ltd. Dewas, Madhya Pradesh. India, as Mentioned in Sustainable Soy newsletter, February 2015, Vol. 2 Issue 1 February 2015, a Quarterly Newsletter of National Platform of Sustainable Soy.

Prasad, H. A. C., N. K. Sinha, Riyaz A. Khan – Performance of Major Social Sector Schemes: A Sample Survey Report – Working Paper 3/2013 DEA, Department of Economic Affairs, Ministry of Finance, GoI, November 2013.

Presentation on TNSDC, Made to National Skill Development Agency, New Delhi on 8th January 2015, TNSDC,2015, Available at: https://c27web2.saas.talismaonline.com/NSDA/.

Presentation to Performance Review Committee, 9 July 2015, DDU-GKY, MoRD. GoI, 2015, Available at: http://ddugky.gov.in/ddugky/DocumentsForDownload/PRC_9_July_2015.pdf

Producer Companies in India: A Study of Organization and Performance, Sukhpal Singh, Tarunvir Singh, Centre for Management in Agriculture, Indian Institute Management, Ahmedabad, 2013.

Producer Companies in India: Potential to Support Productivity Profitability of Poor Smallholder Farmers, Helen Leitch, World Bank, 2014.

Programme Guidelines DDU-GKY, Ministry of Rural Development, Government of India. 2015.

Quarterly Report on Changes in Employment in Selected Sectors (Oct, 2014 to Dec, 2014), Ministry of Labour and Employment, GoI, 2015, Available at: http://labour.gov.in/content/reports/QES_24th_final.pdf

Rao, C.K., Felix Bachhman, Vishnu Sharma, P. Venkataramaiah, Jitesh Panda, Raja Rathinam,

Smallholder Dairy Value Chain Development in India and Selected States (Assam and Bihar): Situation Analysis and Trends, ILRI, July 2014.

Ration Balancing Programme, NDDB, 2015, Available at: www.nddb.org/services/animalnutrition/rationbalance

Reaping India's Promised Demographic Dividend, Industry in Driving Seat, Ernst & Young LLP and FICCI, 2013.

Reaping India's Promised Demographic Dividend, Industry in Driving Seat, FICCI, 2013.

Report of the XII plan Working Group on Animal Husbandry, Planning Commission, 2011, Available at: planningcommission.gov.in/

Report to the People – MGNREG Act 2005, MoRD GoI February 2015, Slowdown compounds India's Job-Creation Challenge, CRISIL Insight, CRISIL Research, January 2014.

Saha, Akash and Adhikary M. M., The Effects of Rural Labour Migration Process on Occupational Distribution, Family Facilities and Livelihoods, *International Journal of Environmental and Agriculture Research*, July 2015.

Saikia, Sailajananda, Development of Rural India and the Significant of Rural Nonfarm Sector: A Case Study of Dhemaji District, Assam, *International Journal of Multidisciplinary Research and Development* 1 (7) 2014.

Sharma, Pravesh, Transforming Agricultural Markets and Value Chains in the 21st Century: Farmer Producer Organisations and Policy Challenges, 2014, Available at: http://www.ggkirma.in/discussionforum/blogdetail.php?id=15&catid=2

Singh, Saurabh Kumar and Kumar Devashish Chandragupta, An Independent Evaluation of the Performance of STAR, Institute of Management, Patna, NSDA, 2014.

Singh, Sukhpal, Tarunvir Singh, Producer Companies in India: A Study of Organization and Performance, Centre for Management in Agriculture, Indian Institute Management, Ahmedabad, 2013.

Skill Development in India–Present Status and Recent Developments, Swantini, Available at: www.swantini.in.

Skill India, Government of Tamil Nadu, 2015, Available at: www.pibchennai.gov.in/

Skill Training Can be Next Fundamental Right, Rudy, Sanjib Kumar Baruah, *The Hindustan Times*, 20 July 2015, Available at: http://www.hindustantimes.com/india-news/skill-training-could-be-the-next-fundamental-right/article1-1371060.aspx

Skilling Indian Workforce, A Blueprint for Setting up National Institutes of Skill Development, a White Paper, Technopak, 2014, Available at: http://phdcci.in/image/data/Upcoming%20Event%202014/Dec-2014/PHD-Chamber-Technopak-Skiling-Whitepaper2014.pdf

Sood, Jyotika, New Milky Way, 15, February, 2015, Available at: (www.downtoearth.org.in)

Srija, A., Shrinivas V. Shirke, An Analysis of the Informal Labour Market in India, Special Feature CII, October 2014.

State of India's Livelihoods Report, 2013–14, Chapter No. 5, Farmer Producer Companies, Vijay Mahajan, Access Development Services, 2014.

State of India's Livelihoods Report, 2014, Chapter No. 5, Farmer Producer Companies, Vijay Mahajan, Access Development Services, 2014.

State of India's Livelihoods, Access Development Services 2014.

State of India's Livelihoods, Access Development Services, 2012.

State of India's Livelihoods, Access Development Services, 2013.

States Finances: A Study of Budgets 2014–15, Reserve Bank of India, May 2015.

The Establishment of Maitree, A Producer Company of Women, A Case Study by Stutilina Pal and Debasish Pradhan Under The Guidance of Sankar Datta and Ved Arya, 2013, Srijan.

The Milky Way: Baif Way of Dairy Development, BAIF Development Research Foundation, 2012.

The NSDC Had No Accountability, 10 August 2015, Outlook, 2015, Available at: http://www. outlookindia.com/article/the-nsdc-had-no-accountability/294976

Transforming Agricultural Markets and Value Chains in the 21st Century: Farmer Producer Organisations and Policy Challenges, Pravesh Sharma, 2014, Availabale at: http://www.ggkirma.in/disc, Vol. 2 Issue 1, February 2015, a Quarterly Newsletter of National Platform of Sustainable Soy.

Twelfth Five Year Plan (2012–2017), Faster, More Inclusive and Sustainable Growth Volume I, GOI, 2013, Available at: http://planningcommission. gov.in/plans/planrel/12thplan/pdf/12fyp_vol1.pdf

Union Budget 2014, Ministry of Finance, Government of India, July 2014.

Union Budget 2015, Ministry of Finance, Government of India, February 2015.

Union Budget 2015–16, Central Plan, NITI Brief 2, National Institution for Transforming India (NITI), February 2015.

Viswanathan, Brinda, Enumeration of Crafts Persons in India, Monograph 24/2-13, Madras School of Economics, February 2013.

Will Producer Companies Act Change Farmers' Fortune? Sanjay Gupta, Rural Marketing, June 2015, Available at: www.ruralmarketing.in

Index

About the Authors

Girija Srinivasan is an expert in development finance and rural livelihoods with extensive international experience in consulting, technical assistance and studies. She has been a development banker for 12 years and has written documents and books on community-based approaches in finance livelihoods and microfinance. She has also authored the *Social Performance Report* for the years 2011–14 and serves on a few trust boards of governance.

N. Srinivasan has been pursuing his personal interests in financial inclusion, rural finance and livelihoods since 2007, after a career spanning about 30 years in RBI and NABARD. He is currently active as an expert adviser and international consultant for different entities, including the World Bank, ADB, Consultative Group to Assist the Poor (CGAP), IFAD, GIZ, Kreditanstalt für Wiederaufbau, Bill & Melinda Gates Foundation and MicroSave. He also authored the well-known publication on microfinance called *State of the Sector Report on Microfinance in India* for four years. He has also written a book on rural finance which is to be shortly released. Apart from this, he has jointly authored books and contributed to edited volumes in development finance and development economics. He also serves several industry forums on the themes of financial inclusion, microfinance and responsible finance.